Sibling Romance in American Fiction, 1835–1900

Sibling Romance in American Fiction, 1835–1900

Emily E. VanDette

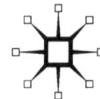

SIBLING ROMANCE IN AMERICAN FICTION, 1835–1900
Copyright © 2013, Emily E. VanDette.

A portion of Chapter 2 appeared in a different version in VanDette, Emily E. "It Should Be a Family Thing: Family, Nation, and Republicanism in Catharine Maria Sedgwick's *A New-England Tale* and *The Linwoods*." *ATQ* (March 2005): 51–74. (Used with permission.)

A version of Chapter 4 appeared as VanDette, Emily E. " 'A whole, perfect thing': Sibling Bonds and Anti-slavery Politics in Harriet Beecher Stowe's *Dred*." *ATQ* (June 2008): 415–434. (Used with permission.)

The National Endowment for the Humanities provided some support for this publication. Any views, findings, conclusions, or recommendations expressed in this publication do not necessarily reflect those of the National Endowment for the Humanities.

All rights reserved.

First published in 2013 by
PALGRAVE MACMILLAN®
in the United States—a division of St. Martin's Press LLC,
175 Fifth Avenue, New York, NY 10010.

Where this book is distributed in the UK, Europe and the rest of the World, this is by Palgrave Macmillan, a division of Macmillan Publishers Limited, registered in England, company number 785998, of Houndmills, Basingstoke, Hampshire RG21 6XS.

Palgrave Macmillan is the global academic imprint of the above companies and has companies and representatives throughout the world.

Palgrave® and Macmillan® are registered trademarks in the United States, the United Kingdom, Europe and other countries.

ISBN: 978–1–137–28718–2

Library of Congress Cataloging-in-Publication Data

VanDette, Emily E.
  Sibling romance in American fiction, 1835–1900 / Emily E. VanDette.
    p. cm.
  ISBN 978–1–137–28718–2
  1. American fiction—19th century—History and criticism. 2. Brothers and sisters in literature. 3. Attachment behavior in literature. 4. Love in literature. 5. Social values in literature. I. Title.
  PS374.B77V36 2012
  813'.509355—dc23   2012030474

A catalogue record of the book is available from the British Library.

Design by Integra Software Services

First edition: February 2013

10 9 8 7 6 5 4 3 2 1

Dedicated to Scott, Joseph, and Elspeth
for their *awes-tacular* love

Contents

List of Figures ix

Acknowledgments xi

Introduction 1

1 Sibling Pedagogy: The Brother–Sister Ideal in Domestic Advice and Children's Periodical Literature 23

2 Remembering Resistance and Resilience: The Revolutionary Sibling Romances of Sedgwick, Simms, and Kennedy 49

3 "She carried the romance of sisterly affection too far": Sibling Love and Violence in Caroline Lee Hentz's *Ernest Linwood* 85

4 "A whole, perfect thing": Sibling Bonds and Anti-slavery Politics in Harriet Beecher Stowe's *Dred* 109

5 Reconstructing Family in the African American Nadir: The Trope of Sibling Affiliation in Works by Harper, Chesnutt, and Hopkins 127

Epilogue: Sibling Romance in/and the Canon; Or, the Ambiguities 149

Notes 159

Works Cited 185

Index 197

Figures

I.1 Brother and Sister (Mary and Gerald Thayer), Abbott Henderson Thayer. Courtesy of Smithsonian American Art Museum/Art Resource   2

1.1 Masthead of *The Youth's Companion* in 1866, illustrating what appears to be a brother and sister sharing the magazine. While the masthead changed many times over the course of the magazine's century-long existence, it usually depicted a brother and sister reading together   33

1.2 The image of a brother and sister leaning upon one another and rapturously pouring over an issue of the magazine, sharing physical space as well as the literacy experience, was an extremely prevalent one on the covers of nineteenth-century children's periodicals. This image is from the cover of *The Youth's Dayspring*, June 1851   34

1.3 The sibling pair depicted on the illustrated masthead of *Burke's Weekly for Boys and Girls* places the girl figure in the primary reading position, with her brother deferentially sharing the magazine from behind his seated sister, his hands resting on her shoulders   35

1.4 An illustration of the valiant Donald rescuing his sister Dorothy (accessed via Project Gutenberg, www.gutenberg.org). Mary Maples Dodge, in her manifesto for editorial reform in children's magazines, emphasized the importance of high-quality illustrations, which, she said, "should be heartily conceived and well executed; and they must be suggestive, attractive, and epigrammatic" (*St. Nicholas and Mary Maples*

Dodge, 17). Here, the heroic image of Donald bravely saving his sister from a nearly fatal horse-riding accident is suggestive indeed of the context of brotherly devotion as the context for manly heroism   45

Acknowledgments

This book began in the margins of my doctoral dissertation, when my committee at Penn State recommended that I develop in a separate project the sibling strain that had emerged in my research. For making that suggestion and for guiding my doctoral research, I would like to thank them: Susan K. Harris, Deb Clarke, Robin Schulze, Bob Burkholder, and Anne C. Rose. Susan has continued to provide me support throughout this process, especially helping me navigate the terrain of book publishing. Over the past couple of years, my colleagues in the Harriet Beecher Stowe Society, Charles Chesnutt Society, Catharine Maria Sedgwick Society, and the Society for the Study of American Women Writers have provided helpful and probing feedback in annual conventions of the American Literature Association. Generous support from SUNY Fredonia, from grants from the United University Professions, and from the Mary Louise White Foundation has allowed me to travel to those conferences. I thank the anonymous reviewers of my manuscript for their collegial and expert suggestions and Palgrave editor Brigitte Shull for her interest in this project. I am grateful to Pat Pflieger for granting me access and permission to use images from her outstanding collection of children's magazines, and to *ATQ* for permission to reprint portions of two of my articles. I was fortunate to be able to focus full-time on completing this book during the summer of 2012 with the support of a National Endowment for the Humanities Summer Stipend award.

I am thankful to Andrea Herrera for igniting my interest in the nineteenth century, and for her mentoring and love. For his collaborative spirit and friendship since graduate school, I thank my dear friend Howard Rambsy II, who will always be *my* Penn State. For reading a paragraph or a chapter, for sharing their personal time, wisdom, and warmth, and for their generosity in letting me ramble on about sibling love, psychology, and literature, I am grateful to the many friends I am also lucky enough to call colleagues at SUNY Fredonia: Aimee Nezhukumatathil, Ann Siegle Drege, Bruce Simon, Dustin Parsons, Christina Jarvis, Jeanette

McVicker, Dawn Eckenrode, Dave Kinkela, and, especially for her support as a trusted reader, Emily Straus. I am grateful to Dean John Kijinski and President Virginia Horvath for their generous support of this book; to Amy Cuhel-Schuckers for her assistance with my NEH application; to the staff at SUNY Fredonia's Reed Library for their assistance throughout my research for this book.

It may have taken a while for academic fields to respond to Freud's "blind spot," and to come around to the power of sibling attachment, but that fact was the first thing I ever knew for sure. My earliest conscious recollection—the warm, sweet breath of my newborn baby sister against my cheek—is always with me; the memory of Katie is a source of inspiration for this book. I thank my siblings, especially John, Keri, Lisa, Brendan, and Andrew, for teaching me the importance of our dynamics in real life and for their loving support and interest as I pursued it as a literary subject. I am one of those lucky academics who have the rare benefit of having a family support system in town, and I thank my parents-in-law, Dennis and Judy VanDette, for being parents to me and the world's best grandparents to my children.

If my childhood taught me my first lesson about the significance of the sibling bond, the wonderful pair that I get to mother continues to affirm that on a daily basis. The friendship between Joey and Ellie is simply the most beautiful facet of my world, and watching them each grow as individuals—their courage to learn new things, their curiosity and creativity—always motivates my best effort. My husband, Scott, has traveled with me throughout my academic journey, from encouraging me to major in English as an undergraduate, and a few years later driving me to my graduate school interview, to listening patiently to my latest fascination with Margaret Mitchell's vanished sibling novella. For all of that and all that he means to me I dedicate this book to him, as well as to our sweet children, as all together they are my greatest source of strength and inspiration.

Introduction

"A Beautiful Picture of Sisterly and Fraternal Love":
Sibling Culture in Nineteenth-Century America

THE BROTHER–SISTER BOND HELD A PROMINENT PLACE in the nineteenth-century American imagination, and it played an important role in the shaping of national ideologies and culture. American artist Abbott Handerson Thayer's 1889 portrait "Brother and Sister" (figure I.1) wonderfully captures the complex place of the sibling bond in American cultural history, as it reveals the nuances of the private and personal significance of the brother–sister bond on the one hand, while engaging, on the other hand, the artist's public anxieties about the decline of his national culture. Thayer's own children, Mary and Gerald, modeled for this portrait, during a sorrowful period when their mother was hospitalized for severe depression, shortly before she would die of tuberculosis. From the time of his wife's illness and especially after her death, Thayer turned to his three surviving children, Mary, Gerald, and Gladys, for emotional succor, a personal history that is reflected in his extensive use of the children as models for his prolific portrait output.[1] Whether posing for the several Angel portraits for which the artist would become most famous, naturalistic Virgin Mary scenes, or ideal human figures, Thayer's children served as his main study, suiting his various subjects and scenes and revealing his artistic, psychological, and social anxieties.

Given Thayer's approach to art as a process of idealization, in which the artist treats his subjects as human types, or "representative beings,"[2] his portrait of his children in "Brother and Sister" has profound relevance to the cultural stature of that family dynamic. In keeping with nineteenth-century expectations for opposite-sex siblinghood, the pair is depicted in a loving embrace, she leaning dependently upon her brother for support, passive beneath his clasp, his diverted gaze suggestive of his

Figure I.1 Brother and Sister (Mary and Gerald Thayer), Abbott Handerson Thayer. Courtesy of Smithsonian American Art Museum/Art Resource.

protective charge. The romantic ideal of brother–sister love resonates with the artist's outspoken deploring over what he saw as declining morality in the Gilded Age, the sordid consequences of industrialization, the loss of purity in the human and the natural worlds around him. Such social realities this artist, an admirer of Emersonian duality and German idealism, protested not only through his determinedly pristine landscapes, modestly clothed human portraits, and spiritual depictions, but also in his impassioned written discourse and in the Thoureauvian naturalism of his lifestyle, as well.[3] Perhaps nostalgically, at a time when such social ideals were rapidly eroding and unraveling, in "Brother and Sister" Thayer restores the romantic vision of a traditional family bond that held rich symbolic potential throughout the nineteenth century.

If Thayer's artistic rendition of the sibling bond performed cultural work, though, at the same time it exposed the most personal of anxieties, too. Sister Mary's swollen, wet eyes and her brother's downcast, distracted gaze certainly speak volumes of the real grief and worry these children experienced during the crisis of their mother's illness. Beyond their representation of model brotherly protection and sisterly dependence, their mutual melancholy and clinging embrace suggest the intensity with which this brother and sister relied upon each other during their distress. Sharing the same home environment, parents, family governance, life trials, Mary and Gerald Thayer would have identified with each other above anyone else, even their passionately devoted father. The reality of their intense, mutual emotional experience, combined with the representational agenda of their socially conscious artist-father, makes this portrait of their bond a remarkable visual symbol of the importance of the brother–sister dynamic in American history.

The cultural and psychological significance of sibling love that is so vividly on display in Thayer's portrait provides a crucial context for understanding the nineteenth century American imagination. It is the goal of this book to demonstrate the importance of the brother–sister bond in American literary history. In particular, this book suggests that sibling love was a meaningful premise for many novels of the family, especially in the context of national crisis. The impressive recent recovery of domestic fiction and its role in American literary history has firmly fixed the family as a central theme and context and sentiment as a powerful aesthetic for disseminating ideas about the family and the nation.[4] Notwithstanding the rich focus on family and sympathy in new narratives of American fiction traditions, the significance of the sibling bond to that history has for the most part escaped substantive notice.[5] With the success of the nation perceived as hinging upon the success of individual families, a notion that has retained its rhetorical power throughout American history,[6] the idea of a tightly knit, insular, self-contained family unit made sibling relationships in the first century of nationhood especially important.[7] As the work of emotional fulfillment, socialization, and education were increasingly relegated to the family, the siblings who were raised together shared intense social experiences and expectations, and the result of that emphasis pervaded the psychology and culture of nineteenth-century America.

Sibling attachment represented for nineteenth-century American novelists a relationship that modeled mutual obligation, loyalty, and affection, ideals that were as tantalizing as they were elusive to a nation struggling to maintain unity and solidarity while preserving the rights and identities of individuals. While scholarly inquiry into how Americans were experiencing and imagining national kinship during times of sectionalism, disunion, and reconstruction has established sympathy as a dominant mode of constructing affiliation, the conversation usually attends to filial loyalty and parental authority as well as to the correlations between marriage and the nation.[8] Recently, literary scholars have given special attention to the plot of courtship and marriage as allegorical representations of national union, particularly within the contexts of reconstruction and reconciliation.[9] But sentimental constructions of affiliation were not limited to parental and spousal dynamics. Nineteenth-century American authors also turned to opposite-sex sibling pairs in their efforts to picture union, as the sibling bond represented an opportunity for them to envision dynamics that balanced loyalty and affection with individual autonomy, as well as to portray the implications of lateral dysfunction in representations that fall short of the sibling ideal. Romanticized brother–sister pairs reflect a range of possibilities that American authors imagined for resolving the crisis of individuality and unity, and, in some cases, for regarding such conflict as irresolvable and endemic to familial (and, by extension, national) affiliation. With their spotlight on sibling pairs, which are more central than the traditional courting couples of their domestic plots, the fictional works this study identifies as "sibling romance" novels engage the social exigencies of sectionalism, loyalty, and national and racial identity formation that preoccupied the culture of the United States in the nineteenth century. While some of the sibling romance novels of this study perform that engagement more overtly than others, the basic striving for affiliation amid difference and separation serves as a constant backdrop to sibling representations in this fraught era of identity building. In many ways, sibling romance novels support, but also complicate, the national project that Peter Coviello calls the "dream of affiliation," in which whiteness in antebellum fiction gestures toward a "state of being-in-relation, a way of being attached ... a quality of inborn connectedness to others" (4).[10]

Historically, correspondence between real siblings reveals the intensity of their interdependence, as they counted on each other to navigate such key social imperatives as developing friendships, responding to authority, collaborating and competing with others, and balancing the boundaries of dependence and independence.[11] American discourse traditions reflected and reinforced such social importance of sibling love. Even such early and significant shapers of Euro-American affiliation as John Winthrop invoked the egalitarianism and mutuality of brotherly love and cooperation in his famous exhortation to his fellow Puritans on board the Arbella in 1630 that they "must entertain each other in brotherly affection" in order to realize the dream of forming a "city upon a hill." But

Winthrop's hint of a lateral design for social order only anticipates the large-scale discursive shift that would take place just after the Revolution, when the "new political and economic systems of the United States... led Americans to dispense with hierarchical metaphors for world order and embrace the ideal of equality."[12]

C. Dallett Hemphill locates in post-Revolutionary discourse, particularly in the proliferation of advice literature of that era, the emergence of the significant sibling spotlight in American culture, a tradition that would become engrained and passed down from generation to generation through literary and social experiences throughout the nineteenth century. Given the special attention to sibling love and solidarity in domestic advice books and children's literature, a trend I will explore in the next chapter, the writers of antebellum domestic fiction could count on their contemporary readers to recognize the codes of sibling love, and to identify and sympathize with brother–sister pairs, making that mode of affiliation an especially powerful and salient device for imagining civic unions. As brothers and sisters increasingly had separate expectations and lives by the middle third of the century, reflecting the culture's escalating gender differentiation, social and discursive traditions stipulated reciprocal edification between opposite-sex siblings, a system that demanded, basically, protection from brothers, moral guidance and domestic servitude from sisters, and a solid pact of mutual confidence between a brother and a sister.[13]

Brother–sister bonds apparently held more cultural weight in family governance than same-sex sibling dynamics, and the reason for that special interest in opposite-sex siblings has to do with increasing gender differentiation. Rotundo explains that the reinforcement of gender inequality counterbalanced the reciprocity of the brother–sister dynamic: "The girls became accustomed to serving their brothers, and grew reliant on fraternal protection in dealing with the world; as they did so, many developed a habit of adoration toward their brothers." In turn, the brothers who were accustomed to protecting their sisters and receiving their adoration in return, "developed that sense of loving, fraternal consideration which their parents had hoped to breed in them" (94). The result of this social fixation on opposite-sex sibling love, for Rotundo, was that it "taught inequality and encouraged love at the same time, and nurtured a separation of the sexes even as it fostered intimacy between them" (95). Hemphill traces the emergence of prescriptive ideology for opposite-sex sibling dynamics specifically to the antebellum era, when "along with the rise of the general cultural ideology of male and female spheres, a sense of strongly gendered but complementary brother and sister roles had emerged in conduct literature." Hemphill interprets this surge of interest in the mutually reinforcing codes for brothers and sisters as a sign that "democratic culture allowed Americans to embrace and celebrate sibling relations as never before" (130). The emphasis on opposite-sex sibling love the emphasis on opposite-sex sibling love that would develop a ubiquitous presence in the antebellum United States manifested not only in public discourses, but also in private writing, where it appears that actual brothers and sisters closely conformed to the social ideal for sibling love. Whether reinforcing the expectations of sibling solidarity and reciprocity, or exposing the consequences of breaches of those codes, or even navigating the nuances of sibling attachment in relation to filial duty, fiction of the nineteenth century frequently adopted sibling love as a mode of exploring a range of possibilities for social order, which have particular significance within historical contexts of national crisis.

Given the emphasis on sibling love in the nineteenth century[14]—both in the real lives of siblings and in cultural representations—it stands to reason that novels of the family would often feature prominent sibling couples. Steven Mintz has argued that throughout the nineteenth century, "in a period of rampant change, fluidity, and self-seeking, the bonds between siblings acquired enormous symbolic significance as a tangible representation of duty, unity, and continuity" (*A Prison of Expectations*, 149). Mintz suggests the sibling representations of the nineteenth century as a site of cultural preservation of intimacy, loyalty, and duty, in the face of increasing individualism. Indeed, the sibling bond has the capacity to represent stability, belonging, and coherence in a world fraught with the paradox of individual identity struggles on one hand and the anxious longing for affiliation on the other, but I contend that fictional siblings themselves often reify the nuance and conflict that typifies the tumultuous culture of nineteenth-century America. While the sibling pairs of nineteenth-century American fiction typically performed an idealized and reciprocal love and devotion, theirs was a love as fraught as their contemporary worlds were with the struggles to achieve individual and social identity, to negotiate the terms of their affiliation to each other and to their social worlds, and experience self-identification without annihilating their own quests for distinct identities.

Having exhausted the trope of rebellious children overthrowing the tyranny of patriarchal parents during the epoch of the revolution, the nation-sustaining Americans turned to the lateral dynamic of brothers and sisters to resolve the crisis of their identities, attachments, obligations, and filial duties. As a more apt paradigm for civil relations during the era of national identity building, the sibling dynamic provided a fitting site for civic-minded writers to imagine the sort of egalitarian social order they found in the anti-paternalism of enlightenment philosophy. Ubiquitously influential on American civic ideology during and after the Revolution, the educational philosophies of John Locke encouraged affectionate, noncoercive governance, both of families and of nations, as an alternative to patriarchal paternalism. Locke's consent-based model of social order, especially as he articulates it in his two works *Essay Concerning Human Understanding* and *Some Thoughts Concerning Education*, not only shaped polemical discourses of the new nation, but was also widely disseminated among early American didactic fiction and children's literature.[15] Absorbing Locke's theories into literary tradition, early Americans naturalized and idealized the idea of the independent child, especially in relation to the appropriate limits of parental authority. When Gillian Brown points out that, "[r]ather than standing as the conceptual figure that Locke imagines, the consensual child quickly becomes a literal entity, being endowed with the full capacities and rights of self-determination" (24), she engages the profound cultural legacy of Locke's consent theory, which denied the natural authority of parents and extended agency to the individual child. The unprecedented emphasis the Lockean parenting model placed on parental affection and solicitude for children posed a potential conflict, though, with the philosophy's emphasis on raising children to be independent-minded and self-defining citizens.[16] The paradox thus presented at the very ideological root of the family-as-nation paradigm, as well as of models for American familial and national governance, would furnish a fundamental crisis for domestic fiction, a riddle that would come to dominate not only literary and social studies, but also psychological discourse: How can the family serve as a site of engendering attachment, belonging, affiliation, and conformity on the one hand, and developing and nurturing individual identities and self-consciousness on the other?

While literary studies have tended to limit the scope of their inquiry into this historical controversy to depictions of parent–child dynamics, nineteenth-century American authors located among the lateral dynamics of siblings the capacity for imagining, and sometimes for resolving, the tensions between independence and solidarity. Ideally, siblings could identify with one another without the question of subservience, they could remain loyal to one another while seeking independent paths, and they could practice an unbounded and lifelong mutual affection while pledging affection and loyalty to others. Such an egalitarian union of the most intimate and authentic affiliation that nevertheless accommodates individualism presented fiction writers with a representational opportunity rich with exigency to the fraught political and social experiences of antebellum and postbellum America. Sibling love would retain its civic relevance as the nation faced the crisis of sectionalism in the middle third of the century and the challenges of recuperation late in the century. While sibling affiliation would come closer to an egalitarian ideal than parent–child, it would continue to present such conundrums as the boundaries of individual autonomy and the terms of loyalty. Even the ideal paradigm of a lateral bond would leave negotiations of identity, power, and agency open to the American literary imagination.

While Locke's antipaternalism harmonized with the egalitarian potential of sibling affiliation, Enlightenment thinking was not the only philosophical influence on the sibling fixation of the nineteenth century. Hegel's philosophy of the brother–sister dynamic and its role in shaping civic relations provides another key context for understanding fictional representations of sibling love.[17] Establishing principles of gender difference and consciousness development that dominated philosophical debate over the last two centuries,[18] Hegel's *Phenomenology of Mind* (1807) posits the supremacy of opposite-sex sibling love in a section titled "The Ethical Relation of Man and Woman as Brother and Sister." For Hegel, the brother–sister relation provides the highest realization of familial ethicality because it is neither contingent nor voluntary, as the marriage relationship is.[19] Hegel would turn to the most classical literary figure of sister love, Sophocles's Antigone, as a source for his influential theories of the ethical scope of familial duty as well as of gender difference.[20] Daughter of the accidentally incestuous bond between Oedipus and Jocasta, Antigone rebels against the tyrannical Creon, her maternal uncle, by burying the body of her brother, Polyneices. Defying Creon's injunction to deprive Polyneices of a proper burial and leave his body exposed as posthumous punishment for his treason, Antigone twice buries her brother. Antigone's repeated rebellion serves to perpetuate the familial and political crisis, including the sacrifice of her own marriage to her fiancé, Haemon, the son of Creon. Given her selfless devotion to her brother and defiance of her king, Antigone represents a model of familial loyalty on one hand, and radical social rebellion on the other, making her an apt interpretive subject in the midst of such conflicting social movements as the rise of individual rights and the increasing relegation of women to the domestic sphere.

The Hegelian understanding of gender difference rests upon an interpretation of Antigone's rebellion as essentially unreflective and apolitical.[21] Most importantly, Hegel's reading of Antigone asserts the sister figure's lack of consciousness, an impossible gesture should the interpretive agency shift from her loyalty to her brother and God to her active rebellion against her uncle and king, or even should the very categories of lateral and vertical affiliation shift to accommodate the chaos of an identity that occupies the spaces of both a sister and a daughter of Oedipus. For Hegel, Antigone serves as the epitome of sisterly loyalty, circumscribed to a space of unconscious and unreflective devotion to her brother's honor and to her pious observation of religious rite and ritual. Hegel's denial of Antigone's independent consciousness is crucial to the long-standing presumption of feminine passivity, especially as a requisite sacrifice for the development of the active male psyche.

The way that Hegel understands the key differences between brother and sister, and of their interrelatedness, or "equilibrium," justifies the separating of genders for the family and the nation in the nineteenth century, an especially crucial rationale for experiments in democracy struggling to locate the conditions of independence. Central to Hegel's explanation of an ethical life modeled in the family is the sister's lack of consciousness, a phenomenon he deems essential to the formation of her brother's individual identity. The conundrum of the family, then—the very puzzle psychoanalysis would take up a century later with Hegel's legacy at the center of its gaze—is that it both demands its members' loyalty and attachment in order to ensure their safe and insulated development and invests its subjects with the right and obligation to detach in order to participate functionally in the world outside of it. For Hegel, the sister figure serves as a safe and static deposit for her brother's ethical welfare, and her lack of individual consciousness spares her from the developed detachment expected of her brother. Devoid of the interference of her own consciousness, the sister stabilizes and sustains the ethical capacity of the nuclear family.

The achievement of mutual identification and attachment demanded for the successful development of the brother's consciousness hinges upon the absence of passion in sibling love, as "the moment of individual selfhood, recognizing and being recognized, can here assert its right, because it is bound up with the balance and equilibrium resulting from their being of the same blood, and from their being related in a way that involves no mutual desire" (477). The incest taboo, therefore, assures the secure development of the "individual selfhood" presumed to depend upon the siblings' capacity for mutual identification.[22] The ultimate performance and outcome of that reciprocal attachment and identification nevertheless is reserved for the brother's development. The pervasiveness of this notion of the brother's necessary detachment from his sister, and the mandatory condition of siblings' abandonment of mutual desire for the attainment of such self-consciousness, makes literary depictions of opposite-sex enmeshment and violence particularly significant; I will explore that line of inquiry in my analysis of the dysfunctional siblings of

Hentz's *Ernest Linwood*, a novel that emphatically situates its title character's stunted psychological development within the context of his sibling attachment.

Hegel's invocation of Antigone resonates with American audiences, who were captivated by this classical Greek tragedy and highly invested in interpreting it.[23] Paradoxically revolutionary in her subversion of her uncle-king's authority and conservative in her familial devotion, Antigone's appeal for antebellum American audiences lies in her capacity for representing radically opposing social agendas during an era burdened with contradictions over the balance of independence and authority and the role that family and gender could potentially play in resolving (or foreclosing) those conflicts. Indeed, the timeless controversy over Antigone's role (that is, whether it signifies the familial devotion and piety appropriate to her gender, or whether it reflects an act of independence and rebellion that defies conservative femininity) epitomizes the power of literary interpretation. The stakes of this particular interpretive war were especially high for nineteenth-century Americans struggling to define the relationship between individual rights and social obligations, with gender circumscription squarely at the heart of those discursive battles. While celebrating the Sophoclean plays as an exemplary body of democratic national literature, American commentators interpreted within more conservative margins Antigone's rebellion against her king.[24] That is, American editors and reviewers cast the heroine according to their standards for the ideal woman—self-abnegating, pious, and devoted to her family at all costs, including the cost of disobeying her king. Both catering to and perpetuating the nineteenth-century American value systems that restricted women from political activity,[25] these writers insisted that Antigone's actions were apolitical, and that the heroine "dragged herself into conflict with the state with extreme reluctance, only when it threatened family and conscience" (Winterer 78). The evidence that Antigone was perceived by antebellum Americans as both the product of an ideal democracy and an exemplary apolitical woman signifies the cultural potential of the sibling bond in domestic fiction, particularly in politicized domestic fiction, of the same time period in America.

Over and over again, the bold sisters of domestic fiction would provoke apathetic or anxious brothers to political and militant activity, while remaining dutifully attached to home, family, and especially fathers. Nevertheless, just as American perspectives would insist upon the apolitical character of Antigone's rebellion, reviewers of antebellum domestic fiction cautiously posited similarly conservative interpretations of the most radically rebellious sister figures to appear in American novels. None other than Edgar Allen Poe, arguably the most influential critical voice to assess Southern antebellum fiction, asserts such an interpretation of Mildred Lindsey, the militant heroine of John Pendleton Kennedy's 1835 *Horse-Shoe Robinson*, a Revolutionary War novel that engages the historic moment of South Carolina's threatened secession from the Union during the Nullification Crisis. Despite sister Mildred's outright rebellion against her Tory father via her surreptitious training of her younger brother for service in the Continental Army and her secret marriage to a patriot soldier despised by her father, Poe claims that, "Mildred Lindsay, in her confiding love, in her filial reverence, in her heroic espousal of the revolutionary cause, not because she approved it, but because it was her lover's, is an admirable and—need we say more?—a truly *feminine* portrait" (523–524; italics in original). Such an oddly placed insistence on the apolitical passivity of "true" femininity—odd in that Poe thus explains the actions of perhaps the most militantly disobedient heroine of antebellum fiction and odd given the novel's repeated use of the label "masculine" to characterize its heroine—suggests both the presumed power of interpretive gestures such as Poe's and the high stakes of characterizing the sister figure's activity. Just as the cultural work of Antigone's rebellion would provide an object of interpretive battleground in the race to define, delimit, and determine enfranchisement and its privileged participants, the dynamics of sibling pairs in domestic fiction suggested social and political possibilities with crucial implications for American civic identity making.[26]

While indeed pervasive, the theory of a sibling equilibrium predicated upon woman's duty to man did not go unchallenged in the nineteenth century. Antebellum philosopher, author, and journalist Margaret Fuller deployed the brother–sister dialectic to reject the notion of masculine superiority in her famous feminist manifesto, *Woman in the Nineteenth Century* (1845).[27] In her argument for the legal enfranchisement of American women, Fuller refutes the general claim that American men will act in the best interests of women, a claim that dates back most familiarly to John Adams's denial to Abigail's plea that he "remember the ladies" in the American Constitution.[28] Fuller insists, "not one man, in the million, shall I say? no, not in the hundred million, can rise above the belief that Woman was made for Man, when such traits as these are daily forced upon the attention, can we feel that Man will always do justice to the interests of Woman?" (25). In her philosophy of equality between the sexes, Fuller repeatedly invokes he concepts of brother and friend as ideal paradigms of opposite-sex relation: "Were thought and feeling once so far elevated that Man should esteem himself the brother and friend, but nowise the lord and tutor, of Woman, were he really bound with her in equal worship, arrangements as to function and employment would be of no consequence" (26–27). She portrays in lateral terms the sort of masculine affiliation that facilitates a woman's growth: "the many men who knew her mind and her life, showed to her confidence as to a brother, gentleness as to a sister" (28). Complaining that the more typical man wants to slow the progress of woman, Fuller turns again to the paradigm of a supportive brother as the preferred model of masculinity: "Man has gone but little way; now he is waiting to see whether Woman can keep step with him; but, instead of calling out, like a good brother, 'You can do it, if you only think so,' ... he often discourages with school-boy brag: 'Girls can't do that; girls can't play ball' " (33). Further, her examples of best-case scenarios for married life all conform to brother–sister equality. Mary Wollstonecraft and William Godwin, for instance, represent an ideal marriage, for "The champion of the Rights of Woman found, in Godwin, one who would plead that cause like a brother.... He acted, as he wrote, like a brother" (63). In an especially pointed demand for sympathetic equality between the sexes, Fuller points out the cultural implications of famous French feminist George Sand's (aka, Amantine Dupin, later Baroness Dudevant) adoption of a male name and identity: "George Sand smokes, wears male attire, wishes to be addressed as "Mon frere;"— perhaps, if she found those who were as brothers indeed, she would not care whether she were brother or sister" (63).

Like Hegel, Fuller looks to brother–sister dynamics in ancient Greek art and literature to understand gender difference. But Fuller's theory presumes equilibrium premised on equality and balance in the sibling dynamic, an interpretation of brother–sister potential certainly at odds with the Hegelian theory of sibling equilibrium. As symbolic of such an ideal, she describes "a zodiac of the busts of gods and goddesses, arranged in pairs. The circle breathes the music of a heavenly order. Male and female heads are distinct in expression, but equal in beauty, strength and calmness. Each male head is that of a brother and a king,—each female of a sister and a queen. Could the thought thus expressed be lived out, there would be nothing more to be desired. There would be unison in variety, congeniality in difference" (43). Indeed, Fuller even alludes to Antigone in an interpretation that challenges, if indirectly, the more pervasive one offered by Hegel. As sisters, and not wives, Iphigenia and Antigone represent for Fuller the purest ideal of woman's potential: "you did not love on earth; for the poets wished to show us the force of woman's nature, virgin and unbiased." Lamenting that the materialistic culture of her own era precluded such feminine strength, she asks, "Were brothers so dear, then, Antigone? We have no brothers" (185). In keeping with her rhetorical insistence that nineteenth-century woman's social equality would demand a drastic reform of society's assumptions about gender difference, Fuller's interpretation of femininity in Sophocles and Euripides emphasizes the fraternal equality that she reads as inspiring the actions of the Greek heroines—a "brotherly" open-mindedness about female agency that she bemoaned as absent in her own society. "Iphigenia! Antigone! you were worthy to live! We are fallen on evil times, my sisters! our feelings have been checked; our thoughts questioned; our forms dwarfed and defaced by a bad nurture. Yet hearts, like yours, are in our breasts, living, if unawakened; and our minds are capable of the same resolves" (185).

Turning to the brother and sister relationship for a model of lateral equality, Fuller urges enfranchisement for women, insisting "[t]hat now the time has come when a clearer vision and better action are possible— when Man and Woman may regard one another as brother and sister, the pillars of one porch, the priests of one worship" (157). In Fuller's alternative understanding of men and women as brothers and sisters lies a compelling exception that affirms the pervasiveness of sibling love to competing theories of gender and of individual and social development. Hegel's engagement with Antigone as the most classic literary representation of a sister's love for her brother, his assumptions about the limited and subservient capacity of woman's role in the family and in society, and his controversial application of the brother–sister dynamic in perpetuation of the separation of the sexes would continue to be salient theoretical assumptions in nineteenth-century American intellectual discourse.

With its ubiquity in art and philosophy, its capacity for representing an egalitarian ideal, and its containment of the psychological paradox of difference and sameness, the brother–sister paradigm had special appeal to nation-conscious novelists in the tumultuous nineteenth century. Take, for example, a significant narrative moment in the 1856 novel *Ernest Linwood* by the popular Southern author Caroline Lee Hentz:

...Edith occupied a low ottoman at [Ernest's] feet. One arm was thrown across his lap, and her eyes were lifted to his face with an expression of the most idolizing affection. And all the while he was talking, his hand passed caressingly over her fair flaxen hair, or lingered amidst its glistening ringlets. It was a beautiful picture of sisterly and fraternal love,—the fairest I had ever seen. The fairest! it was the first, the only one. I had never realized before the exceeding beauty and holiness of this tender tie.

This setting of rapturous affection between a brother and sister would introduce the novel's first-person narrator, the orphaned Gabriella, to sibling love in all its glory. But it would also serve as a context for Gabriella's introduction to the title character, who would become first her adopted brother and then her violently jealous husband. Hentz, best known as the author of the most famous novel of the anti-Tom tradition, *The Planter's Northern Bride*, and for her vehement defense of slavery and of Southern domestic culture in her prolific fiction career, would thus imagine an intricate romantic triangle, at the heart of which lay the rich possibilities for affiliation and crisis contained within sibling love. Especially within the context of her public reputation as a protector of domesticity, Hentz's deployment of the sibling romance trope to expose violent consequences of enmeshed family attachment complicates the author's otherwise narrow legacy.

In their depictions of intense dynamics between brothers and sisters, the sibling romance novels of this study were engaging the discourse of intense sibling bonds advocated throughout the century. The cultural work of disseminating an idealized opposite-sex sibling love throughout the culture occurred largely through such popular genres as domestic advice manuals and children's literature, sites of sibling discourse that I will explore separately in the next chapter. This study looks at novels that portray intense brother–sister dynamics from the antebellum and postbellum eras, because the opposite-sex sibling bond was an apt narrative trope during antebellum sectionalism and throughout the historical struggle to define racial and national identities after Reconstruction. As the central national crisis throughout this long period of tension revolved around the quest for unity and solidarity, the idea of a mutually devoted, supportive, affectionate sibling pair provided writers with a salient familial dynamic for imagining the possibilities and conditions of lateral affiliation and union. The sibling bonds of some of the more nationalistic novels in this study indicate visions of egalitarian harmony and union. Catharine Maria Sedgwick's *The Linwoods*, for example, presents sibling solidarity as an unshakeable force that can inspire a more affectionate and tolerant paternal authority. In other cases even the most ardent sibling attachment would be riddled with dysfunction, suggesting a bleaker outlook on the fate of a union dependent upon lateral solidarity and goodwill. Particularly suspicious of the limitations of brotherly love, especially as it has been historically determined and circumscribed by racial hierarchies, Charles Chesnutt's turn-of-the-century novel *The House Behind the Cedars* suggests the dystopian futility of a brother–sister attachment in the context of a Reconstruction setting. Chesnutt's bleak adoption of the sibling romance trope contrasts contemporaneous race writer Pauline Hopkins's more optimistic version of an early black nationalism that appropriates the historically white-centric terms of lateral affiliation.

Given the relevance of national identity quests and fissures to the literary traditions I examine, the historical circumstances of the national struggle to remain unified—the basic realities of sectionalism and reunification—serve as prominent contexts for the sibling romance tradition. While the century's largest national crisis, the Civil War, certainly was fraught with lateral tension, this study focuses on the sibling love and attachment that had a ubiquitous presence especially during the antebellum struggle to retain national unity amid increasing difference, as well as throughout the sometimes wistful quest to restore a sense of national unity after the failure of Reconstruction. In both the era leading up to the Civil War, and the period following it, national union was an actual, if vulnerable, reality, making the romance of sibling love particularly salient and interesting within those contexts. In the next chapter, my survey of the cultural pedagogy that established sibling love includes some relevant instances of brother–sister attachment in children's Civil War literature, but the remaining eight novels that occupy this study respond to a range of pre–Civil War historical struggles, such as states' rights and slavery debates, as well as post-Reconstruction controversies over racial and national belonging. While the sibling bond often functions metaphorically for nation when read within the context of social crisis, it tends to interrogate and complicate, rather than standardize, the ideas of nation and nationalism. In this way, my interpretations of politicizing sibling romance align with Robert S. Levine's move to "dislocate" the history of nation and race, when he asserts that "[d]uring the nineteenth century, there were numerous and competing nationalisms and no sure sense of which (if any) would become *the* defining nationalism" (241). Therefore, while I seek to place the sibling romance in conversation with historical struggles to locate and define particularly national union, I strive to appreciate and acknowledge the active agency of the literary texts and perspectives themselves, which often defy the neat and tidy compartments of historical narrative. While Kennedy's anti-patriarchal sibling pair may well reflect the staunchly unionist voice that he maintained throughout his entire political career, for example, his novel's remorsefully nostalgic treatment of the siblings' defeated tyrant-father betrays some anxiety over the conditions and consequences of a reformed South.

While the family is broadly recognized as a model for representing nation in fiction, intensely attached, enmeshed opposite-sex siblings have particular implications in narratives of family and nation. This book examines novels that develop family and courtship narratives with prominent opposite-sex sibling dynamics that are central to their representations of individual and social identities, the terms and conditions of affiliation within and beyond the sibling bond, and the crisis that ensues with the urge to identify and belong while self-determining and distinguishing. I suggest that, by significantly shifting the romantic focus of their narratives from courtship to sibling attachment, these novels respond and contribute to historical and literary conversations about affiliation in the context of national union and crisis in antebellum and postbellum America.

The usual site of sibling attention in literary criticism has been gothic romance, whose incestuous siblings have provided a wealth of representational material for psychoanalytic discovery.[29] The scope of this book includes the tradition of popular, domestic fiction, often overtly propagandist, which reveals the exigencies of sibling attachment to the crisis of identity in the new nation. I examine sibling plots in domestic, sentimental novels, a tradition with a diminished legacy in American literary history. This nearly exclusive treatment of non-canonical works contends that the tradition of popular domestic fiction establishes cultural relevance as well as literary modes that should impact critical understandings of such canonical legacies as Poe's Usher siblings, Melville's incestuous Pierre and Isabel, Hawthorne's Clifford and Hepzibah Pyncheon, and even Faulkner's Compson family dynamics and Toni Morrison's recurring narrative attention to sisterhood and siblinghood. My epilogue suggests that those celebrated stories of attachment and violence among brothers and sisters have a lineage rooted in the sibling romance plots from the sentimental tradition, especially given the firm ground domestic novels would establish for the capacity of brother–sister dynamics to capture and respond to social identity quests in a democratic society. As both a metaphor and an institution, the family has represented an apt mode for fiction writers to engage in identity debates, and the sentimental treatment of the core sibling dyad would contribute significantly to the social potential of literature.

This book engages methods of historical, theoretical, and literary analysis to pursue its analysis of the social and political significance of sibling representations in nineteenth-century American fiction. I examine primary sources to establish two key contextual frameworks: the prevalence and definitions of the brother–sister ideal and the particular national crises that the different novels of this study engage. As this is predominantly a work of literary studies, throughout the book I engage various theoretical lenses to respond to the exigencies of close reading. Whereas some novels' more overt engagement with political upheaval warrants a thorough historicizing of their response to national crisis, a psychoanalytical approach teases out the significance of sibling love in the more subtly politicized works. By acknowledging psychological alongside historical implications of sibling love, I seek to destabilize such typically static critical categories as genre and identity; I will consider how "women's fiction" often dwells compellingly on the psychological self while also engaging the exigencies of the social world, and how such classic traditions as the historical novel could contain overt, if conflicted, social responses, even while contributing to a transcendent literary tradition. Also, depending upon a given novel's stature in literary history, more or less attention is devoted to such essential close reading tasks as explicating plots and analyzing characters, as well as to situating works within the context of literary traditions. While all of the novels included in this study were well known in their day, most of them, particularly the Southern antebellum works (Kennedy's *Horseshoe Robinson* and William Gilmore Simms's *The Partisan* in Chapter 2 and Hentz's *Ernest Linwood* in Chapter 3), have been destined to relative obscurity in the history of American literary studies. Individual chapters, therefore, vary in the extent to which they engage historicism, psychoanalytical and philosophical lenses, and close reading. The important constant is the book's insistence on the capacity of fiction to complement and complicate our understanding of affiliation and crisis in American literary and cultural history.

While *The Sibling Romance* focuses mostly on the relationship between fiction and history, the legacy of psychoanalytical theory plays two important roles in this study: it provides exigency for the recovery of sibling romance in novels of family and nation, and it offers a lens for considering the potential motivations, implications, and consequences of lateral love. The need for this book in the twenty-first century stems at least partly from the enduring cultural fixation on parents' influence over their children and on children's rebellion against that influence, a fixation at the cost of acknowledging and understanding the historical, social, and psychological implications of lateral affiliation. To a large extent, the preoccupation with parent–child paradigms across all fields of twentieth-century discourse can be explained by the tenacious legacy of vertically aligned psychological inquiry and heightened individualism.[30] With its ubiquitous inquiry into the implications of the "Oedipus complex," the tradition of understanding the human psyche has been universally occupied by this masculine-centric point of view. As Juliet Mitchell recently hypothesized in her revisionist psychoanalytic study, *Siblings, Sex, and Violence,* "... the dominance or near-exclusiveness of our vertical paradigm has arisen because human social and individual psychology has been understood from the side of man." Shifting the object of study from parent–child to sibling psychology, Mitchell insists, restores critical attention to femininity, just as, for instance, "Sibling relations prioritize experiences such as the fear of annihilation, a fear associated with girls, in contrast to the male fear of castration. They involve fear of the loss of love which is usually associated with girls; an excessive narcissism which needs to be confirmed by being the object, not subject, of love. Siblings and femininity have a similar overlooked destiny" (3–4).[31] Similarly, I believe that shifting the interpretive focus of fictional families from parent–child to the sibling couple will bring to the fore the imagined potential, limitations, and negotiations of female agency within lateral dynamics, in particular, as well as other areas of psychological and social activity and representations that vertically aligned approaches may fail to make visible. By examining the implications of opposite-sex sibling pairs in fiction, I hope to assert the importance of a major family romance trope—the sibling bond—to our understanding of nineteenth-century efforts to grapple with the crisis of individual identity and social responsibility. That writers would turn to the lateral dynamic to resolve (or, to expose or dramatize) the conflicting priorities of attachment and independence reveals the frustrating limitations of the hierarchical paradigm of parent–child, which, by the antebellum era, had worn out its immediate salience for many socially engaged American imaginations.

While most of this book focuses on examples of sibling romance novels—that is, novels that portray sibling couples as their central character dynamic—it begins with a chapter that examines the pedagogy of sibling love in nineteenth-century America. The popularization of codes and expectations for sibling love establishes an important context for the exigency of sibling romance novels. Chapter 1, therefore, examines the brother–sister ideal as it was disseminated in domestic advice manuals and children's periodical literature. The prolific representations of values related to opposite-sex sibling dynamics reveal the cultural investment in mutual obligations, duties, and attachment between brothers and sisters. The widespread pedagogy of sibling love in the nineteenth century meant that writers of politicized domestic fiction could depend upon their readers' shared sense of the importance of the bonds between brothers and sisters, giving that dynamic a powerful rhetorical salience.

Chapter 2 embarks on the sibling romance novel tradition by exploring the remarkable presence of sibling pairs in three novels of the Revolutionary War, all published in 1835, all adapting Walter Scott's historical novel to an American version of the genre, and all arguably resonating with and responsive to the contemporary crisis of the Nullification Controversy, in which South Carolina's threat to secede from the Union presented the biggest public spectacle of national disunion prior to the Civil War. The Revolutionary novels of Catharine Maria

Sedgwick, John Pendleton Kennedy, and William Gilmore Simms engage the widespread anxiety over the balance between individual rights and the limits of justified authority that was dramatized in the states' rights debates during the 1830s and throughout the entire antebellum period. That brother–sister dynamics occupy the central position of their novels' interventions in that historic crisis underscores the rising relevance of that lateral dynamic in the American imagination at the time. As states struggled to determine and protect their independent identities and rights while preserving their attachment to the national union, sibling solidarity would provide antebellum authors an apt model for imagining the capacity, limitations, and conditions of filial loyalty and lateral identification.

Chapter 3 turns to a mostly neglected novel, which, while less overt in its social engagement than the three Revolutionary War sibling romances, nevertheless contributes compellingly to the spectrum of fictional sibling love in the context of crisis and affiliation. The sibling love and violence that dominates Caroline Lee Hentz's *Ernest Linwood* suggests the darker implications of lateral enmeshment, with special historical significance given the author's legendary investment in Southern family and culture. Most notorious for her famous fictional apologias for Southern domesticity, Hentz would produce, in her 1856 novel *Ernest Linwood*, a remarkable portrayal of the violent implications of manic and unrestricted lateral attachment. Although not directly engaging in the context of the growing sectional division, given her otherwise explicit and staunch defense of slavery and Southern family (her novel, *The Planter's Northern Bride* continues to be the most famous of the anti-Tom tradition), the compelling narrative of sibling love, sexuality, and violence that she develops in one of her only novels to eschew direct political or social agenda provides this study with an opportunity to delve into the capacity for domestic fiction to reflect the psychological complexities and implications of individualism and attachment. Read within the context of the writer's famed anxiety to preserve the dying patriarchal culture of the South, *Ernest Linwood* presents a bleak outlook upon a laterally aligned social order that fosters jealousy, dysfunction, and violence, and that is nevertheless inevitable.

Returning to a more overt response to national crisis, Chapter 4 examines the significant mixed-race sibling dynamics of Harriet Beecher Stowe's second abolitionist novel, *Dred* (1856). In that chapter, I suggest that, by extending the exclusive lateral bond of siblings to a white mistress and her half-brother and slave, Stowe responds to critiques of the strict parameters of nuclear family and race in her *Uncle Tom's Cabin* and attempts to complicate the legacy of her representations of family and race. *Dred* represents an early model of the potential for the sibling romance trope to expose the very presumptions of union and solidarity, a lateral affiliation that was typically affirmed in antebellum America, setting the stage for alternative and competing constructions of race and family that would come later in the century, with the growing tradition of African American literary voices.

While Stowe's effort to introduce mixed-race family lineage to the discourse on American domesticity was indeed provocative, it would not be until African American writers participated fully in the project of representing nation, family, and race that the very sibling bond trope that epitomized white national union in the antebellum era would serve to expose its costs and limitations in the period after Reconstruction. Chapter 5 demonstrates how three postbellum African American writers, Frances E. W. Harper, Pauline Hopkins, and Charles Chesnutt, appropriated the trope of sibling love to resituate the project of Reconstruction as one that centers on African American affiliation and to criticize the limitations of (white) brotherly love in Jim Crow America. In this chapter, I argue that the sibling union trope, as it appears in fiction by African American writers, reveals the complications of civility in post-Reconstruction America. Harper's *Iola Leroy* (1892), Chesnutt's *The House Behind the Cedars* (1900), and Hopkins's *Contending Forces* (1900) each adopt the romantic sibling trope to imagine the possibilities for recuperation, reunion, and reconstruction. In response to white-centered visions of a Reconstruction movement that would reunite North and South at the expense of the civil rights of ex-slaves, African-American-authored romances of Reconstruction adopt the sibling trope as a nucleus not of (white) national union, but of black-centric consanguinity, solidarity, and nationalism. Concluding this study of the ways in which fiction writers deployed the romance of sibling attachment to respond to national crisis, the final chapter will close with Hopkins's representation of siblings at the heart of a black nationalistic movement, a gesture that intervenes in the project of white national identity making, which Peter Coviello has recently articulated as a "dream of affiliation," which he locates in the "sudden rise of whiteness as a vehicle for ... nationalist intimacy" (7). If, as Coviello suggests, antebellum writers of nation adopted "whiteness ... as a premier vehicle for the nation's unifying cohesion ... a kind of inborn connectedness between mutually unknown citizens" (27), Hopkins's *Contending Forces* performs a compelling critique of the "poetic dream" of white brotherhood and posits a radically subversive lateral solidarity by highlighting the lineage and struggle of multiple generations of opposite-sex sibling pairs. In suggesting the potential for the sibling bond to challenge racial hegemony and the narrative of white affiliation, Hopkins posits brotherly affiliation as central to black nationalism and, in experimenting with the simultaneously cohesive and disruptive power of the family in fiction, she thus anticipates the far-reaching capacity of the sibling romance trope in American literary and cultural history.

CHAPTER 1

Sibling Pedagogy: The Brother–Sister Ideal in Domestic Advice and Children's Periodical Literature

> What can be a more lovely sight than that of brothers and sisters who truly love one another, and who seek to elevate, adorn, and improve each other?[1]
>
> William Alcott

WITH HIS CLAIM FOR THE UNSURPASSED LOVELINESS of sibling devotion in his 1850 book of advice for American boys, William Alcott, one of the most prolific American domestic educators of the nineteenth century, articulated a social fixation that predominated in advice literature, fiction, and the real lives and correspondence of brothers and sisters in nineteenth-century America. The tradition of American family values discourse that emerged with unprecedented emphasis throughout the nineteenth century placed a special spotlight on sibling dynamics. As the trope of tyrannical parents and rebellious children that dominated Revolutionary discourse wore out its salience in the era of national identity building, an era more conducive to the antipaternalism and egalitarianism of Enlightenment thinking, American discourse increasingly invoked the lateral dynamic of brothers and sisters to resolve crises of identities, attachments, obligations, and filial duties. At once evocative of sameness (generational, familial, biological, cultural, and hierarchical) and difference (namely, and significantly, gender), the opposite-sex sibling pair presents the richest potential within the family for interrogating the extent and boundaries of individual identities and their bonds and duties to others. It is the goal of this book to demonstrate how American writers, especially from the antebellum era through the movement of the African American nadir, seized upon that potential in their fiction. Beyond its capacity for allegorizing social and political identities and dynamics in fiction, representations of the love between brothers and sisters had a resounding role in the moralizing discourse of domestic instruction as well. In this chapter, I will trace the popular dissemination of ideal sibling love through the traditions of domestic advice manuals and children's periodical literature, genres that share a widespread popularity and appeal, as well as a rich capacity for disciplining family dynamics. The sibling pedagogy that emerges in these prolific fields of discourse establishes the cultural salience and rhetorical appeal of the sibling affiliation that writers of American fiction would seize upon in their depictions of lateral affiliation.

"Now, my young friends, be 'what a sister should be'": The Ideal Opposite-Sex Sibling Bond in Domestic Advice Literature

When they imagined American civic and social relationships through the paradigm of sibling dynamics, writers of nationalizing domestic fiction were tapping into a family ideology widely articulated in the advice literature of the day. In their depictions of intensely attached and mutually devoted brothers and sisters, nineteenth-century novels reflected a cultural trend that posited the opposite-sex sibling pair as the ideal, reciprocal, and unsullied social dynamic.[2] The popular genre of domestic advice literature gave special attention to codes of conduct for opposite-sex siblings throughout the nineteenth century. Resembling the traditional heteronormative marriage values of the day, the advice to young adults often defined the brother's responsibility to protect and serve his sister, and the sister's duty to confide in and depend upon her brother. As Hemphill has established in her history of siblings in America, "By the 1830s, brothers and sisters were advised directly to spend time with and confide in each other, and that they were properly a great influence on each other." The antebellum advice for siblings encouraged young men to protect their sisters and asserted as a particular charge to young women the moral improvement of her brothers. Brother–sister pairs were raised to practice the sort of dynamic they were to aspire to as married adults, as their sibling relationship allowed children to test their skills and feelings in an intense, affectionate relationship with the opposite sex.[3] Mintz attributes the cultural trend of encouraging marriage-like closeness between siblings to the reality that, as the typical marriage age was increasingly older due to socioeconomic pressures, many Victorian parents would not live to see their children married and settled into adulthood, and were therefore anxious to foster sibling solidarity to ensure familial support. Mintz also points to "the ethic of purity that discouraged early love affairs," as well as the tradition of educating children at home, which placed siblings in constant contact and fostered their intellectual and emotional attachment to one another.[4] Particularly given that the literature for American children historically reflects a strong attachment to Lockean principles for consent-based and antipatriarchal governance and education, the emphasis on sibling love presented a fitting opportunity to reinforce egalitarian dynamics, solidarity, and cooperation.[5]

That some of the most popular and prolific writers of domestic fiction also contributed to the growing discourse of family conduct reinforces the emphatic role of sibling love in both of those genres. In her historical novel *The Linwoods* (1837), Catharine Maria Sedgwick would allegorize the imminent danger of Southern secession signaled by the historic Nullification crisis of the 1830s in the story of a Revolutionary-era family fraught with a divisiveness that could only be repaired by the passionate attachment between the Linwood brother-and-sister pair. If sibling affiliation would signify the terms of national recuperation in that novel (a reading that I will expand upon in the next chapter), Sedgwick would promote the more practical codes of sibling attachment in her conduct book for young women, *Means and Ends, or Self-training* (1839), in which she presents to her young readers ideal womanhood through the model of a sister's devotion to her brother. In *Means and Ends*, "Mary Bond," the young woman whose manners Sedgwick implores her young readers to emulate, exhibits impeccable industry, conscientiousness, familial devotion, as well as piety in a central chapter that describes Mary nursing her sick brother back to health during their parents' extended absence from home.

By showcasing Mary's devotion to her brother in the setting of a sick room, Sedgwick draws upon a particular expectation that sisters serve their brothers in this capacity. As one of Sedgwick's contemporaries articulated in an 1837 conduct book, "As woman seems formed by nature to execute the offices of a nurse, *sisters should be particularly kind and tender to sick brothers*; for there are few things which tend more to conciliate affection, than sympathy with us in our sufferings, and all those gentle and willing efforts, which, if they cannot mitigate our pains, have such a power to soothe our minds and divert our attention from the sense of suffering."[6] The importance of Mary's competence in this context underscores the exclusivity of her sisterly love and care, as she learns to take full responsibility for her brother's care when all others who take turns as "watchers" risk the invalid's life with their absurd and careless bedside blunders. When even the family doctor declines credit for Raymond's recuperation and admits to the grateful parents that "Raymond owes his recovery to Mary," Raymond's sentimental expostulations affirm the power of his sister's devotion: " 'Oh, mother!' exclaimed Raymond, bursting into tears, 'she is the best sister in the world!' 'She is the best sister in the *two* worlds!' cried little Gracie Bond, a child of five years old." Not only does the main recipient of Mary's loyal and competent care validate her fulfillment of ideal sisterhood, but Mary's success also serves as a model for the younger sister looking on. The moralizing voice of the narrator articulates the broader implications of Mary's conduct: "A source of true comfort and happiness is such a child, and such a sister, as Mary Bond!—a light in her parent's dwelling, and destined to be the central sun of a little system of her own" (140). By practicing her domestic skills, devotion, and selflessness upon her brother, the primary object of her familial love and devotion during her childhood, Mary exhibits her capacity for assuming the role of wife and mother in "a little system of her own" after her eventual separation from her brother.

While the practice of sisterly devotion as training for domesticity was standard enough family pedagogy, Sedgwick returns to Mary Bond, a name rich with affiliation-laden significance, to make a compelling case for the relationship between sibling love and the campaign for women's rights in a chapter titled "Might Makes Right." While she demurs against placing women in some of the higher offices of "man's sphere," claiming that women were never intended to "lead armies, harangue in halls of legislation, bustle up to ballot-boxes, or sit on judicial tribunals," Sedgwick urges her readers to uplift the social status of women through their own intellectual development, which will qualify them for a closer intercourse with the men in their families. Although not quite as radical in her agenda for women's rights as to demand equal enfranchisement to men, Sedgwick advocates for the reform of property rights as well as divorce and custody laws, and she insists upon the importance of women elevating themselves intellectually in order to make private interventions in the public sphere. She asks, " . . . may we not hope there will be less folly and corruption in the places where men most do congregate, when women are so educated, that men may hold more communion on their great social duties with their mothers, wives, and sisters?" (271) It is the last of those familial roles that Sedgwick will draw upon to illustrate for her young readers the power of "women's work" in her extensive example of Mary Bond's capacity for influencing her brother.

In this illustration of a woman's sisterly devotion equipping her to influence her brother's character, Sedgwick explains the ideal mutuality of the relationship between a loving sister and her brother, as the sister who inspires her brother's admiration and respect may count on gaining educational advantages beyond the conventional sphere of womanhood. Her rationale invokes the idea of the supremacy and intensity of sibling love:

> The tenderest friendship existed between [Mary] and her brother Raymond. The love of a brother and sister has been called the only Platonic love; and if by that is meant an affection with the tenderness of love, and the purity and disinterestedness of friendship, it is so. Mary was next to Raymond in age, and they were bound together by that bond of sympathy which often unites particular members of a family, when, not loving the others less, they love each other more. Raymond saw Mary's accurate and intelligent performance of her domestic duties; he saw that nothing in her "woman's sphere" was neglected or slighted. Her habitual, thorough personal neatness, excited his respect, and her delicacy, and the perfect purity of her mind, his reverence.

As a reward for Mary's model execution of domesticity, she shared the masculine privileges of her brother's world: "Mary was not confined to 'woman's sphere.' Raymond, as far as was possible by the communication of letters, participated his studies with her; and, during his vacations, they studied and read together, and talked on those intellectual subjects that most interested him" (272). While not advocating for such social reform as would extend educational access and political agency directly to women, Sedgwick encouraged her young readers to earn access to their brothers' world through the virtue of their domestic prowess, which would render young women, and their domestic sphere, irresistible safe havens to men. "Believe me, my young friends," she insists, "there is no spell of enchantment like that wrought by domestic love" (273).

For Sedgwick, a more important reciprocity a brother could offer his sister than the sharing of his formal education, and an ultimate goal of such domestic pedagogy, is his public-sphere stewardship over the rights of women. Extending her example of Mary Bond's successful application of ideal domesticity to the purpose of securing her brother's love and respect, Sedgwick follows the Bond siblings to their young adulthood, when Mary exhibits her intellectual capacity to manage their father's estate for their widowed mother, while educating and nurturing the younger siblings of the family, "and, in the midst of all these new cares, and multiplied responsibilities, preserving the sweetness and cheerfulness of her temper, the modesty and deference of her manners, and the unpretendingness of her conversation" (273). Sedgwick credits such an impressive balance of domesticity and intellectual capacity with inspiring the brother to act on behalf of women's interests in the public sphere:

> What, think you, was the effect of the conviction of his sister's competency and goodness upon his character, and upon his views of the rights of women? Would he not have a faith in the capabilities of women which no argument could shake, and no ridicule could touch? If called upon to legislate in the matter, would he not maintain a married woman's right to her own property? Would he not allow that she and her husband were equal partners in their pecuniary concerns, and that in case of survivorship, she was competent to manage the property? Would he, above all, deny her right to separate from a tormenting or drunken husband, and to retain the custody of the children she had borne to him? (274)

Taking a more conservative approach than such radical contemporaneous feminists as Margaret Fuller, whose *Woman in the Nineteenth Century* would demand women's right to participate fully in the shaping of public policy, Sedgwick nevertheless uses her domestic advice as a vehicle to advocate for the reform of women's rights in divorce and property cases. Revealing the loaded social significance of her book's title—that is, that domesticity functions as the "means" to the "ends" of women's elevation in society—Sedgwick would turn emphatically to the potential that lies in the affectionate loyalty between a brother and sister for reforming woman's status in the social world.

The example of Mary Bond illustrates that a sister's love represents the power to influence her brother's political righteousness as well as his moral character, crucially interrelated civic virtues for Sedgwick's ideal American man. In their instructions for the mutual obligations between a brother and sister, domestic-advice literature typically places the brother's moral life, especially as it will be reflected in his eventual marriage choice, as a particular charge to his sister. The disciplining voice of Sedgwick's *Means and Ends* asks, "Would a young man who had enjoyed an intimate intercourse with such a sister as Raymond's, be in danger from the allurement of vicious women? Would he not disdain the society of emptyheaded, frivolous, and gossiping girls, and with the image of actual living excellence cut into his heart, would he run the slightest risk of yoking himself to an uneducated girl, however beautiful, high-born, rich and fashionable she might be?" (274). To reinforce her argument for a sister's moral influence over her brother, Sedgwick shares the ostensibly first-hand testimony of a letter from a "college-boy . . . to his sister" (presumably a letter to the author from her own brother), which declares, " 'One who has an affectionate and loveable sister who can sympathise with him, and show an interest in his welfare, has a greater safeguard for his own character, than he ever could create within himself. If all sisters were aware how much power they exert over their brothers, if the sisters of the present day were what they should be, we should see a much higher standard of character and principles among the young men of this generation.' " (274) Imploring her readers to "be 'what a sister should be,' what Mary Bond was, is to her brother," (275) Sedgwick insists that by such means the present generation of women may become "competent to exercise all the rights which your friends claim for you; and when you are thus competent, they will not, as I have said before, long be withheld from you." Despite the militant overtones of her concluding declaration that "Your might will enforce your right," Sedgwick's optimistic estimation of the social power of women's strict application of sibling codes interestingly echoes the conservative rationale for the gradual emancipation of slaves that trickled into abolitionist debates of the same era. Perhaps seizing upon the reciprocal capacity for sibling devotion that she experienced in her own life[7] and represented over and over again in her nationalistic fiction, Sedgwick would reinforce in her conduct literature the social importance of nurturing strong attachments between the brothers and sisters of a family.

As the central figures of the domestic world, siblings represented the potential of the family to inculcate and insulate, a socializing process deemed critical in a nation of self-determining citizenry. In the dynamics parents were to encourage between opposite-sex children lay an opportunity not only for instructing the accepted gender roles and dynamics, but also for perpetuating and protecting the self-contained, insular, private family unit. To that end, domestic manuals urged brothers to protect and serve their sisters, who were in turn expected to depend upon and confide solely in their brothers. Mutuality is the most pressing lesson for this dynamic. As one conduct book author firmly instructs, "*Mutual respect should be shown by brothers and sisters.*" The same author insists that gender difference does not authorize brothers with unchecked power over their sisters: "Brothers ought not, even in lesser matters, to be *tyrants over their sisters*, and expect from them the obsequiousness of slaves."[8] Especially relevant to antebellum fiction writers grappling with an increasingly divided citizenry and striving for a sense of national kinship was the strict confidence domestic advice books typically required between opposite-sex siblings. One domestic conduct book that stresses the importance of mutual sympathy between a brother and sister articulates the role that confidence plays in such mutuality:

> Confide in each other, and be intimate with each other. I do not deem it a beautiful thing when a sister is ready to make a confidant of almost any one rather than her brother; nor for a brother to be more intimate

and confidential with almost any one's sister rather than his own. There should be such an interest shown each in the other that they will be ready mutually to speak and consult about thing which would be confided in no one else. A sister may get the counsel and the help of a brother, when she can, perhaps, properly seek it from no other male friend; and a brother may avail himself of the womanly tact and instinct of a sister, when no other lady friend can be called upon to his assistance. [9]

Also relatable to fiction writers of the day who grappled with models of egalitarian civic consanguinity was the typical domestic advice that positioned the opposite-sex sibling bond above even the hierarchical parent–child dynamic: "Between brothers and sisters there is generally more confidence than between parents and children; and the reason is obvious. A nearer equality of age, a freer intercourse, a unity of pursuits, all conduce to less restraint and more open deportment with each other."[10] As a result of its perceived potential for generating intimacy, confidence, and insularity, the opposite-sex sibling relationship was the subject of much attention and interest, and the prescribed codes for brothers and sisters functioned as both a value system that fiction writers could tap into for rhetorical exigency, credibility, and legitimacy, and a model for nuclear consanguinity that would be especially accessible and adaptable within the tradition of nationalizing domestic fiction.

Echoing Sedgwick's suggestion to young women for their moral influence over their brother, Alcott's *The Young Man's Guide* places special emphasis on the potential for sisters, especially older sisters, to shape the character of young men. In a section titled "Society of Sisters," he instructs, "Try to deserve the character of her friend. She will sometimes look to you for little services, which require strength and agility; let her look up to you for judgment, steadiness and counsel too. You may be mutually beneficial. Your affection, and your intertwining interest in each other's welfare, will hereby be much increased." (220) The mutuality of the brother–sister dynamic Alcott encourages presumes a sister's ability to serve as a moral compass, in exchange for her brother's protection and respect. Alcott explicitly defines the opposite-sex sibling relationship as a vehicle for the moral education and experience of young men, urging his readers to acknowledge and profit from the evaluative and critical perspective of sisters.

> A sister usually present, is that sort of second conscience, which, like the fairy ring, in an old story, pinches the wearer whenever he is doing any thing amiss. Without occasioning so much awe as a mother, or so much reserve as a stranger, her sex, her affection, and the familiarity between you will form a compound of no small value in itself, and of no small influence

if you duly regard it, upon your growing character. Never for one moment suppose *that* a good joke at which a sister blushes, or turns pale, or even looks anxious. If you should not at first perceive what there is in it which is amiss, it will be well worth your while to examine all over again. Perhaps a single glance of her eye will explain your inconsiderateness; and as you value consistency and propriety of conduct, let it put you on your guard. (220)

Alcott's emphasis on the special role that a sister plays in a man's life credits the unique intimacy that exists between siblings. Evoking neither the "awe" of a mother nor the "reserve" of a stranger, a sister may function as a safe relationship for a man to practice relating to the opposite sex, to develop moral values, and to enjoy confidence and trust. For his young male reader, Alcott repeats a commonly held assumption that sisters serve an important social function in relation to the development of a man's character, in addition to, as Hegel would theorize, his psychological consciousness and eventual maturation out of his original family.

Like most antebellum-era domestic instruction regarding a man's duty to the women in his family, Alcott reinforces the assumption that young men should escort and protect their female kin, and he suggests that such practice at home will prepare men for suitably interacting with women in the world. Alcott explains, "There is a sort of attention due to the sex which is best attained by practising at home. Your mother may sometimes require this attention, your sisters still oftener." (221) Urging his readers to attend to their sisters "when their safety, their comfort, or their respectability require it," Alcott rationalizes that "It is their due," presumably for the sacrifice of serving as a second conscience to facilitate their brothers' participation in the world outside of the home. Repeatedly, Alcott couches his advice in terms of how a man can profit from the experience of serving his sister, whether in the development of his social habits or as an impressive reflection upon his own character: "Your sister could, indeed, come home alone, but it would be a sad reflection on you were she obliged to do so. Accustom yourself, then, to wait upon her; it will teach you to wait upon others by and by; and in the meantime, it will give a graceful polish to your character." (221)

Alcott's target audience may account for his framing of the brother–sister dynamic as particularly serving to shape a man's character, but his emphasis on the unique intimacy, mutual confidence, and reciprocity of this bond aptly captures the social assumptions about the importance of brother–sister relationships in nineteenth-century America. Another domestic advice author, Rev. John Angell James, would even extend this typical family instruction to insist that adult brothers and sisters maintain that intense mutual attachment throughout their lives. He promotes regular correspondence between siblings as a method of keeping close during periods of separation. He warns that, "Flames burn brightest in the vicinity of each other. An affectionate letter, received from an absent friend, tends to fan the dying spark of affection. They who can be long separated without such a bond as this, are already in a state of indifference to each other, and are in rapid progress to still wider alienation."[11] He also urges siblings to remain close to each other after the death of their parents, a period in which he fears siblings are at special risk of estrangement. He offers detailed guidelines for how dutiful brothers are to protect their sister's inheritance and "to consider themselves as the natural guardians of unmarried sisters; their advisers in difficulty, their comforters in distress, their protectors in danger, their sincere, tender, liberal, and unchanging friends, amidst all the scenes and vicissitudes of life."[12] Taking his codes for sibling intimacy from early childhood, youth, and adulthood, James's deep interest in the welfare and sustainability of this family bond represents his culture's value for the supremacy of brother–sister attachment.

Sibling Salience in Children's Periodicals

The domestic advice genre derives its cultural impact from its wide net, with its varied audiences of mothers, fathers, and children of both sexes. While the narrower rhetorical situation of children's periodical literature limits its readership, its sharper focus certainly intensifies its moralistic purposes and cultural messages.[13] Children's periodicals serve as an especially significant site of cultural dissemination given their regularity and their proliferation throughout the nineteenth century, and the relationships that thus developed between their contributors, editors, and readers. R. Gordon Kelly points out that publishers of children's periodicals in the second half of the nineteenth century "considered themselves custodians of morals and culture acting in proxy for the nation" (*Mother Was a Lady*, 10).[14] Moreover, the personal relationships that editors fostered with their readers through columns, letters, and even contributions from the young readers themselves fortified the cultural weight and impact of this powerful genre. Michelle H. Phillips has argued that one periodical, the celebrated and long-lived *St. Nicholas Magazine*, even extended the sense of community to the effect of a shared agency between children and the adult producers of the periodical. *St. Nicholas*, Phillips asserts, "invites its readers and contributors, regardless of age, to imagine themselves as members of a hybridized community, capable of inhabiting and communicating across such vast sociological interiors" (85).[15] The intimacy established between the creators and readers of children's periodicals made it an especially rich ground for the promulgation of religious instruction, civic virtue, and family values. Given the salience of the sibling bond to those two parallel social agenda, the frequent and emphatic presence of brothers and sisters in children's periodicals, as signaled by the recurrent representation of a boy and girl, apparently a brother–sister pair, on the covers and mastheads of the magazines (see figures 1.1–1.3), has special significance.

Sibling love furnished the contributors to children's periodicals with a model of affiliation that their young readers could easily relate to, a mode of identification that allowed the genre to connect with the lived experiences of its audience. Given the high rate of infant and childhood mortality, the experience of losing a sibling was all too common for nineteenth-century readers, and contributions to periodicals frequently engage and reflect this intense life moment.[16] Published in 1846 in *The Youth's Companion*, a periodical known for its heavily moralistic content,[17] "A Child's Grief" shares the experience from the point of view of a first-person child narrator, who mourns the death of his infant sister. The narrator establishes his instant attachment to the newborn—"a *"little baby*...a little *sister* for me" (190)—and describes the intimacy of the family, who would gather "round the coal fire in mother's chamber," singing hymns and laying the young narrator down next to the sleeping infant. Such an emphasis on the child's early bond with his little sister may have disrupted any cultural tendency, because of the high rate of infant death, to diminish the significance of a baby's role in the family. At any rate, the narrator shares the lasting impact of this loss, mourning that "I shall never forget my little sister, I do not love to play now, I do not care for my sleds or skates.... Next summer, the flowers will grow again, and so will our honeysuckle vine, and the robins will build their nest in

Figure 1.1   Masthead of *The Youth's Companion* in 1866, illustrating what appears to be a brother and sister sharing the magazine. While the masthead changed many times over the course of the magazine's century-long existence, it usually depicted a brother and sister reading together.

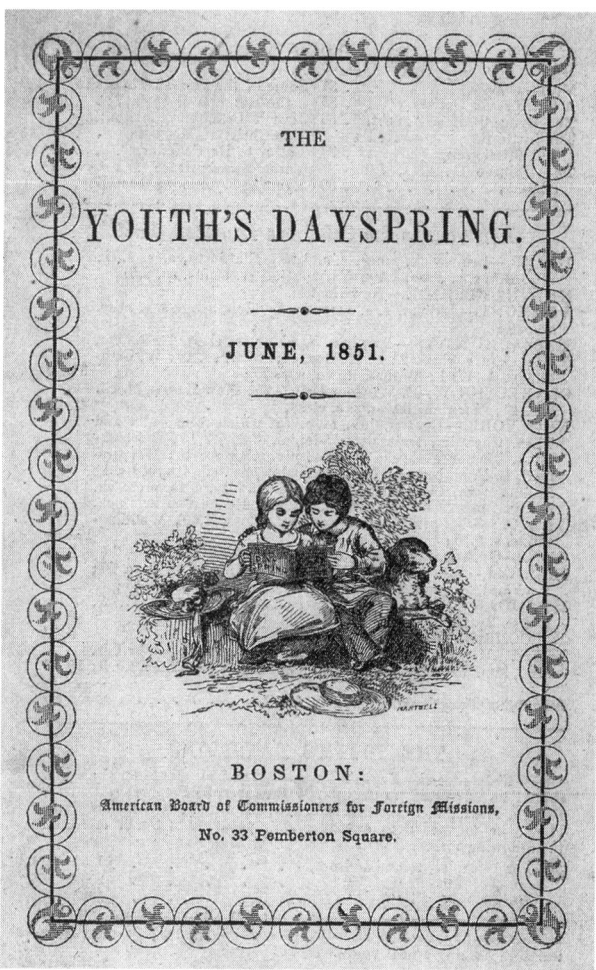

Figure 1.2 The image of a brother and sister leaning upon one another and rapturously pouring over an issue of the magazine, sharing physical space as well as the literacy experience, was an extremely prevalent one on the covers of nineteenth-century children's periodicals. This image is from the cover of *The Youth's Dayspring*, June 1851.

the old pear tree again, but I shall not care for the birds, nor flowers, as I used to." The narrator repeats his pathos-laden declaration "I shall never forget my little sister" three times in this concluding paragraph, dramatically reinforcing the impact of this sibling love and loss to his world and giving expression to the child audience's shared experience with a loss too often diminished or dismissed for the impact it had on surviving siblings.

Figure 1.3 The sibling pair depicted on the illustrated masthead of *Burke's Weekly for Boys and Girls* places the girl figure in the primary reading position, with her brother deferentially sharing the magazine from behind his seated sister, his hands resting on her shoulders.

The loss of a sibling had the capacity to reinforce and test religious faith and devotion, a socializing agenda that retained relevance to children's periodicals even throughout the genre's evolution in the second half of the century. Typifying the role of mourning in children's literature of the era is a story by Charles Dickens, published in *Household Worlds* in 1850 and republished for American audiences in *Merry's Museum* in 1867. An overtly religious tale of sibling mourning, "A Child's Dream of a Star" traces the impact of a sister's death throughout the life span of her surviving brother, whose repeated dreams of his deceased sister's spirit in the image of a star function to mark successive deaths of loved ones whom he imagines joining his sister in the afterlife. The visions of his angel sister follow each death experienced by the brother: first of the sister herself (the brother pines to accompany his departing sister, "Oh, sister, I am here! take me!"); then of another sibling (an infant brother); later, their mother; and eventually, the "maiden daughter" of the man who lost his sister in his childhood. Significantly, while the story's titular "child" ages into an old man, he marks his successive familial losses with his anticipation of his own reunion with his sister, his patience to join her in heaven serving as a testament to his religious faith. With each loss, the angel-sister of his dream asks, "Is my brother come?" and the brother's resignation of another loved one signifies and reinforces his loyalty and faith. Seizing upon the bond that has the most immediate presence and relevance to the periodical's child readers, the story recognizes life's inevitable losses through the lens of the rhetorically exigent sibling attachment. In another example typical of how sibling love may signify an enduring testimony of religious faith, a simple poem published in *Our Young Folks* (1872) shares the narrator's reminiscence, 20 years later, of his "little blue-eyed sister" interceding on his behalf to prevent his beating by a brutal schoolmaster. The narrator reveals his sister's death through a retrospective aside ("O the darling! How we've missed her/ Since she joined the angel band!"), and reflects as a grown man upon her manner of defending him against the teacher's brutality, with "Love illuming every feature" (Howard, 296). Counting on his sister to repeat in heaven her pleading that "Brother dear is good sometimes," the narrator draws upon this sibling connection to reinforce and testify to his faith that "... angels gather /Round the throne of God above,/ Making intersession ever/ For the objects of their love"; (297). That he has cherished the memory of his sister throughout his life qualifies this brother-narrator to expect his sister's "intersession" in the afterlife, an expectation that places the sibling bond at the very center of the spectrum of familial bonds within and beyond the space of a person's life.

The sentimental endorsement of sibling love in children's periodicals reflects the genre's inclusion of domesticity, alongside the competing traditions of sensationalized fiction and adventure stories. Domestic children's literature presented an alternative particularly to codes for masculinity that were embedded in boys' novels. Taking as his example the prolific and popular children's author Lydia Sigourney, Ken Parille traces the nineteenth-century American masculinity to competing traditions of boys' literacy. Parille asserts that "An important theorist of antebellum domesticity, Sigourney conceives of the boy not as a figure who stands in opposition to the domestic sphere and its virtues (as Twain, Aldrich, and others frequently did) but as a critical part of a home-centered value system that endorses masculine self-sacrifice and social obligation" (5). According to Parille, domestic children's authors like Sigourney objected not only to sensational novels, but also to popular histories that tended to sensationalize military glory and present boy readers with unattainable and dangerous heroic ideals. In a significant moment in her own revisionist history of Roman emperor Marcus Aurelius, Sigourney would commend the historical hero's family devotion over his military accomplishments: "when a child, he was...attentive to his mother... [and] when a boy, he was careful to teach and protect his sister" (quoted in Parille, 11). Given the apparent consciousness and vigilance of her pedagogy for boys' literacy, Sigourney's emphasis on family love and duty as an intervention in the masculinizing of American boys reinforces the salience of the sibling bond, which would have had special presence and relevance for children readers, as they had yet to grow up and leave the family fold to embark upon their own independent lives.

Historians of children's periodicals note the impact of the Civil War on the evolution of the genre, especially as editors and contributors would shift their attention from the religious conversion that predominated before the war to the more socially pressing urgencies of educating children about the war and securing their loyalty and participation in the Union effort.[18] Sibling love, particularly sisterly love, dominates the most famous children's Civil War novel, and its author served as a beloved and influential contributor to children's periodicals. *Little Women* exemplifies not only sibling affiliation, but also the tradition in children's literature of representing domesticity and sibling relations in response to the crisis of the Civil War. The resonance of sibling love in children's literature with the era's dominant metaphor for the War—"brother against brother"—is no coincidence.[19] Perhaps somewhat paradoxically, though, the crisis of the nation divided, and its stock allegory as a family divided, seems to have reinforced rather than weakened the exigency of the sibling bond in children's literature. That is, while the metaphorical "family" or "house" of the nation was divided, literature for children emphasized the duties of brothers and sisters to one another as a microcosm of their civic duty. While their father was away at the battle front serving as a Union chaplain, the March sisters of *Little Women* confronted such private challenges as resisting the temptations of vanity and materialism, overcoming passions of anger and jealousy, accepting poverty with dignity, and practicing Christian charity and benevolence. The novel situates the sisters' various trials as the domestic parallel to the Union fight. Famously, Mr. March's letter to his wife in the opening chapter reminds his children that he expects "that they will be loving children to you, will do their duty faithfully, fight their bosom enemies bravely, and conquer themselves so beautifully that when I come back to them I may be fonder and prouder than ever of my little women"; tomboy heroine Jo's response to her father's words reinforces the effect of the parallel, when she reflects "that keeping her temper at home was a much harder task than facing a rebel or two down South," in turn invoking the same metaphor of the Civil War as her father did. Appropriating the war as a metaphor for the challenges of home-life simultaneously legitimizes the social weight of the domestic sphere and feminizes the traditionally male-centered sphere of war, a representational act that conflates or makes interchangeable the categories of family and nation.[20]

While *Little Women*'s emphasis on sibling love in the face of national crisis makes it a compelling contributor to the discursive contexts of the sibling romance,[21] it is not the only site of Alcott's representation of reciprocal sibling devotion in response to the Civil War. Before the serialization of *Little Women* in 1868, Alcott was already an established contributor to the successful new children's magazine, *Our Young Folks: An Illustrated Magazine for Boys and Girls*.[22] Although the first issue appeared just as the war was coming to a close, the Civil War remained alive in the imaginations of the magazine's contributors (a list that included such prominent authors as Harriet Beecher Stowe, John Greenleaf Whittier, Henry Wadsworth Longfellow, and Thomas Bailey Aldrich).[23] Set in the home of a recuperating Union soldier, Alcott's "Nelly's Hospital" showcases the power and reciprocity of sibling love, as the wounded veteran inspires his little sister to establish her own "Sanitary Commission" for sick and injured animals, and little Nelly's charity and perseverance in turn inspire the moral courage and patience of her elder brother. The story's conclusion emphasizes the reciprocal success of the siblings' relationship: "No more idle days for Nelly, or fretful ones for Will, because the little sister would not neglect the helpless creatures so dependent upon her, and the big brother was ashamed to complain after watching the patience of these lesser sufferers, and merrily said he would try to bear his own wound as quietly and bravely as the 'Commodore' [a wounded turtle] bore his" (276). Alcott seizes upon the dual significance of the sibling bond within the context of the Civil War, moralizing not only upon the mutuality and loyalty that brothers and sisters should perform for each other, but also upon the sense of loyalty crucial to a national brotherhood. When Nelly hesitates to rescue a snake, reflecting that "He is a rebel, I wonder if I ought to be good to him," she recalls that "Will said there were sick rebels in his hospital, and one was very kind to him." Having made the righteous decision to save the "rebel" reptile, Nelly "was thoughtful after that, and so busy puzzling her young head about the duty of loving those who hate us, and being kind to those who are disagreeable or unkind" (273). A timely call for Christian charity and benevolence as a premise for national reunification, Alcott's conflation of the story of the national crisis with the mutual bond of a brother and sister reflects a paradigm that would pervade children's literature as much as the other popular discourses of the era.

Perhaps inspired by the enormous popularity of *Little Women*, Mary Greenleaf Darling's *Battles at Home*, serialized in *Merry's Museum* in 1870 before its publication as a book, develops another domestic tale as an allegory for the Civil War.[24] With both parents absent from the narrative, the sibling dynamics in Darling's novel achieve even more emphasis than they did in Alcott's *Little Women*. The novel opens with a minister father's announcement to his five children that he intends to spend a year in Europe in order to recuperate from some vaguely defined illness, and that he can only afford to take along their mother and youngest sister, leaving the four boys behind to fight their own personal battles, that is, the various weaknesses of their own characters. When a passionate Bob, a misunderstood middle child, complains, "I wish I was old enough to go to the war," his father's response reinforces the titular metaphor of this moralizing family story: " 'O, you'll find fighting enough to do at home' " (31). Later, the father's letter to his sons (his "little band of warriors," as he calls them) encourages them to "Fight on, my little soldiers, and let me find that you have gained ground in this year of depending on yourselves" (115). The story proceeds to develop a range of personal conflicts and challenges, all cast in parallel terms to the Union's struggle with Southern rebellion. During the year that they spend at the conspicuously country home ("though so near Boston, it is not at all city-like," 46) of the elderly Osbornes, their maternal grandparents, the Stanley brothers make the acquaintance of their grandfather's ward, Union Colonel Guy Dalton, and his younger sister, a child whose presence virtually replaces the Stanleys' own absent little sister (a narrative device made all the more insistent for the story's double use of the name "Lillie" for both the real and the proxy sister).

While the Stanley brothers each strive for moral improvement throughout the plot of this simple children's tale, the novel's most vivid conflict centers upon Lillie Dalton's "battle" to conquer her passionate nature, an undesirable trait that manifests in her self-centered attachment to her brother. When she suspects her brother's blossoming love for "Sue," her governess and an elder cousin to the Stanleys, Lillie exhibits a most unladylike hostility and jealousy that shame her noble brother. The narrative explains that "when her soldier brother came back to her, the brother whom she had hardly known before, Lillie's ardent fancy made a hero of him, gloried in his wounds and his honors, and secretly idolized him" and that when Lillie "saw, or fancied she saw, that Guy cared for Sue Osborne, her undisciplined little heart was filled with the bitterest jealousy, and she almost hated Sue" (88). Just as Sigourney's domesticity for child readers counters the hero-worship of military histories that she perceived as harmful in the education of American boys, here Darling couches Lillie's most serious flaw, her passionate jealousy, in terms of her misguided glorification of her brother's battle experience. Lillie's "ardent fancy" dangerously distorts her feelings about her brother; instead of maintaining a proper sense of mutual affection and support expected between siblings, she acts upon possessiveness and vain pride of her hero-brother. A crucial narrative device for the explanation of such a dramatic misapplication of sisterly devotion lies in the separation between the brother and sister for most of Lillie's childhood, as she was raised by a materialistic and shallow aunt in the city while her brother's manly character was nurtured in the more morally conscientious and wholesome atmosphere of the Osborne's country homestead.

The narrative marks Lillie's dramatic awakening to the errors of her ways with an outpouring of sentimental remorse and affection that strongly resembles similar dialogues in the sibling romance novels featured in the remaining chapters of this book. Reflecting upon the precariousness of her wounded brother's life, and her own narrowly self-centered behavior, Lillie wondered, "what had she ever done to make him love her?" Overcome with the thought of losing her brother and her remorse for her ill behavior, "she threw herself upon his breast in a perfect storm of sobs and tears." Following Lillie's private outburst, the siblings engage in a sentimental exchange significant for its typical mutuality and reciprocity, signaling an important shift into normative sibling love for this brother and sister:

> "Guidie! O my own dear, dear brother Guy!"
>
> "Why, Lillie, what is all this?" said her brother, feeling the tears start to his own eyes as she clasped him in her arms.
>
> "I wish you wouldn't hate me!" sobbed Lillie.
>
> "And why should I, my dear little sister?" said Guy, getting the troublesome arm out of the way, and putting the other round Lillie." [. . .]
>
> "But you don't care for me," she said, mournfully; "and it is my own fault, because I don't take the best way to make you. But I do love you dearly, and you're all I've got!"
>
> "And you're all I've got—aren't you?" said her brother, playfully, pulling her head down to his shoulder. "But, Lillie, dear, I don't believe we either of us take the best way to make ourselves loved. Can't you try, my little sister, to be less petulant and passionate, and try to *seem* to care for other people as much as I believe you really do? . . . . I know each of us is all the other has; so we ought to take care to make that all a great deal—oughtn't we?" (90–91).

This resolution of the fissured sibling bond concludes with the conventional exchange of physical affection, as "Guy kissed her cheek as he spoke, and Lillie clasped her arm around his neck," and the sibling pair fell asleep in each other's arms. Throughout the remainder of the novel, Lillie's character proceeds to improve under the influence of her brother, who in turn moderates his own gravity and adopts a more expressively affectionate rapport with his younger sister.

After several trials and lessons, Lillie learns how to moderate her passion in response to her brother's loving guidance, and the success of their mutual quest is marked by Lillie's quiet submission to brother Guy's return to the war late in the novel. As a testament to their reformed sibling relationship, a functionally loving brother–sister pair more marginal to the story, Fanny and Jack (cousins of the Stanley boys), serve to parallel and reinforce the Dalton siblings' dynamic. When Jack joins Colonel Dalton's regiment and together the brother figures leave for the war, Fanny and Lillie share a sympathetic bond over their sisterly sacrifice. "Fanny Osborne was very often at Lakeside Hill, now that her brother was in camp, and she and Lillie were much drawn together in their common feeling for their brothers." Together, the "little maidens" would spend their days sewing "all sorts of comforts or keepsakes for the soldiers" (228). Especially affirming of Lillie's successful reform, Fanny admires her friend's fortitude, as she "secretly wished she could wear as brave a front as her little companion, when she thought of the approaching departure of that regiment in which both were so interested" (230). In a final test of Lillie's reformed character, the formerly jealous and possessive sister readily accepts Sue as Guy's betrothed wife and her own new sister, an especially significant gesture, as sacrificing her brother to another woman had even greater personal implications for Lillie than to lose him to war. While Guy awaited ("a little anxiously") his sister's response to the news of his engagement, Lillie's ready reply that she was "so glad and so happy, *sister* Sue!" rewarded her brother with the only gesture "that had been wanted to make his happiness quite complete" (239–240).

While the siblinghood of Lillie and Guy thus proved its successful recuperation and capacity for mutual support and endurance, the novel concludes with an even more emphatic note of sibling love. Rather than letting the romantic wedding of Guy and Sue close the scene of the final chapter, the narrative offers the last words to the happy sibling pair Fanny and Jack, who affirm, though light-heartedly, their life-long commitment to one another. In flip disregard of the traditional post-wedding expectation for maidens to sleep with a piece of wedding cake under their pillows in order to dream of their future husbands, Fanny instead reasserts her sisterly monogamy: " . . . Fanny, turning quickly to Jack, who stood behind her, drew his arm over her shoulder, saying, in her impulsive fashion, as she threw aside the crutch, whose place she had taken, 'I mean to dream of nobody, then' " (328–329). Literally assuming the physical support of her brother, disabled by battle wounds, Fanny symbolically rejects the social expectation that she aspires to the role of wife and avows her sisterly loyalty instead. Brother Jack's response makes this gesture even more overt: " 'Till death do us part, Fanny?' said Jack, smiling at her." The narrative follows that significant matrimonial vow with a final statement that brings to a full circle the reciprocal metaphor of family and war: "But that is a hint of the future, and few of us, as we fight our home battles, would care to look forward in our lives and know just how it is to go with us when we are fairly out in the world!" (329). The "hint of the future" that lies in Jack and Fanny's mutual expression of support and attachment for one another underscores the power of sibling affiliation in this domestic response to the nation's crisis. The marriage-like intensity of Jack and Fanny's mutual devotion and commitment reflects the key social function of the opposite-sex sibling dynamic in domestic pedagogy of the day.[25]

Sibling affiliation would retain its appeal to American children throughout the post-bellum era, as illustrated in a famous serialized novel by the century's most beloved and celebrated children's periodical editor, Mary Maples Dodge. Credited with radically transforming the genre in her role as editor of the premier children's magazine *St. Nicholas* from 1873 until her death in 1905, Dodge presented a consciously innovative pedagogy for the children's periodical tradition. Dodge's particular intervention lies in her insistence that editorial practice reflect the pleasure-seeking, and not simply the moralistic, interests of young readers. That is, Dodge sought to provide children with literature that they would truly enjoy, not just reading that their parents would deem edifying. In her 1873 letter to Roswell Smith of Scribner and Company, a letter that Smith found so compelling that he published it in *Scribner's Monthly* (and promptly hired her as editor of the new magazine that would become *St. Nicholas*), Dodge urged a new editorial policy for the burgeoning market of children's periodicals, one that would "let there be no sermonizing . . . no wearisome spinning out of facts, no rattling of the dry bones of history. A child's magazine is its pleasure-ground" (*St. Nicholas*, 17).[26] Rather than shaping a children's magazine according to the typical adult magazine reader's value for edification, education, and the defining of literary taste, Dodge insists that child readers "do not want to be bothered, nor amused, nor taught, nor petted. They just want to have their own way over their own magazine." While she carefully affirmed the need for children's reading to be morally healthy, and she vigorously objected to the dangers of sensationalism, Dodge urged that a good editor "must give just what the child demands, and to do this successfully is a matter of instinct, without which no man should presume to be a child's editor and go unhung (17)."[27] Such a decidedly child-centered and aesthetically minded editorial pedagogy certainly should indicate the consciousness of Dodge's decisions as an author as well as an editor. Eschewing overt didacticism for children, Dodge sought simply to give child readers what they want. That philosophy, combined with her proven awareness of the interests of children given the supreme success of her magazine, makes her emphasis on sibling romance in *Donald and Dorothy* especially compelling for the logical implication that nineteenth-century American children found the story of sibling love enthralling and captivating.

Published in 1893 after its serialization in *St. Nicholas, Donald and Dorothy* would become one of Dodge's most famous and beloved children's novels (rivaled only by her 1865 novel *Hans Brinker; or the Silver Skates*). The novel's plot develops around the intense bond between the titular pair of twins, whose union is under siege by an evil outsider to the family who claims Dorothy as his own kin. Rescued from a shipwreck as infants, the twin brother and sister grow up under the guardianship of their doting paternal uncle. Upon her blossoming into a young adult, Dorothy's identity raises suspicion, as the infant daughter of an adopted sister of the twins' uncle (and of their own father) was among the victims lost at sea, and various similarities to "Aunt Kate," mostly in Dorothy's mannerisms and personality, provoke her uncle's deepest fears and anxiety, especially because he lacked conclusive evidence that the female baby he inherited was in fact the child of his brother and not of his adopted sister. Meanwhile, the emergence of the adopted sister's villainous biological brother exacerbates the crisis of Dorothy's mysterious identity, as his legal (and, as the family interprets it, ethical) claim upon Dorothy looms over them, threatening to tear apart the inseparable twins. The hero whose actions resolve this domestic crisis would be none other than Donald himself, of course, and, though just 15 years old, he would embark upon a solo adventure to Europe and collect evidence confirming Dorothy as his real twin sister.

As sibling attachment furnishes the basic premise of the plot, the novel appears somewhat liberated from the task of establishing the intensity of the brother–sister bond through an exaggeratedly sentimental aesthetic. Dodge tones down the sentimental language of sibling love that would characterize so much sibling romance, adopting for her child readers a simpler representation of her brother and sister characters' mutual sense of love and loyalty. The narrator introduces the twins with a brief caveat about their differences (Donald was of a "somewhat livelier temperament" and Donald "more self-possessed"; she "was ahead of him in history, botany, and rhetoric," while in "algebra and physical geography he 'left her nowhere' "[28]). It goes on to affirm their sibling attachment: "But never were brother and sister better friends. 'She's first-rate,' Don would say, confidentially, to some boon companion . . . And many a time Dorothy had declared to some choice confidential friend . . . that Donald was 'perfectly splendid! nicer than all the boys she had ever seen, put together' " (7). While their own exchanges tend to presume the intimacy of their relationship without overly demonstrative outpourings of verbal or physical sentiment, the notion of their separation, even for such a socially normative suggestion that Donald attend boarding school, disturbs both of the siblings. While Donald finds the adventure of leaving home tantalizing, he reflects, "but then how strange it would be to live without Dorry! Oh, if she only were a boy!" (34). Meanwhile, in response to their uncle's decision to defer boarding school for a while, as Donald was still needed at home to help protect Dorothy from a mysterious villain who was lurking around the family, Dorothy's private reflections reveal the magnitude of her sisterly attachment: " 'Needed here?' thought Dorry. 'I should say so! Uncle might as well remark that the sunshine, or the sky, or the air was needed here as to say that Don was needed.' A big tear gathered under her lashes." Mingling with Dorothy's sadness, though, is her indignation over her own diminutive stature as the sister who would be left behind in her brother's path to adulthood: " 'Besides, she was no more his little sister than he was her little brother. They were just even halves of each other—so now. And the tear went back' " (35). Dorothy's internalized narrative would send her first on the brink of sentimentality, signified by the gathering tear, only to moderate or complicate that emotional response as her sense of indignation curtails the tear. The novel portrays an intensely attached sibling pair, an attachment that serves as the central plot premise, without asking its young readers to accept the utter absence of rivalry or difference or to digest an excessive amount of sentimentality, as much of the twins' emotional expression remains in the unspoken privacy of their thoughts and reflections.

Dodge contextualizes Donald's heroic role completely within his character's righteous brotherly devotion. Foreshadowing the great act of heroism that would lead to the validating of his sister's identity, he demonstrates his selfless valor when he risks his own life to save her from a wild horse ride, an adventure highlighted with a significant illustration of the brotherly rescue (see figure 1.4). Breaking away from the friends who attempt to restrain him, Donald "had heard Dorry scream, and somehow that scream made him and his pony one" (69). In a dramatic scene of courage and fortitude, the brother succeeded in seizing the wild horse that held his sister; "Don was master of the situation." Donald's modest response to his success reflects not only the ideal manliness of his brotherly character, but also the novel's moderation with sentimentality: " 'Good for you, Dot!' was Donald's first word, 'you held on magnificently' " (69). Even while she allowed the valiant Donald the romantic privilege of catching his sister in his arms as she teetered toward a faint after climbing off the horse, Dodge withheld the conventional outpouring of a brother's pathos-laden anxiety over his sister's

Figure 1.4 An illustration of the valiant Donald rescuing his sister Dorothy (accessed via Project Gutenberg, www.gutenberg.org). Mary Maples Dodge, in her manifesto for editorial reform in children's magazines, emphasized the importance of high-quality illustrations, which, she said, "should be heartily conceived and well executed; and they must be suggestive, attractive, and epigrammatic" (*St. Nicholas and Mary Maples Dodge*, 17). Here, the heroic image of Donald bravely saving his sister from a nearly fatal horse-riding accident is suggestive indeed of the context of brotherly devotion as the context for manly heroism.

life or a sister's tearful clinging to her brother's neck and covering of his face with kisses. Indeed, Dodge gave her child readers the adventure she knew they wanted, as well as the sort of affectionate attachment they could relate to, with neither extraneous sentimentality nor excessive moralizing.

Donald's ultimate heroic act, his journey to Europe to search for evidence of Dorothy's identity, reflects Dodge's pedagogy for boys, in particular, comparably to Alcott's and Sigourney's interventions of domestically centered contexts for boyish adventure.[29] Donald's story features all of the aesthetic and romantic appeals of a boy's adventure plot: he leaves his home, journeys on his own across the Atlantic, braves new settings and encounters exotic people and places, and faces unforeseen dangers. His adventure even evokes the exciting conventions of the detective genre that was gaining popularity in the late nineteenth century, as Donald pieces together clues to locate the only survivor of the shipwreck who could confirm Dorothy's real identity. Dodge firmly couched the story of Donald's heroic escapades, though, within the precincts of his duty to his sister, avoiding not only excessive sentimentality but also dangerous sensationalism.

By depicting her hero as a loyal brother, Dodge balanced her moral obligation to youthful readers with her sense of responsibility to her child reader's literary imaginations and taste. A revealing 1890 review of the impact of *St. Nicholas* on children's literature asserts the importance of such serial stories as *Donald and Dorothy* for their ability to appeal to children's "diverse tastes" without being of "the hot, unhealthful sort— the sort that tends to produce a harvest of renegades, highwaymen and pirates."[30] The author of this celebratory review of the magazine quotes Dodge herself on the subject of sensational boys' novels: "Now, it will not do to take fascinating bad literature out of boys' hands, and give them in its place Mrs. Barbauld and Peter Parley[31]; or, worse still, the sentimental dribblings of those writers who think that any 'good-y' talk will do for children.[32] We must give them good, strong, interesting reading, with the blood and sinew of real life in it, heartsome, pleasant reading, that will waken them to a closer observation of the best things about them." Dodge's words, as cited by this reviewer, further emphasize the importance of allowing boys to enjoy experiencing the world through "good" literature:

> It is right and natural for a boy to want to see the world. It is right and natural for him to wish to read books that, according to his light, show him what the world is.
>
> The evil is the impression given to young minds that *seeing the world* means seeing the badness of the world. Let a boy understand that to *see the world* in a fair, manly way, one must also see its *good* side, its nobleness and true progress, and you at once put his soul in the way of a wholesome growth.
>
> Vile writers and worse publishers are fattening on this tendency of boys, and the culpable carelessness of parents in not helping them to satisfy it properly.
>
> Good writers and honest publishers are offering the means of remedying the great evil, and are showing the boys of this country how they may see the world and yet remain pure and true.

This contention with the authors and publishers of sensational stories for boys characterized and motivated Dodge's editorial and authorial legacy. In *Donald and Dorothy*, she offers children readers a model but realistic sibling bond, one that motivates and morally justifies the exciting exploits of the hero, through whom child readers could "see the world" within the safe and healthy context of familial devotion. Even while the aesthetics of sibling pedagogy itself would evolve to accommodate different generations of readers, the construct of brother–sister love provided a model of consanguinity unmatched in constancy and emphasis in nineteenth-century family values discourse. While the fiction writers who would invoke that bond in their grappling with social crisis would imagine nuanced implications of lateral love and attachment, they drew upon a concrete and widely disseminated idea that they could count on their readers to know.

CHAPTER 2

REMEMBERING RESISTANCE AND RESILIENCE: THE REVOLUTIONARY SIBLING ROMANCES OF SEDGWICK, SIMMS, AND KENNEDY

THE SALIENCE OF SIBLING LOVE TO THE AMERICAN LITERARY IMAGINATION and to dialogues of American nationalism would manifest in the era that marks both the first flourishing of those histories and the first large-scale jeopardy to the national union. In 1835, as the Nullification controversy, arguably the forerunner to the Civil War, was at its peak, at least three different novels published in the United States developed their romantic plots within Revolutionary War settings. Catharine Maria Sedgwick, William Gilmore Simms, and John Pendleton Kennedy, all supporters of the Union at the time of the Nullification crisis, employed significant sibling pairs in their representations of the Revolutionary War. Adopting the historical fiction genre popularized by Sir Walter Scott and, following Scott's example, American frontier novels,[1] Sedgwick, Kennedy, and Simms give sibling love the spotlight in their Revolutionary romances, and their sibling depictions resonate compellingly with contemporary debates over loyalty, unity, and individual rights. The novels' opposite-sex sibling couples, more developed and central than the courting couples in the novels (or, in the case of a quasi-sibling pair in Simms's novel, actually furnishing the courting couple), reveal complicated political responses to the possibility of South Carolina's secession from the Union. More broadly, they experiment with the potential and limitations of lateral dynamics, loyalties, and obligations between siblings and states, as well as among the hierarchies of paternal and national governance. Appropriating Scott's historical novel genre to the dual services of responding to American national crisis and of establishing an American literary tradition, Sedgwick, Simms, and Kennedy would position the sibling dynamic among American historical and political contexts to imagine and weigh the costs, means, and value of filial, fraternal/sororal, regional, and national allegiance.

With a national history founded on revolution, and in the self-consciousness evoked by such international criticism as Sidney Smith's infamous "who reads an American book?" gibe, the genre of the historical novel was an ideal response for political- and social-minded novelists aspiring to contribute to American literary nationalism whilst grappling with the very real possibility of Southern secession from the Union.[2] Scott's historical fiction formula employs historical figures as prominent actors within the plot, striving for historical accuracy in delineating their characters and the historic events that made them famous; but its main plot develops around fictional characters who play imaginary, supporting roles in those historical moments, and whose interpersonal dynamics, especially romantic entanglements, provide the main focus of interest in the novel. Thus fusing historical conflicts and romance, and allowing much license for imagining interpersonal dynamics and conflicts as elements of the historical narrative, the genre lent itself to both political intervention and romantic literary experimentation.[3] Facing the growing likelihood of Southern states threatening to secede from the national union, the setting of the Revolutionary War, with its rich potential as a backdrop to mingled, conflicting, and confusing fraternal and filial attachments and betrayal, was an apt context for American writers to intervene in contemporaneous debates over states' rights and relationships to one another and to the central government. The three writers featured in this chapter all favored the solidarity of the Union over the secession of Southern states at the time they wrote their 1835 Revolutionary War novels, and the historical novel provided a fitting outlet for their anxieties over both the possibility of secession and the costs of remaining united.

The employment of fiction for their political expression in 1835 functioned in interestingly different ways for these three writers. Around this time, Simms would abandon his aspirations for a political career in light of recent and unrelenting public humiliations and discouragements, and commit himself more fully to his literary career. He would resort to fiction as the main venue for his political intervention, eventually publishing eight Revolutionary War novels before and after the Civil War, among many other novels, short fiction, poetry, and histories. Conversely, Kennedy's budding and promising career as a novelist was abruptly terminated with the rising and all-consuming success of his own political career, and his critically acclaimed and popular *Horse-Shoe Robinson* would be the second of only three novels he would author. Finally, while clearly espousing her own vehement political views, Sedgwick's gender precluded her from participating in political debates in virtually any arena outside of the world of letters, but her unconventional resistance to marriage and motherhood afforded her commitment to her impactful, prolific, and at times overtly political, literary career. That each of these novelists would respond to the sectional crisis by adopting the historical novel and imagining familial conflicts and resolutions amid the backdrop of the Revolutionary War speaks to the salience of that genre to the exigencies of American romantic fiction. Moreover, that sibling dynamics would play prominent roles in these narratives of the Revolution reveals the intrigue and relevance of the lateral dynamics between brothers and sisters, especially the conflicts that would arise between their attachments to each other and their obligations to authority figures, for antebellum writers imagining national crisis and affiliation.

Although all basically supporting the national union, Sedgwick, Kennedy, and Simms each maintained strong regional attachments to their New England, border-state, and Southern native regions, respectively, and their depictions of sibling dynamics in their novels offer complicated reflections upon the apparently conflicting interests of national (and filial) devotion and regional and local (and fraternal/sororal) loyalty. *The Linwoods, Horse-Shoe Robinson*, and *The Partisan* each emphasize sibling relationships, with Revolutionary soldiers whose activity depends upon the support, encouragement, and motivation of strong sister characters. Although they each locate sympathy firmly with their rebellious sibling pairs, their narratives' nuances of sibling loyalty and filial duty and conflict complicate rebellion and attachment, independence and loyalty. While Kennedy's sister character would actively rebel against her father's loyalism, training her younger brother to become an American soldier and crossing battlefields herself to defend her patriot lover, the sister of Sedgwick's novel would motivate her brother's patriotic military duty while staying by the side of her loyalist father; Simms would reinforce the need for a sister's motivation by replacing the Revolutionary hero's dying, vocally pacifist sister with a militantly patriotic first-cousin lover, but their bond would hinge upon their mutual filial devotion. The novels present various degrees of attachment and deference to paternal figures, despite the unwavering mutual support among siblings. While all of the novels would ultimately affirm rebellion against tyranny as well as a brotherly sense of nationalism, their sibling dynamics expose the nuanced conditions and implications of severing filial ties. Rather than confirm any coherent argument for national unity at the cost of states' rights, local loyalties, or individual independence, taken together, the three novels, and especially their representations of central sibling couples, reveal the intricacies and nuances of debates about nationalism and independence, which too often have been reduced to historical narratives of binary opposition. As this intriguing instance of the three sibling romances of Revolution in 1835 affirms, especially given the shades of different anxieties and values from novels that essentially share a unionist sentiment, affiliation and nationalism in antebellum America were anything but simplistic constructs.[4]

The pressing contemporary crisis that Sedgwick, Simms, and Kennedy engaged in their 1835 novels was the national drama surrounding South Carolina's movement to nullify a federal tariff, in effect threatening to secede from the national union, and Jackson's forceful authority in suppressing that gesture of rebellion. The Nullification crisis, which one historian has said "created the most serious constitutional crisis to take place in the United States in the period between the adoption of the Constitution and the Civil War,"[5] brought to a head the tension between the power of the federal government and the extent of states' rights. In 1828, just before the start of Andrew Jackson's presidential term, the federal government passed a tariff, raising the cost of imported goods sold in the United States and fueling a controversy about the relationship between the federal government and states' governments. In 1832, South Carolina responded by passing the Nullification Act, which declared the federal tariff act null and void and contended that each state government had the right to nullify any federal law that it deemed unconstitutional. South Carolina threatened to secede from the Union if the federal government challenged the state's new law. The Nullification crisis subsided in 1833, when Congress passed a compromise tariff proposed by Henry Clay, just in time to prevent military conflict, as Congress gave Jackson permission to use federal troops to compel South Carolina's compliance with force. While the compromise plan would conciliate the Nullifiers and preserve the national union, the five-year-long dispute over the tariff and, more significantly, states' rights versus federal power, left a strong impression on the citizens of the still-young nation: the Union was not invincible. Moreover, the controversy brought to the surface conflicting definitions of state sovereignty as well as unresolved questions surrounding the right of individual states to secede from the national union.[6]

The Nullification crisis inspired a prolific and passionate public response. During and after the period of Nullification debates, Americans grappled with their anxieties over the solidarity of the nation, as they tried to come to terms with the nature of states' rights and the extent of the federal government's power.[7] Participants in the debate over South Carolina's secession frequently invoked the popular metaphor of the nation as a family. During the controversy's peak in 1830, an article in the famous medium of American literary nationalism, *The North American Review*, articulated the widespread public anxiety over the potentially catastrophic consequences of a state's secession. The editorial voice expostulates, "God preserve us from the day, when ... any member of the common family, in war or in peace, shall separate from the Union." The dissolution of the national union, to this writer, "would be on the grandest scale and in the extremest exasperation, a comprehensive family quarrel, in which a thousand natural bonds of union would be so many causes of unappeasable and remorseless hatred and hostility."[8]

The leading political voices of Nullification adopted a particular emphasis on the rhetoric of brotherhood and sisterhood in their incendiary arguments. In one of his earliest and most notorious public speeches in favor of Nullification, James Hamilton, Jr. denounced "the grasping avarice, and unconquerable injustice of those whom we have hitherto regarded as brothers of one family, hitherto bound to us by the natural ties of a common origin, by the association of united labours and confederate triumphs, by all that can consecrate and endear the sympathies of a common country—one people and one home!"[9] Expressing his accusation of what he saw as the northern states' greed and betrayal in terms of a breach of brotherly solidarity, Hamilton tapped into a rhetorical trope that both sides of the debate would adopt. Anticipating the inevitability that Nullification would lead to Civil War, unionist William Drayton, a US Congressman from South Carolina who represented the state's political moderates, engaged the family rhetoric favored by the nullifiers; in his speech at the Fourth of July Unionist Celebration in 1831, Drayton warned that as a result of such a rebellion against federal authority, "we [might] witness the spectacle of brother armed against brother, of parent against child, and of the child against his parent."[10] Reflecting the general opposition to Nullification by all of the other Southern states, a special committee of the Mississippi state legislature submitted an official response to the crisis, which, in its denunciation of the ordinance of Nullification draws heavily upon the language of sibling unity and filial devotion: "Your committee deeply deplore the alarming crisis in our national affairs; they regret it the more as proceeding from the unwarrantable attitude assumed by a sister of the South, whose best interests are identified with our own. In the spirit of brethren of the same family, we would invoke them to pause—to hearken attentively to the paternal, yet ominous, warning of the Executive of the Union." While proclaiming Mississippi's loyalty to the Union as "precious above all price" and affirming that they "heartily accord in the general political sentiments of the President of the United States... and that [they] stand firmly resolved, at whatever sacrifice of feeling, in all events, and at every hazard, to sustain him in enforcing the paramount laws of the land,"[11] this revealing report nevertheless admits its authors' fear of Jackson's "parental, yet ominous" threat of military suppression. With such a compelling mingling of exhortations for lateral cooperation on the one hand, and anxious deference to executive authority on the other, this resolution aptly reflects that the stakes of the debate over South Carolina's Nullification and secession were grounded in complex and conflicting interpretations of lateral solidarity and filial duty.

Not merely a superficial or cursory rhetorical device, the pervasiveness of the family metaphor in political discourse represented a powerful instrument in the mobilization of the Nullification movement in South Carolina, which gives it added salience to the arguments on both sides of the controversy. While the rest of the nation progressively embraced a more democratic social order throughout the first half of the century (albeit with marked limitations, namely defined by race and gender), a rigorous adherence to patriarchal hierarchies continued to dominate the social systems of the South. South Carolina was particularly attached to the idea of patriarchal family order, and its political and social institutions were strictly defined by family lineage.[12] The presumptions of white, masculine privilege that the system of slavery reinforced provided rich fodder for political agents to promote volatile resistance to perceived tyranny.[13] "As Nullification was to reveal," Stewart asserts, "planter [candidates] faced an electorate which they could easily arouse and manipulate... [and they] would protect traditional customs that South Carolina voters of all stations held most dear: familial supremacy and patriarchal power, female subservience, and the subjugation of blacks." The most important aspect of this social system to the mobilization of support for Nullification was "the sense of independence that each white male, rich or poor, valued most and feared losing above all else."[14] If South Carolinians regarded localized authority as supreme and clung to their sense of paternalistic control over their own affairs, the prevalence of family metaphors in the Nullification controversy held special rhetorical importance. The invoking of lateral solidarity has conflicting implications when the nullifiers use it to invoke their sense of the betrayal of sister states that either wield greater Congressional power in the North or decline to join their resistance movement in the South, versus the unionist's insistence that brothers and sisters remain united, even sometimes in deference to filial authority, and that such a laterally defined Union would serve to democratize the society. This spectrum of implications for lateral and filial devotions provides a crucial context in which to consider the three Revolutionary novels that engage the contemporary controversies surrounding their authors and readers in the 1830s.

In their 1835 novels, Sedgwick, Simms, and Kennedy each allegorize the nation as family, and they each highlight the role that sibling affiliation plays in that family union. The Revolutionary War provided an apt setting for their narration of resistance and domestic strife, and the lateral attachment between siblings more closely approximated the new stakes of resistance, independence, and solidarity in the United States of the 1830s. While these three authors would imagine varying degrees and conditions of sibling attachment and independence, all of their novels would highlight brother–sister pairs and explore the potential and implications of a sibling couple's resistance to paternal authority. With sibling bonds that persevere during familial crisis, the lateral alignment of affiliation in Sedgwick's and Kennedy's novels reflects those authors' unionism and staunch opposition to patriarchal social order. In contrast, the deference of the siblings of Simms's novel to filial authority reflects the South Carolinian author's consciousness of his native state's deeply engrained patriarchal culture, a value system to which he would appeal in his insistence on the urgency of lateral affiliation in support of, rather than in opposition to, filial authority.

"...THERE CAN BE NO STRONGER NOR TENDERER AFFECTION THAN THAT OF BROTHER AND SISTER": SIBLING SOLIDARITY IN SEDGWICK'S THE LINWOODS

As the daughter of Theodore Sedgwick, a Revolutionary War major, US Senator, famous defender of slave Elizabeth Freeman/Mumbet's rights to freedom and equality, but also a staunch federalist and suppresser of Shay's Rebellion, Catharine Sedgwick grew up with a first-hand glimpse into the complicated ideological debates surrounding the balancing act of natural rights, independence, and authority. Bridging her father's Federalism and the Jacksonian democracy of her own generation, Catharine Maria Sedgwick disseminated her own brand of republican virtue throughout her prolific career as a writer of domestic advice literature and fiction. A federalist-turned-democrat, and a Calvinist-turned-Unitarian, Sedgwick clearly embodied processes of synthesis and transformation. She sought to bring together the republican values of virtue, selflessness, and patriotism, and the democratic principles of equality, opportunity, and independence. Throughout her career, she grappled with the clash between the restrictive codes of her Calvinist upbringing and the post-Enlightenment appeal to human reason and rationalism that informed the nation's founding.[15] In her fictional depictions of the American family, its values, dynamics, and governance, Sedgwick imagines resolutions to these ideological conflicts, which were at their peak during the successful 1835 publication of her novel, *The Linwoods*, in which Sedgwick experiments with the fraught balancing act between the rationalist right to self-government and the necessity of authority for the sake of the Union.

When she interrogated the limits and conditions of justified authority and the terms of filial duty in *The Linwoods*, Sedgwick was revisiting a line of inquiry that occupied her earliest novels, beginning with her first Unitarian tract-turned-novel, *A New-England Tale* (1822), which exposes the harsh tyranny of Calvinist parenting and advocates for a more rational, Locke-inspired parental authority. In response to the nation's sectional crisis, *The Linwoods* returns to the theme of familial governance, particularly considering the extent to which a functional family (or government) can actually allow its children (citizens) to be self-determining. More overtly than any of her other domestic fictions, *The Linwoods* grapples with the seemingly conflicting republican values: the rationalist ideals of independence and individuality and the perceived need for the filial love of children and patriotism of citizens. Drawing upon Lockean prescriptions for parental governance, Sedgwick imagines the recuperation and healing of a divided family by means of rational, non-coercive governance. Moreover, the novel represents the dynamics that emerge to keep nuclear families, and, by extension, republican nations, resilient and unified in the face of threats of estrangement or secession. Finally, while Sedgwick's main objective, the recuperation and preservation of the familial or national union, reflects a conservative political agenda, the circumstances under which she will allow the Linwood family to reunite reveal that her political position is actually somewhat more complicated than is usually assumed. Neither as liberal as many of the nationalists of her generation, nor as strictly conservative as her federalist father, Sedgwick, in her most overtly political novel, reveals her moderate ideas about how the citizens and government of the new nation should interact.

It was Sedgwick's willingness to provide literature and literary morality aimed at a distinctly American audience that earned her special recognition with nineteenth-century American readers, particularly during the 1830s.[16] The perceived lack of democratic, American literary traditions and the corresponding erosion of republican values concerned many during the era of Jacksonian democracy. For example, the famous coiner of "Manifest Destiny" himself, John L. O'Sullivan, complained in his debut issue of *The United States Magazine and Democratic Review* that, "Our 'better educated classes' drink in an anti-democratic bit of feeling and thinking from the copious... fountain of the literature of England; they give the same spirit to our own, in which we have little or nothing that is truly democratic and American. Hence this tone of sentiment of our litera[ture]... poisoning at the spring the young mind of our people" (15). Sedgwick's writing answers that widespread plea with its self-consciously republican agenda and its reliance on American rhetorical trends. As Maria Karafilis points out, Sedgwick "depicts for her readers what she considered to be appropriate models of democratic behavior in a post-Revolutionary society, a society whose republican foundation was eroding and whose national self-imagining was thereby threatened."[17] Truly, the responses of Sedgwick's contemporaries speak to the effectiveness of the novel's republican messages: for at least one reviewer of Sedgwick's day, *The Linwoods* reveals "the marks of a true genius for commencing a literature for the mass of the American people, which shall bring up their moral tone to the spirit of their institutions. Her mind appreciates the peculiar dignity of republicanism, and her heart rejoices in its enacted poetry."[18]

Already appreciated by her contemporaries for her careful preservation of republican values, Sedgwick would address the urgencies of sectional crisis in *The Linwoods* by showcasing the dynamics of the title American family as it battles through its private trials and reaches reconciliation during the Revolutionary War. Beyond the clear allusion to Walter Scott's most famous historical novel, *Waverley, or, 'Tis Sixty Years Since*, Sedgwick's title and subtitle, *The Linwoods; or, "Sixty Years Since" in America*, enact the very parallel the novel presents between an American family and the American nation: this novel tells the story of an American family, or, the story of a young nation. Certainly, the familial paradigm for national political discourse was not new; the family metaphor dominated Revolutionary-era debates, whether the crown was configured as the tyrannical or the betrayed parent and the Americans as rebellious or abused children. But the vertical power struggle of parent–child that was typical to Revolutionary discourse did not entirely serve the exigencies of the nation's major antebellum political battles, including abolition, expansion, sectionalism, and states' rights, crises that called into question the terms and potential for the Union, solidarity, and individuality among states and the extents and limits of obligation and loyalty. As the event encapsulated so much of that friction, the Nullification crisis gave special significance to the lateral dynamics between siblings, and the novels of Sedgwick, and her contemporaries Simms and Kennedy, place special emphasis on this nuclear family relationship in light of its relevance to states' rights, sectionalism, and national unity. As the first large-scale threat to the authority of the Constitution, the crisis of Nullification was an especially salient provocation for Sedgwick, whose own father fought to ratify that binding contract.

The portrayal of the Linwood family's disunion and reunion allows Sedgwick to imagine the repair of her cherished republic. In the shadow of the first major threat to the national union, Sedgwick offered her readers a resolution to national crisis through the reconciliation of a family torn apart by private and public revolutions. Karafilis sums up the cultural work of *The Linwoods* with the premise that the metaphor of the family as nation achieved Sedgwick's conservative goal of preserving the national union: "Sedgwick's novel allowed her readers to 'intervene in' and re-imagine the pending Nullification crisis, to retell a story of profound discord that eventually results in conciliation. It is 'imaginative intervention' that explains in great part why the novel resonated so deeply with its contemporary audience" (xxvii). But rescuing the nation from crisis is only one aspect of the novel's cultural work. While *The Linwoods* apparently performs the conservative task of preserving the national union, it nevertheless makes space for political difference. Even while finally accepting his children's American patriotism in the final chapter, Mr. Linwood remains a staunch loyalist, mournfully watching the British leave New York. Just as in *A New-England Tale* Sedgwick carefully avoids sectarianism and calls for a sense of Christianity that will tolerate diverse denominations,[19] in *The Linwoods* she imagines a family/nation that will allow diverse political positions. In both novels, Sedgwick's utopian Unions feature humanitarian leadership, mutual respect, and goodwill among the various members of families, nations, and communities. In *The Linwoods*, Sedgwick imagines a republican Union that accommodates, to some extent, political dissent and self-determination. Though *The Linwoods* reinforces conservative republican standards for virtue, then, it also explores a liberal model of familial/national governance. Sedgwick may have desired the preservation of the Union, but only with a rational, fair leadership and independent citizenship. The latter criterion, the independence of citizens, is showcased through the several sibling pairs of the novel, particularly the brother and sister of the title family, whose unity and perseverance compel their father's eventual yielding of patriarchal authority.

The narrative of the Linwood family's involvement in the Revolution is, above all else, a story of sibling resilience, solidarity, and collusion. Set mostly in the New York scenes of the Revolution, the novel follows the young Herbert Linwood through his excruciating decision to go against his father's staunchly loyalist position and join the Continental Army. Notwithstanding his passionate patriotic convictions, Herbert hesitates to join the American side of the war, until his sister, Isabella, who is at this early point in the narrative an avowed loyalist like her father, urges him to act independently of their paternal authority and to claim his masculine right to a political opinion. Herbert's eventual decision to join Washington's army, protracted and dramatized to highlight his conflicting filial anxieties and eventually only resolved upon the influence of his sister (significantly, despite her political differences), provokes his father to exile him from the family. Throughout the various scenes of war, Herbert's filial duty brings him back to beg his father's forgiveness and seek the comfort and aid of his sister, who is gradually coming around to the side of the Revolution while maintaining her steadfast devotion to her father. Meanwhile, Isabella's romantic entanglements parallel her evolving sense of nationalism, as her affections shift from the Tory lover of her youth to a New England patriot, Eliot Lee, whose emphatically developed attachment to his sister, Bessie, offers a subplot that reinforces the centrality of sibling romance to the novel. Sustained throughout its turmoil by the enduring and resilient sibling bond between Herbert and Isabella, the only familial bond sustained unwaveringly throughout the narrative, the Linwood family recuperation is achieved upon the resolution of the Revolutionary War, with the Tory father subdued to a more humble and cooperative head to his reunited family.

 The reader learns of the Linwood family crisis through a series of epistolary exchanges between Isabella Linwood, and her friend, Bessie Lee. Isabella's letters underscore the significance of the theme of family to the novel's representation of the American Revolution. Although Isabella's politics will eventually align with her brother, she sides with her father's loyalism in the beginning of the novel, and in her letter to Bessie about her family's crisis, she laments her brother's rebellion against their king and father. Reflecting upon the divisive impact of Herbert's politics on her own family, Isabella adopts the family rhetoric of the day in her references to the war. She refers to the American cause as a rebellious prejudice that "pervades the country, and fires New-England against the legitimate rights of the mother country over her wayward, ungrateful child" (38). Later in the novel, Sedgwick applies that rhetorical trope to the opposite political perspective, in a letter to Isabella from her Revolutionary-minded aunt, Mrs. Archer, whose patriotism, rationalism, and virtuous republican womanhood are the persuasive combination needed to influence Isabella's transition from a Tory to a Whig. Mrs. Archer uses the family metaphor to criticize England's abuse of its power and authority: "Our English mother,

God bless her, too, should have known better than to trammel, scold, and try to whip her sons into obedience, when they had come to man's estate, and were fit to manage their own household" (158).

The novel interrogates the boundaries of patriarchal authority chiefly through Isabella's shifting allegiances and attitudes, which significantly evolve in the direction of her brother's allegiances. In the beginning of the novel, while Isabella's political convictions remain on the side of the "mother country" and her father, she is unable to criticize her father's irrational authoritarian behavior, and, instead, she blames her brother's rebellion for her family's trials. She complains to Bessie that the "stormy miserable week" since she wrote the last letter "has ended in Herbert's leaving us, and dishonouring his father's name by taking a commission in the rebel service" (39). Even at this point, though, Isabella acknowledges the role of affection in family dynamics. She continues to express love for her brother and insists that her father's affection for his son will prevail. In closing a letter that fiercely opposes her brother's rebellion, she says, "Ah, Herbert!—but I loved him before; and once truly loving, especially if our hearts are knit together by nature, I think the faults of the subject do not diminish our affection, though they turn it from its natural sweet uses to suffering" (39). Moreover, she doubts that her father's authority can overpower his affection for his son: "[Papa] says he has for ever cast Herbert out of his affections. Ah! I am not skilled in metaphysics, but I *know* that we have no power whatever over our affections" (39).

The conflict Sedgwick portrays between filial devotion and the value placed on a child's independence reflects the tension between the affection-based, nuclear-family ideal and the Lockean paradigm in the new nation. The Lockean notion of raising children to think and act independently, so that they will become healthy, productive adults, conflicts with the emergent emphasis on close, private family life.[20] In many ways, the Linwood family fulfills the affectionate, private, nuclear family ideal, a portrayal that is reinforced by the family's complete insulation, as the family never appears together in the narrative outside of their home. Moreover, affection has a strong enough presence in the Linwood family dynamics to serve as a lure to win back the wayward son. In a desperate attempt to convince Herbert to abandon his role in the Revolution and return to the family unit, Mrs. Linwood appeals to her son's love for the family. She pleads, "Oh, my dear, dear son, . . . if you but knew how much we have all suffered for you, and how happy you can now make us, if you only will, you would not hesitate, even if the rebel cause were a good one: you are but as one man to that, and to us you are all the world" (148). Significantly, Herbert's dilemma lies between the comforts and love of his family and home and his own adult independence, a predicament that typifies the conflict between the ideologies of nuclear family and Lockean childrearing. After his mother's pathetic plea, he considers his options: "It was a moment of the most painful vacillation; the forgiveness of father, the ministering, indulgent love of his mother, the presence of his sister, the soft endearments of home, and all its dear, familiar objects, solicited him" (148).

While dramatizing the conflicting priorities of independence and familial attachment, Sedgwick is careful to preserve the supremacy of the family and to envision alternative modes of authority capable of tolerance, forgiveness, and love amid difference. Even while its authority is resisted, overtly by Herbert and surreptitiously and vicariously by Isabella, the supremacy of the nuclear unit is never fully ruptured in this narrative of rebellion. In fact, given the centrality of sibling children to the insulated nuclear family, their resilience and solidarity despite differences and turmoil reinforce the Union. Rather than sacrifice the nuclear family for the sake of a child's independence, the parent's guidance and education of his young children evolves into a loving respect for the adult children. The story of the Linwoods imagines the potential compatibility between a Lockean education and an affectionate, private family. Sedgwick points to the love between Mr. Linwood and his children as the chief factor in the reunion and recuperation of the family. Although Mr. Linwood's political allegiances never change, his approach to family governance alters significantly, shifting from unconditional obedience to unconditional love and pride as the sources of family happiness. Near the end of the novel, at Mrs. Linwood's suggestion that the farewell "should be a family thing" (353), the Linwoods gather to watch the defeated British leave New York. Just as the representatives of the old, patriarchal British authority depart, Mr. Linwood expresses to Isabella his own, newly awakened sense of his role as a father. He insists that, although he remains as loyal as ever to the king, he can tolerate his children's different view, because they have been loving, virtuous children:

> ... Belle, I'll tell you what it is that's kept the sap running warm and freely in this old, good-for-nothing trunk of mine. My child," the old man's voice faltered, "you have been true and loyal to me through all this dark time of trial and adversity; you have been a perpetual light and blessing to my dwelling, Belle; and Herbert—if a man serves the devil, I'd have him serve him faithfully—Herbert, in temptation and sore trials, has been true to the cause he chose—up to the mark. This it is that's kept me heart-whole. And, Belle, if ever you are a parent, which God grant, for you deserve it, you'll know what it is to have your very life rooted in the virtue of your children, and sustained by that—yes, as mine is, sustained and made pretty comfortable, too...." (354–355)

Mr. Linwood's new sense of authority features his newly acquired tolerance for diverse political values, a republican requirement modeled by the bond between brother Herbert and sister Isabella, who functionally collaborate and support each other despite their initial political differences. Furthermore, the "virtue" that sustains Mr. Linwood is no longer grounded in obedience and submission but in loyalty, consistency, and love. Isabella's father has come to accept her political independence from him because she has remained loving and faithful to their family. He accepts Herbert's independence because he recognizes his worth as a respectable, loyal adult and a good citizen.

As compatriots even while politically different, the Linwood siblings represent civic loyalty and duty, especially timely in the face of the potential secession of Southern states in the United States of the 1830s. The lesson of the siblings' solidarity reinforces the civic virtue of patriotism, which translates to filial loyalty in Sedgwick's family/nation allegory. Even while they disagree with their father, the Linwood children remain loyal, loving, and respectful. The Lockean value for "filial esteem," which was also a key moral of Sedgwick's *A New-England Tale*, holds the Linwood family together through political crises. Even when Herbert seems to be defying his father by joining the American forces, Sedgwick carefully maintains the son's continued respect for his father as well as his angst over his father's disapproval. In a conversation with his friend, Eliot, Herbert agonizes over his father's "curse" against him: "you really have no conception how miserable my father's displeasure makes me... certainly my conscience acquits me, yet I suffer most cruelly for my breach of filial obedience" (105). While Herbert ultimately chooses patriotic duty over "filial obedience," his continued reverence for his father and love for his family make him go to extreme lengths to regain his role in the family union. Indeed, reconciliation with his father is only possible when he temporarily abandons his military duties. Only after sneaking back into New York against Washington's orders, and being held prisoner by the British army, does Herbert eventually regain his relationship with his father and his status in his family.

When Herbert's politics clashed with his father's, he chose the route of involuntary "secession," sacrificing his role in the family union in order to preserve his independence. Isabella, on the other hand, developed an independent position while remaining on good terms with her father and preserving her role in the family. As a daughter, Isabella's filial obedience was especially crucial in the eyes of Sedgwick's contemporaries. A virtuous young republican woman, Isabella stayed by her father's side, nursing him during illness, and entertaining him when he was lonely. Sedgwick keeps Isabella from even uttering her strong patriotic inclinations to her father until the climactic moment of the British army's departure from New York and Mr. Linwood's announcement of his new-found appreciation for his children's virtue. Isabella enacts her most effectual subversions via her interventions on behalf of her brother, and her repeated efforts to reinforce Herbert's masculine resolve and action allow her to perform rebellion vicariously, all the while maintaining her feminine filial devotions. Even while attending dutifully to her father's illness midway through the novel, Isabella, aware of her brother's imprisonment in a nearby British camp, writes a letter and sends it through her Tory lover, Jasper, to implore the commanding officer holding her brother in custody to release him.

More resounding in this novel than the virtue of the individual Linwood children, though, is that the bond between brother and sister remains unconditional and invincible. If Sedgwick configures the reconciliation of the nation through the Linwood family, she stresses the importance of cooperation and sympathy among compatriots Herbert and Isabella. In fact, the strength of the brother–sister bond is even more effective in repairing the family union than the father's slowly improving style of authority. Although she was still a loyalist at this point in the novel, it was Isabella who reminded Herbert of his patriotic duty when their parents tried to persuade him to switch sides and rejoin the family. " 'Herbert,' exclaimed Isabella, and her voice thrilled through his soul, 'is it possible you waver?' He started as if he were electrified: his eye met hers, and the evil spirits of doubt and irresolution were overcome. 'Heaven forgive me!' he said, 'I waver no longer' " (148). Herbert's independent resolve, fulfilled successfully in the eventual victory of his cause, is completely dependent upon his sister's encouragement. Even while he was imprisoned within a British camp, suspected of violating a truce agreement, Isabella intervened in his fate. Besides composing the letter to the commanding officer on his behalf, she also carefully restricted the manner in which her loyalist suitor presented to Herbert the predictable conditions of his release. Revealing her full consciousness of her brother's personal weaknesses and exhibiting her own capacity for manipulating him into the righteous (and manly) course of action, she urged Jasper to avoid persuading Herbert to abandon his cause: "He may—it breaks my heart to think it possible—but he may—his spirit broken by imprisonment and desertion... he may yield to the temptation you offer, and abandon a cause that he still believes, in the recesses of his heart, to be just and holy" (188). Absorbing a gargantuan share of the work of nurturing and developing her brother's psyche that Hegel charges to the ideal sister figure, Isabella appears to know and accommodate her brother's moral and mental limitations more fully than he does himself, and she facilitates his effectual maturation while remaining purposefully within the domestic realm. Interestingly, though, Sedgwick carefully invests Isabella's active intervention in her brother's path with the consciousness that Hegelianism denies the theoretical sister.

While the persevering bond of Herbert and Isabella represents the potential for sibling love to prevail over the conflicts and strife of familial division, the more romanticized dynamics between siblings Eliot and Bessie Lee reinforces the sentimental capacity of the sibling bond. A letter from Eliot to Bessie upon his departure to join the Revolutionary army strongly evokes the antebellum codes for opposite-sex sibling love:

> My sweet sister Bessie, nothing has afflicted me so much in leaving home as parting from you. I am inclined to believe there can be no stronger nor tenderer affection than that of brother and sister; the sense of protection from the one part, and dependance (sic) on the other; the sweet recollections of childhood; the unity of interest; and the communion of memory and hope, blend their hearts together into one existence. So it is with us—is it not, my dear sister? (63)

Later in that letter, Eliot further insists that no other relationship, including a romantic one, could be more important than the one between a brother and sister, a sentiment echoed in Sedgwick's correspondence with her own brothers.[21] True to his word, Eliot stands by his sister during her mental breakdown, an episode provoked by the romantic betrayal of Jasper Meredith, the red-coat rake of Isabella's youthful romance. Bessie's downward spiraling mental condition is revealed in a series of letters addressed confidingly to her brother, in which she confesses her fall to the romantic ploys of Jasper and shares her increasingly disordered sense of reality that resulted from his deception. In a scene in which Bessie consummates her obsessive wish to return to Jasper the "charms" he used to seduce her (dried flowers, jewelry, notes, and knots of hair), Eliot compels Jasper to stay and allow Bessie to give full vent to her mad compulsion, a scene that concludes with her fainting into a near-death fever. Eliot's devotion to Bessie during her melodramatic illness is rewarded by her recovery and, significantly, her unmarried fate in the novel's conclusion.

Each of the brother–sister pairs of *The Linwoods* strictly adheres to the contemporary expectations for close sibling bonds. Besides being intensely affectionate, each pair overcomes a test to their solidarity. Isabella and Herbert proved the strength of their relationship when it was tested by divergent politics and Herbert's exile. Bessie and Eliot are first separated by war, and then by Bessie's breakdown. Also, in an interesting subplot that develops around Isabella and Herbert's patriotic aunt Mrs. Archer, her twin, blind children, Lizzy and Edward, are literally ripped apart by Tory robbers. In both the cases of Bessie's breakdown and attack on Lizzy Archer, the sisters end up on the brink of death, and in each situation it is her brother whose intense love and attentiveness save her and sustain her. Overall, Sedgwick's repeated depictions of brother–sister dynamics strictly adhere to the gender differentiation in antebellum sibling codes, most explicitly revealed in Eliot's statement that the brother offers "a sense of protection," and the sister, one of dependence. The portrayals of brotherly protection and sisterly dependence in *The Linwoods* reveal Sedgwick's interest in the social responsibility of the independent republican citizens whose free will she ultimately wants to protect.

The sibling relationships in *The Linwoods* were vital to the continued health and harmony of the family units, a notion that signifies Sedgwick's wish to repair national fissures and restore the Union while protecting rationalist self-determination. For Sedgwick, the functional bond between nuclear-family siblings was crucial to the health of individual families as much as the cooperation of republican citizens was to the recuperation of a divided nation. Sedgwick chooses brother–sister bonds to suggest the roles between the enfranchised and disenfranchised compatriots in the republican nation, as their parallel social circumstances make their political distinctions especially apparent. Sharing parents, filial love, racial and class identities, even education in many cases, the brothers and sisters of *The Linwoods* differ significantly only in their gender-determined political agency. The brother–sister depictions in *The Linwoods* allow Sedgwick to strike a compromise between democratic rights and national hierarchies. Sedgwick argues for the preservation of both the Union and the republican self-determination, by granting the right to think and act independently only to those already enfranchised, and asking them to use that power for the service and protection of their dependent, disenfranchised compatriots. Maintaining the hegemony of white men as the only self-determining, enfranchised republican citizens, Sedgwick asserts that, with the freedom to self-determine comes the duty to act righteously for the service and protection of the disfranchised members of the republican nation. Sedgwick's liberalism in asserting independent rights is limited to inculcating young white republican men with a sense of social responsibility to protect those who, like Isabella Linwood, will keep their political dissent private and obey and honor their fathers. Extending the familial paradigm to focus more exclusively on the power and capacity of the lateral relationships between siblings, Sedgwick's fictional family drama imagines conflicts and resolutions surrounding the raising of nuclear families and the governing of democratic, republican nations. While trapped in the very dilemma she seeks to resolve in her fiction–that is, striving to balance exemplary civic loyalty with the pursuit of democratic rights and freedoms–Sedgwick reveals the circumscriptions of independence and loyalty, thus responding to the timely tensions between independence and loyalty, rationalism and patriotism, individualism and civic virtue that predominated amid antebellum sectionalism.

"Mildred and Henry were inseparable": The Rebel Siblings of *Horse-Shoe Robinson*

Though, as a three-term Congressman (1838, 1840, and 1842) and long-term member and speaker of the Maryland House of Delegates, John Pendleton Kennedy's political career would preclude him from a prolific literary life, his short-lived career as a novelist was marked with his success and impact. In his glowing review of Kennedy's second novel, *Horse-Shoe Robinson*, the influential Southern literary critic Edgar Allan Poe claimed to "feel very little afraid of hazarding our critical reputation, when we assert that [*Horse-Shoe Robinson*] will place Mr. Kennedy at once in the very first rank of American novelists."[22] As Charles H. Bohner records in his biography of Kennedy, the novel went through multiple editions throughout the antebellum period and was adapted into a play and staged successfully in 1836, 1841, and again in 1856. Like so much fiction authored for popular consumption, Kennedy's *Horse-Shoe Robinson*, despite its intriguing response to national history and crisis and its successful adoption of the historical genre that so captivated antebellum audiences, has for the most part been neglected in contemporary critical conversations. Given its emergence during the peak of the Nullification crisis, given its hearty reception by the first flourishing American literary spheres, and given its author's public commitment to political and social interests and his fraught relationship to the historically significant controversies surrounding national and regional affiliations and loyalties, this fascinating novel warrants critical attention. *Horse-Shoe Robinson*, in its account of the American Revolution, blends affection for region with national pride and loyalty. While at times his almost neutral attention to such larger-than-life historical figures as Charles Cornwallis and Francis Marion seem to reveal his non-partisan historical objectivity,[23] his loving attention to Virginian landscapes and his complex portrait of competing familial dynamics and loyalties disrupt and complicate the steadiness of his historical treatment. Such a friction between the author's historical method and literary style parallels the politician's increasingly fraught position as a Union man in the South, opposed to the secession of southern states even during the Civil War, when national loyalty meant painful ostracism for the Baltimore politician. In a compelling picture of a divided family during the Revolution, *Horse-Shoe Robinson* presents the conflicting narratives of a celebrated and heroic independence won at the melancholy cost of a disappearing patriarchal order, authority, and love. The nostalgic undertones of this novel of sibling revolution vividly anticipate the author's own conflicted positions as a loyal southerner and loyal American throughout the antebellum crisis.

Of the three Revolutionary sibling narratives from 1835, Kennedy's *Horse-Shoe Robinson* contributes the most rebellious sibling couple. Like *The Linwoods*, the central sibling narrative in *Horse-Shoe Robinson* emphasizes the mutual support and solidarity among the siblings, with a strong sister figure encouraging her brother's active patriotism in opposition to their father's loyalism. But Kennedy would extend his heroine's rebellion beyond the careful boundaries of feminine filial duty that Sedgwick maintained. While Isabella Linwood would encourage her brother's rebellion from the sidelines, where she maintained her dutiful service to her father, Kennedy's Mildred Lindsay would not only influence her brother to take sides with the patriotic cause in defiance of their father, but she would also serve as brother Henry's military trainer, teaching him classical philosophies and techniques of warfare; in return, Henry steadfastly supports and enables his sister's ultimate act of rebellion, her romantic attachment to a patriot soldier who is the particular object of their father's most adamant hatred. Given the importance of female submission to the patriarchal system that was so central to the Nullifier's campaign, Kennedy's actively rebellious heroine performs an especially significant rebuke to South Carolina's Nullification movement.

While the structure of sibling collusion and rebellion in Kennedy's *Horse-Shoe Robinson* parallels the sibling narrative of *The Linwoods* (notwithstanding that Kennedy offers a more audaciously rebellious heroine than Sedgwick imagined), its setting is more closely aligned with Simms's 1835 Revolutionary novel. Both *The Partisan* and *Horse-Shoe Robinson* represent roughly the same eventful period in the Revolutionary War, the summer of 1780 in the South (dubbed the "The Tory Ascendancy" in Kennedy's subtitle), with greatly overlapping historical and regional settings; *The Partisan* is set exclusively in South Carolina and culminates with the Battle of Camden in August, while *Horse-Shoe* takes place mostly in South Carolina, but also in North Carolina and western Virginia, and concludes with the Battle of King's Mountain in October. While the authors would portray basically the same set of historical circumstances, namely the downfall of Southern resistance to British occupation, their narratives would emphasize different implications of the crisis and its outcomes, and their divergent interpretations and renditions of this significant moment in Revolutionary history are reflected in the different uses they would make of sibling bonds in their novels.

Horse-Shoe Robinson shares the adventures of the title character, a Natty Bumpo-like frontiersman patriot who serves as a guide to the chivalrous Continental Army major, Arthur Butler. But certainly the role of the adventurous heroine, Mildred Lindsay, warrants the title status Kennedy gave to her in earlier drafts of the novel, before settling instead on Horse-Shoe.[24] Upon Butler's capture by a party of violent Tories who frame a phony charge against the major, his lover, Mildred, and her brother Henry, brave enemy lines (with Horse-Shoe's guidance) to confront the historically famous General Cornwallis with the false charges made against Butler and to urge the general's leniency. Throughout the novel, Henry sustains his dutiful attachment to his sister, facilitating her secret rendezvous with Butler as well as her adventure to intercede with Cornwallis on her lover's behalf, in open defiance of their father's increasingly wrathful, eventually deranged opposition to the match between Mildred and Butler. By the end of the novel, when Mildred and her brother follow Butler into battle to facilitate his rescue, we learn of the irrevocable union of their forbidden romance by a secret marriage the year before, the ultimate performance of a daughter's rebellion against an irrationally prohibitive father. Mr. Lindsay follows his daughter and son to the battle field, where he is mortally wounded, managing before his death to forgive his children for their defiance. The novel concludes with the rebellious couple settling into their married life in the Lindsay's Virginia plantation.

From its beginning and throughout the entire plot, the solidarity between Mildred and Henry is central to the novel's development. Even while Mildred's most passionate attachment is to Butler, because his imprisonment keeps the lovers separate throughout the plot, and because the main plot follows the rescue adventure of Mildred and Henry, the sibling romance occupies the central focus of the novel. While not as sentimental in their outpourings of love for each other as Sedgwick's Bessie and Eliot Lee and as Simms's Emily and Robert Singleton, Mildred and Henry nevertheless share a bond that defines and determines the development of the plot, namely in Mildred's rebellious marriage to Butler and Henry's becoming a patriot soldier. Mildred's clandestine meeting with Butler was coordinated by Henry, who deliberately hunted in an area of woods where he hoped to cross paths with the soldier and then sounded off a bugle signal to beckon his sister when he found her lover. In the multiple scenes of their father's violent outbursts prohibiting Mildred's attachment to Butler, Henry serves as comforter and confidant, reinforcing his sister's spirit in the face of their father's aggressive opposition. The narrator emphasizes the sibling attachment that accounts for Henry's active role in the secret romance of Butler and Mildred: "There was a confidant in all their intercourse: no other than Henry Lindsay, who united to the reckless jollity of youth an almost worshipping love of his sister. His thoughts and actions were ever akin to hers" (91). Significantly, too, the narration of Henry's role as confidant and conspirator directly associates his involvement in his sister's rebellious romance to his alignment with her lover's (and her) politics: "... as he could not but think Arthur Butler a good and gallant comrade, he determined that his father was altogether on the wrong side in respect to the love affair, and by a natural sequence, wrong also in his politics" (91). Thus passively assuming the political stance to which his own father vehemently opposed, Henry defines himself entirely through his lateral affiliation with his sister and her lover.

Beyond his apparently instinctive political alliance with his sister and her lover, Henry's more vivid identity development, his military training, is directly attributed to his sister's influence. Although introduced comically as an overgrown boy playing soldier in garishly fancy attire and accoutrements, Henry, at 16, was certainly of age to participate in the war, and the novel traces his eventual growth into an active soldier. Henry's attachment to his rebellious sister, combined with his father's unwillingness to recognize his son's growth into independent manhood, gave Mildred the upper hand in the shaping of Henry's identity. While their father persisted in denying his son's inevitable maturity, considering his attraction to the neighboring Whig military activities "no other than a gewgaw that played upon the boyish fancy of Henry without reaching his principles," Mildred seized upon Henry's childish curiosity about the romance of warfare and of independence and nurtured his political and militant leanings. "She had inspired Henry with her own sentiments, and now carefully trained him up to feel warmly the interests of the war, and to prepare himself by discipline for the hard life of a soldier. She early awakened in him a wish to render service in the field, and a resolution to accomplish it as soon as the occasion might arrive" (92). Periodically throughout the novel's progression toward their climactic adventure to Cornwallis, at which point Henry would be a fully consummated patriotic soldier, Mildred would challenge and test her brother's knowledge and preparedness for warfare, alluding to her instruction of classic Roman military heroes, as well as the famous Revolutionary military trainer and author of Revolutionary War drill manual, Friedrich von Steuben. When Henry hesitates to spend the night outside alone, a final test before embarking on their dangerous adventure through enemy lines, his sister firmly insists, "You must go alone... before I shall think you fit to be promoted," to which Henry chides his sister for being "forty times more severe than the German Baron's at Richmond" (346).

But Henry's gradual coming of age would hinge upon his sister's audacious heroism and independence, traits that Kennedy's narrator unapologetically acknowledges as "masculine." In its portrait of this brother–sister duo, the novel conspicuously blurs and swaps defined gender categories; even the transformation of Henry's feminine passivity into manhood is attributed to his sister's masculine spirit of adventure and rebellious activity. Whether falling asleep on his horse, complaining to his severe sister that he prefers Shakespeare to Steuben, or self-referencing as "Sleeping Beauty," Henry's comically feminized identity starkly contrasts his sister's powerful horsemanship, endurance, and classic military literacy. At the outset of the journey Mildred and her brother undertake to confront Cornwallis on behalf of Butler, the narrator notes the unsexing implications of Mildred's resilience and courage: "Mildred, so far from sinking under the weariness and increasing hardships of her present toils, seemed to be endued with a capacity for sustaining them much beyond anything that could have been believed of her sex" (392). Beyond the sense of bravery, adventure, and endurance that disrupt the femininity of her personality, even Mildred's physical stature is cross-gendered: while she is conventionally beautiful and graceful, her figure features "a degree of steadiness and strength that might be denominated masculine" (373).

In a chapter titled "The Companionship of Brother and Sister," the narrative interrupts its lively action to explain the implications and causes of the Lindsay children's gender confusion. The narrator assiduously credits Mildred's masculine traits for the development of her brother's character and point of view. Describing the heroine's magnetically attractive combination of feminine modesty and rare bravery, as she had a "quiet and unostentatious but unvarying current of resolution, that shrank before no perils," the narrator thus rationalizes her persuasive influence over Henry: "It was not wonderful that a mind so organized and accomplished should have acquired an unlimited dominion over the frank, open-hearted, and brave temper of her brother, now just stepping beyond the confines of mere boyhood. Her influence over Henry was paramount and unbounded: her affections were his, her faith was his, her enthusiasm stole into and spread over his whole temper" (340). The consequence of this intense brother–sister attachment, namely, Mildred's influence over her brother, is defined strictly in terms of political persuasion: "Mildred and Henry were inseparable; and, in proportion as his sister's zeal and attachment to the cause of independence became more active, did Henry's inclination to become a partisan grow apace" (340). While Henry renders all of the conventional brotherly services to his sister, escorting, protecting, and defending her, and deferring to her physical comforts and honor throughout the various settings of their mutual adventure, Mildred's single and dogmatic reciprocation of her brother's devotion lies in her effort to train him for patriotic service; as, "her conviction that a time was at hand when Henry might be useful, gave rise to an eager solicitude to see him well prepared for the emergencies of the day, by that necessary mode of education which, during the period of the revolution, was common amongst the young gentlemen of the country" (340).

While at times the narrative points to historical circumstances and the exigencies of the Revolution in its apology for such gender perversion of Mildred's and Lindsay' characters, more significantly it accounts for the queering of the brother and sister by its emphasis on the exclusive enmeshment of their attachment[25]:

> Another consideration may serve to explain the somewhat masculine character of Mildred's pursuits. Her most intimate companion, at all times, and frequently for weeks together her only one, was her brother. These two had grown up together in all the confidence of childhood; and this confidence continued still unabated. Their pursuits, sports, exercises, thoughts, and habits were alike, with less of the discrimination usual between the sexes, than is to be found between individuals in larger associations. They approximated each other in temper and disposition; and Henry might, in this regard, be said to be, without disparagement to his manly qualities, a girlish boy; and Mildred, on the other hand, with as little derogation, to be a boyish girl. This homebred freedom of nurture produced, in its development, some grotesque results, which my reader has, doubtless, heretofore observed with a smile; and it will, likewise, serve to explain some of the peculiar forms of intercourse which may hereafter be noticed between the brother and sister. (341)

Thus preparing his reader for the extremities of Mildred's bravado and her brother's slow ability to match it during the perils they would face on their journey together, Kennedy's narrator accounts for this gender bending by pointing out the remarkable insularity of the sibling pair, and their removal from the "larger associations" that would have more appropriately nurtured their conformity to gender codes. This explanation of the sibling pair's exclusivity reinforces the novel's earlier revelation that the children were even alienated from their emotionally withdrawn father during his extended period of melancholy over their mother's death, an isolation that further solidified their absolute dependence upon each other. The narrator's sardonic, at times even apologetic, treatment of the "grotesque" outcomes of such exclusivity and isolation—that is, Mildred's militant zeal and Henry's fanciful softness—exposes its fraught relationship to the solidarity that would both distort and disfigure the siblings' individual identities while also extraordinarily equipping them to overthrow the patriarchal order. While valorizing Mildred's capacity for bravery and rebellion and for influencing her brother, the novel nevertheless asserts the queerness and perversity of her rare power; while "smiling" at Henry's malleability and impressionability, it nevertheless allows him to exchange the accoutrements that were the "toys of a pampered boy" (34) for a real broadsword and validates the power of his attachment to his sister by graduating him to the stature of a valiant and battle-experienced soldier as a result of his sister's training.

Contributing significantly to this fraught picture of the power and perversity of lateral attachment is the flailing and deranged patriarchal authority of Mr. Lindsay. Philip Lindsay's severe prohibition against his daughter's marriage to Butler, while not an uncommon device for dramatizing national and historical crisis, takes on special significance in this novel, both for its basis in the character's superstitious convictions and for its violent extremity. While Lindsay's initial opposition to Butler grows predictably enough out of his objection to the patriot soldier's politics, his wife's death-bed demand that he prevent their daughter's marriage to Butler, and his later belief that his wife's ghost lingers as a haunting reminder of this promise, leads to his increasingly wrathful and adamant denial of his daughter's love affair. The supernatural episode that thus accounts for Lindsay's repeated outbursts against Mildred upon discovering her persistent attachment to Butler serves to reinforce and foreshadow the extent of the father's morbid fixation on preventing his daughter's romance.

The juxtaposition of his haunting ghost wife reminding him of his duty to the past against the current reality of his daughter's unwavering resolve, "a purpose which now fed all his melancholy" (352), combine to propel Philip Lindsay's increasingly disordered sense of dread of the transformation that a bond between Arthur Butler and Mildred Lindsay would seem to signal. "Ever since his first interview with Mildred on the subject of her attachment, his mind had been morbidly engrossed with the reflections to which it had given rise. There was such a steadiness of purpose apparent in her behavior, such an unchangeable resolve avowed, as seemed to him, in the circumstances of her condition, to defy and stand apart from the ordinary and natural impulses by which human conduct is regulated" (351). Mildred's father thus interprets her resistant behavior as paradoxically supernatural and realistic as the vaguely fluttering image that he accepts as evidence of his dead wife's ghost. Mildred's attachment to Butler meant, for Lindsay, a real-world distortion of familial and social order: "A predominating trait of this superstition was an increasing conviction that, in Mildred's connexion with Arthur Butler, there was associated some signal doom to himself, that was to affect the fortunes of his race. It was a vague, misty, obscure consciousness of impending fate, the loss of reason or the loss of life that was to ensue upon that alliance if it should ever take place." Mr. Lindsay's dread of his daughter's resolve thus reflects upon his sense that such a disruption in the steady and stable stream of power threatens the nature of his identity, power, and history, which, threatened by a dogmatic rebellion, causes him "to decline towards a fearful point; that point was—frenzy" (352). Mr. Lindsay's frenzied resistance to the displacement represented by Mildred's romance motivates his own despotic and possessive restrictions of his daughter; the physical demonstrations of passionate intimacy that follow each of his violent outbursts–her head on his lap, his caressing and kissing her– reinforce the father's perversely conflicted and unsustainable attachment to his daughter. While cast in sentimental terms, Mr. Lindsay's prohibitive attachment to his daughter nevertheless has the impact of parent–child incest, especially in its violent suppression of change.[26]

Mr. Lindsay's downward mental spiral, which gains momentum in reaction to the conquering mutiny of his colluding son and daughter, complicates the novel's antipatriarchal nationalism, especially as it builds nostalgic sympathy for the cultural and historical circumstances of this father's demise. "He was perplexed by the intrigues of politicians, against whom he had no defence in temper nor worldly skill: he was deluded by false views of events: he was embarrassed and dissatisfied with himself: above all, he was wrought upon, bewildered, and glamoured (to use a most expressive Scotch phrase) by the remembrance of a sickly dream" (352). The "sickly dream" that thus haunts and disfigures Mr. Lindsay's imagination, whether it signifies the literal dream of a visitation by his dead wife or the figurative dream of the patriarchal order that he recognized as threatened by his daughter and her lover, is central to the novel's crisis and resolution, and the tragic sympathy it evokes for Mr. Lindsay's sense of loss and melancholy disrupts the otherwise happy coherence of the Union and independence marked by Arthur and Mildred's marriage and Mildred and Henry's sibling love. While the narrative would allow siblings Mildred and Henry to accomplish their dreams of independence with all due heroic valor, it does not fail to notice and reflect upon the sacrifice of their father and affirm his ultimate dread, not only with his own death, but also with the symbolic usurping of his estate by the newlyweds. Such a melancholy loss, especially associated as it is with the decidedly nostalgic figure of the Virginian gentleman in Mr. Lindsay's character, coupled with an affirmation of resilient, lateral solidarity interestingly parallels Kennedy's own conflicted positions as a Southern regionalist writing nation and as a border-state

Union man decrying the disappearance of civilized gentry in the public sphere.[27]

"...THERE WAS ALWAYS ONE TO ME OF WHOSE SYMPATHIES, WHEN OTHERS WERE COLD OR STERN, I COULD BE CERTAIN": THE CONDITIONS OF SIBLING LOVE AND LOSS IN SIMMS'S *THE PARTISAN*

When Simms composed his first best-selling Revolutionary War novel in 1835, he imagined the representation of crisis and error as a crucial intervention in national history. His preface to a revised edition of *The Partisan* explains, "I am decided that a nation gains only in glory and in greatness, as it is resolute to behold and pursue the truth. I would paint the disasters of my country, where they arose from the obvious errors of her sons, in the strongest possible colors." Seeking to record and expose historical foibles in order to enlighten and instruct his readers, Simms consciously evokes the causes and consequences of misguided leadership in the Revolutionary warfare in South Carolina with the hope of intervening in the analogous dangers and potentialities of his own day. "... I have dwelt earnestly upon our disasters," he claims, and, "... the reflecting mind will see the parallel position of cause and effect which I have studiously sought to make obvious, wherever it seemed to me necessary for the purposes of instruction" (viii). Thus reflecting upon the intentions and consequences of the auspicious start of his Revolutionary novel series, Simms retrospectively articulates the value and potential of the novel. "It is in this way, only," he concludes, "that the novel may be made useful, when it ministers to morals, to mankind, and to society" (viii). The novel truly was Simms's most successful and rewarding tool for such political intervention, and *The Partisan*, responding to the urgencies of the Nullification debate, proved for the young novelist the most effective medium of his discursive intervention.

Marking Simms's authorial transition from polemical discourse to political novels,[28] *The Partisan* was the first of a Revolutionary War trilogy that would be followed by *Millichampe* (1836) and *Katherine Walton* (1851), and then by successive additional novels for a total of eight novels set in the Revolutionary War, more than any other American author. By 1860, Simms enjoyed the reputation of being the South's most celebrated man of letters and representative of Southern culture; the Southern magazine *DeBow's Review* would declare that Simms "reflects, in sentiment and character, the moral and intellectual attributes that distinguish the spirit and temper of Southern civilization; announces its opinions, illustrates its ideas, embodies its passions and prejudices, and betrays those delicate shades of thought, feeling, and conduct, that go to form the character, and stamp the individuality of a people."²⁹ But Simms was not always known for such staunch Southern allegiance, and his fame in that regard during the Civil War era reflects a sharp transformation in his politics as we well as his public image. During the period of the Nullification crisis, Simms's outspoken defense of the Union's interests provoked harsh criticism and ostracism from his fellow Southern journalists.³⁰ Driven from expressing his political convictions in newspapers by his opponents' public attacks, Simms retreated from his ambitious journalistic and political career and resorted to the historical novel as an outlet for his cautionary interventions in American politics.

Simms's fraught relationship with the Southern secession movement during the 1830s makes the Nullification crisis and Simms's shifting political allegiances compelling contexts in which to understand the author's first Revolutionary War novel. Although he would eventually support secession and the Southern Confederacy in the Civil War, an evolution of political thought reflected in his later Revolutionary War novels, during the time of the Nullification crisis he vehemently objected to secession. While maintaining his reverence for and loyalty to the South, Simms openly opposed the Nullification movement that was becoming increasingly popular in his native South Carolina. He advocated for a resolution to Southern economic complaints that would empower his beloved South without severing its tie to the rest of the Union, a tie that he believed was crucial for the strength and longevity of the South. When his most hostile opponent, Henry Laurens Pinckney, published in an editorial the sneering suggestion that Simms "eschew politics and confine himself to witticisms, poetry (good luck!), and literature for ladies,"³¹ Simms seems to have subverted the insult into a challenge and inspiration, publishing a successful, and overtly political, novel that represents the costs, implications, and methods of a revolution and the wisdom that would be necessary for independence, in the most timely moment of the Nullification controversy.

Together, Simms's own reservations about the implications of Nullification, alongside his conviction of the novel's capacity to "minister to morals, to mankind, and to society," provide the most essential contexts for interpreting his portrayal of Revolutionary warfare in the South and the interpersonal conflicts and goals he imagines within those historic episodes. Sibling romance would furnish an apt vehicle for his political commentary in his first and most famous Revolutionary novel. The sibling (and quasi-sibling) dynamics of *The Partisan* occupy prominent, if at times tenuous, positions in the development of conflicts and resolutions in this romantic plot. Like Sedgwick and Kennedy, Simms carefully attends to the development of region in his fiction, and his simultaneous devotion to region and loyalty to nation parallels the delicate balance he will develop between lateral bonds of siblings and their filial obligations in *The Partisan*.[32] The first in a trilogy, the novel is nevertheless sufficiently self-contained to warrant its individual critical interpretation; as Simms's preface acknowledges, "But, with a perfect knowledge of the danger which usually attends such an experiment [i.e., of aspiring to write a trilogy], I so arranged my *material* as to make each of the stories independent of the others. Each was to be wrought out to its separate conclusion" (vi). The separate and primary status of this first novel in what would become a celebrated trilogy underscores the importance of the sibling dynamics that would occupy much of its interest. While not investing sibling love with the supremacy and power that it would hold in either Sedgwick's or Kennedy's novels, Simms's employment of lateral bonds rather reinforces their subordinate, and nevertheless crucial, function within the patriarchal order. Brothers and sisters will not undermine and overthrow fathers in *The Partisan*, as they do in both of the other novels, but their bonds will reveal the limitations and costs of filial allegiance. The nuanced implications of sibling love among these three examples of politicized historical fiction reflect that, rather than representing a static and coherent idea of lateral affiliation within the nation, sibling dynamics in fiction reveal a range of responses to the nation in crisis. As the least conflicted unionist of the three authors, Sedgwick imagined the most utopian capacity for sibling love and mutual devotion to prevail, signaled by the significant reformation of paternal love in the Linwood family; Kennedy's unionism subverted the patriarchal cultural prerogatives of his native South, a tension that would manifest in the bleakly nostalgic undertones of his rebellious siblings' successful mutiny against their disordered and disconnected father, whose death at the end of the novel signifies complicated implications of social progress. The sibling dynamics of Simms's *The Partisan* are central to the progress of the novel's Revolutionary plot, but the sibling characters carefully comply with the imperatives of filial devotion. Rather than undermining the importance of lateral affiliation, the deference of the siblings of Simms to patriarchal authority presents a rhetorically savvy engagement with the outdated social order that still predominated in the South, particularly in the Nullification discourse. Maintaining his unpopular position as a South Carolinian opposed to Nullification, Simms's emphasis on filial obligation in his first Revolutionary novel serves as a timely reminder of the civic obligation to respect and honor parental (or, executive) authority, a central premise of the patriarchal order espoused by the Nullifiers themselves. Furthermore, even while the siblings of *The Partisan* defer to patriarchal order, their obedience strengthens their bond, which in turn facilitates and even saves the larger familial (and, by extension, national) union. The result is a union of laterally affiliated members who enjoy reciprocal devotion and affection, while collaboratively following the lead of their authority, a fitting allegory for Simms's Union loyalties during the time of the Nullification crisis.

The Partisan opens with the attempt by Major Robert Singleton, the novel's titular protagonist, to recruit surreptitiously for the American army, with the ambition of reigniting resistance in South Carolina. The chief object of his quest is the patriotic allegiance of his influential, aristocratic uncle, Colonel Walton, who has regretfully accepted "protections" from the British in exchange for his allegiance to the Crown, in order to protect his property and his only daughter, Katherine. When the British break their promise of neutrality and command all proclaimed loyalists in the region to take up arms against their rebel countrymen, Walton, with the influence of his fiery patriotic nephew, abandons his coerced allegiance to the crown and joins Singleton's patriot forces in the neighboring swamps.[33] While seeking the leadership and participation of his uncle in the Revolutionary War, Singleton just as zealously seeks the hand of his uncle's daughter, his own first cousin, Katherine, a romance that is developed in decidedly sibling-like terms, underscored by their near-sibling relation as cousins, and which is delayed and subordinated to the fulfilling of filial honor and obligation. The romance concludes with Singleton dramatically rescuing his uncle from a hanging (sentenced unjustly by an uncompromising Colonel Cornwallis), a service that finally earns him his cousin's promise of marriage, which she had suspended throughout the entire novel.

Sibling love occupies a major portion of this novel's focus and development and provides the basic framework for familial affiliation and insularity, and, although its functionality will be contingent upon filial duty, the sibling bond is ultimately strengthened by the fulfilling of such obligations. The family structure and dynamics of the protagonist furnish the main sites of sibling development. Upon the opening of the novel, the only living member of Singleton's immediate family is his invalid sister, Emily, who, we learn, has been removed to their uncle's plantation, "The Oaks," just in time to avoid witnessing the plundering and burning of their own family plantation. The family retreat to "The Oaks" is rife with significant insularity, indeed: seeking to avoid society during the embarrassment of his regrettable submission to British protection, Uncle Walton "solaced himself in his family mansion with the small circle which widowhood, and other privations of time, had spared him," and thus "studiously estranging himself" (199), he retired from society with his only child, Katherine, his "maiden sister," and another (deceased) sister's daughter, Emily Singleton. Robert Singleton's urgencies at "The Oaks" early in the novel involve the threefold and overlapping interests of securing his uncle's loyalty to the patriotic cause, his cousin's promise of marriage, and his sister's safety. The first object he achieves almost immediately; the second will be an effort protracted throughout the novel and deferred to the primary sense of filial obligation, as Katherine will refuse to accept Singleton's marriage proposal out of a sense of duty to her father; and the third is predicated on half-truths and lies, as Singleton withholds from his beloved, dying sister the knowledge that the home she repeatedly asks him about is in ashes and ruins, even evading her questions about the pet dog that the Tory soldiers shot down.

As the most obvious and immediate sibling attachment in the novel, although it would effectually end with Emily's melodramatic death early in the second volume, the bond between Emily and Robert is enlightening for its role in revealing the capacity for exclusivity and passion as well as the limitations and conflicting interests possible within sibling dynamics. While exhibiting the conventional outpourings of his passionate attachment to his sister (upon meeting her at his uncle's home, " 'Dear, dear Emily!' he exclaimed; 'my sister, my sweet sister!'—and his lips were pressed to her forehead ... ," 269), Robert nevertheless not only withholds from her the ruin of their family home and loss of their beloved servants (the servants figuring as "family" attachments in this Southern novel), but he also misrepresents his own involvement in warfare. After reviving from the fainting fit brought on by her overwhelming reunion with her brother, Emily demands, albeit timidly, to know the extent of his militancy: "you are come, Robert, and with no ill news. You have no harshness on your brow, and the vein is not swollen; and by this I know you have not been engaged in any war or violence. Is it not so?" Robert again equivocates and evades, "He did not undeceive her, and suppressed carefully every allusion to his late adventures; spoke of indifferent things, and encouraged in her that idea of the national peace, which, from a hope, had already grown into a thought of her mind." When even her sisterly cousin (she calls Kate, "my sister, my more than sister") tries to console the dying girl with insisting that "We are all here at peace," Emily reveals to her cousin and brother that she knows the truth: "Why seek to deceive me, Kate, when but a glance at Robert tell a different story? Look at the sword by his side—the pistols in his belt, and say why they are there, if war be not around us—if there be no occasion for strife, and if he is not exposed to its dangers" (270, 271).

Emily's tacit acknowledgement that her brother is concealing the truth from her suggests a schism in their bond, which is further emphasized by their extremely opposing positions regarding the exigency for violence. The patriot's sister would perform her most active and vocal intervention with an impassioned plea against warfare, an outburst climaxing with her exclamation, "Oh, brother, dear brother, wherefore would you engage in this horrid war? What blessing so great will it bring you, as to take from you the thought of the butchery you must go through to secure it? Oh, turn not away, Robert, but hear me!" Emily's argument that warfare was an act against God's will evoked the sympathy of her uncle and brother, but not their complicity. Robert would respond, "Ah! Emily, you only prove how impossible it is, in the present state of the world, to be a Christian" (157). This fundamental difference in the perspectives of these Revolutionary War siblings underscored the familial conflict signified by the novel's representation of the war. Emily and Robert maintained their affectionate mutual bond despite their major difference, until Emily's death released Robert from his conflicted sense of duty and allowed him to pursue the attachment of his sister-like cousin, the daughter of his mother's brother, whose more patriotic, even militant, sympathies made her an apt replacement sister. The sister-cousin that would take Emily's exclusive place in Robert's life would share not only Robert's maternal heritage, but also his fierce sense of patriotism and willingness to fight; in a significant moment highlighting the contrasting sister identities, Katherine even attempts to use Robert's pistol to shoot down the Tory major who sought to invade Emily's bedroom in search of her rebel brother at the very moment of her death.

Indeed, despite his withholding of crucial knowledge from his sister—a gesture that would undermine the basic principles of sibling affiliation—Singleton avows passionate attachment to his sister, and it is that bond that he seeks to replace with his marriage to the daughter of his mother's brother. When Katherine admonishes him for proposing marriage while his sister lay dying, a gesture she deems "irreverent," Singleton asserts his sister's anticipated death as an added exigency for his proposal to his cousin:

> At another time, and with an affliction less severe than this, your rebuke would have been felt. But this to me is no common affliction. It leaves me alone—unaccompanied—desolate in all the wide world of man. You know our history. For years that girl has been all to me: I had her to love; I was her brother—her protector—her all; and upon her I expended a thousand strong feelings and warm affections which, when she goes, must crowd back upon, and overwhelm me. We must have something in life giving us the right to love—something which we can make our own exclusive altar-place, which our loves and cares may hallow to themselves, sacred from all intrusion, all rivalry, all denial from another. While she lived—while

there was hope for her—there was always one to me of whose sympathies, when others were cold or stern, I could be certain. When she leaves me, Kate, I am alone; there is but one to whom I may turn with confidence and trust—but one, and of that one I would be secure in the proffer which I now make to you: it is for you to say, and to say freely, with what hope.

Singleton's defense of his indecorously timed marriage proposal presumes the exchangeable roles of his sister and sisterly cousin. Indeed, Katherine, with her militant sense of patriotism, represents a more sympathetic match for Singleton than his own pacifist sister, whose withering life threatens to stagnate and impede her brother's participation in the action of the Revolution; with his enemy at his heels, Robert lingers dangerously by his sister's deathbed, arrested by her dying gaze. Katherine, on the other hand, ready to use a pistol against an intruding Tory and, eventually, following her own father into his enemy imprisonment, actively engages in and supports Singleton's cause, making her a fit replacement sister for the pacifist Emily.

But Katherine's acceptance of Singleton's persistent marriage proposals would be emphatically contingent upon her fulfillment of filial duty to her father. While owning her "esteem" and love for her cousin, Katherine firmly restates a resolve she asserts over and over again throughout the novel: "... in this season of peril, owing as I do the duty of a child to her parent, I will not, while he may need my attendance, bind myself to other duties, which may be inconsistent with those which I owe to him" (279). Unlike the typical courtship romance, in which the romantic heroine may demur and waiver in her return of her lover's affection, Katherine Walton frankly admits her love for her cousin and flatly rejects romantic attempts by Singleton's Tory rival. Significantly, though, Katherine defers marriage while maintaining her filial obligation, a fulfillment that hinges upon the outcome of her father's participation in Revolutionary warfare. Until the vaguely defined consummation of those filial duties, Katherine's capacity for loving her cousin is confined to sibling status, as she insists in one of the several occasions in which she puts off Singleton's marriage proposal, " '... I shall give you my hand, perfectly and all your own, as fully as I give it to you this moment in sisterly regard. There, take it, and leave me, for the hour is growing late' " (280). Making little distinction between romantic passion and sibling attachment, Katherine's "sisterly regard" seamlessly transfers to a marriage commitment, but not until she claims her filial fulfillment.

Katherine's prioritizing of her father over her lover is suggestive of the zealous daughter of Mozart's classic opera *Don Giovanni* (1787), Donna Anna, a famous icon of filial loyalty who defers her attachment to her lover until he avenges the murder of her father by her would-be rapist. Like Donna Anna, too, Katherine's fulfillment of perceived filial obligations would bring her into active collusion with her lover; rather than passively receiving his service to her father, Katherine would be the agent to initiate and martyr herself to the cause of her father's aid. Upon his arrival at the scene of his father's imprisonment just before his sentenced execution, Katherine, characterized by her marked sense of pride and self-esteem throughout the novel, sacrifices her own sense of self at the altar of her father's honor: "Oh, Robert! I have come to you a beggar—a wobegone beggar. I have no hope but from you—no confidence but in you. To you—to you only—I bend my thought—I turn my eye—I look for life—my life, my father's life—all. Save him—save me!" And when he promises to help, the dutiful daughter insists on playing a role: "But what is your hope, your plan?—tell me all, that I may calculate on your chances, that I may note their progress, that I may pray—that I may assist, if assist I can, in a work which calls for men—for manhood only" (508).

More importantly, having secured her lover's vow to rescue her father (or, in the event that his rescue attempt fails, to spare him the dishonor of hanging by shooting him instead), Katherine finally consents to marrying her cousin: "Now hear me—my hand is in yours—it is yours—I give it you in love, in pledge, in true affection—it is yours, and I am yours for ever. Only save my father—say to me that you will save him, and here, in this solemn place—these thick trees, and the spectre-like stars, only looking wanly down upon us, and bearing witness—I avow myself your wife—yours, at any moment after, that you shall name, to bind me such for ever" (509). When Robert declines her sacrifice and pledges his own oath to rescue his uncle, thus denying his lover the claim to his service, Katherine seizes his role in pursuing their courtship, effectually reversing the balance of power in their romance and consummating their relationship: " 'I will now become the suitor in turn; and, Robert, if the poor charms and the humble virtues of Katherine Walton be not all gone, in the eyes of her cousin, she offers them all—all, without pledge of service, without hope of recompense, without any thing in return, but the noble heart and the true hand which he once proffered to her' " (509). Their first kiss upon this requited commitment, allowed by Katherine's sacrifice to her father's honor, seals the exchange of power, commitment, and collusion between this romantic sibling/cousin couple. While making their lateral commitment contingent upon the fulfillment of honors due to their father, an especially significant gesture in the context of the Southern author's unpopular antebellum unionism, the sharing of power and collaboration performed by this romantic pair is nevertheless strengthened and affirmed by their mutual sense of commitment and loyalty to their beloved uncle/father. While all basically validating and reinforcing the nuclear/national union, the three Revolutionary sibling novels of 1835 perform a wide range of possibilities for the balance of power between laterally related individuals and between the affiliated pairs and their central authoritarians. Whether joining forces to overthrow loyalist fathers, negotiating between gendered possibilities for agency and self-definition, or navigating and redefining the terms and conditions of lateral affiliation—even redefining sites of vertical authority along lateral lines, as in the blurred and interchangeable categories of uncle/father—the novels of Revolutionary sibling attachment reveal the sibling romance narrative's rich potential to engage the complex social riddles emerging upon the landscape of national identity making in the antebellum era. Historically relegated to the status of "precursor," the Nullification crisis provoked a chorus of diverse voices straining for the articulation of filial solidarity and independent identity, in which loyal Southern regionalists sought a ground for sustaining national union. The opposite-sex sibling dynamic supplied an apt representational opportunity for experimenting with the possibilities and stakes of independence and affiliation.

Even while seizing upon the recuperative and reuniting potential in lateral attachment in a moment of national fissure, the Revolutionary sibling romances revealed the complicated cost, loss, and violence associated with the enmeshment of peer identities. In the most optimistic rendering of the potential for lateral solidarity to intervene in vertical systems of authority, Sedgwick's Linwood family survives the divisiveness of the Revolution by the graces of Henry and Isabella's sibling constancy, which models the type of tolerance their tyrannical father will have to embrace in order to restore the family union. Perhaps reflecting their authors' conflicted roles as protectors of the national union and loyal defenders of the American South, the sibling plots of Kennedy's and Simms's novels particularly suggest the crisis of a lateral loyalty that is contingent upon the sacrifice of vertically oriented authority, affection, and protection, a sacrifice that Simms decidedly rejects, while Kennedy mournfully and wistfully exposes. The primary sibling couple of Simms's Revolutionary War novel dissolves in difference and death, only to make way for a more sympathetic lateral marriage that will be contingent upon a strict sense of filial loyalty. Simms's positing of a sibling romance that supports paternalistic prerogative appropriates and reinforces the very patriarchal paradigm to which his native South Carolina clung in its Nullification discourse. Together, Kennedy's rebellious heroine and her dutifully obedient brother successfully overthrow their father, whose disordered sense of commitment to an ancient and decaying order is symbolized by the specter of his wife's ghost, a spirit ostensibly clinging to the same parental control over her family's destiny that occupied the final moments of her life. While the novel bestows all conventionally appropriate glory upon the conquering heroine and her brother, thus ultimately reifying the lateral affiliation that enabled their collaborative rebellion, its narrative pause over the loss of patriarchal order, its sympathy for the father's sense of dread over the change signified by his daughter's rebellious marriage choice, confers a nostalgic remorse over this sibling victory, a melancholy effect not entirely mitigated by the conquering antipaternalism of the sibling romance narrative. Kennedy's wistful acknowledgement of the price of lateral constancy anticipates, to some extent, the morbid clinging to a violent cycle of commitment and enmeshment that another prominent Southern novelist, famous for her defense of the domestic culture of the old South, would showcase in her psychological melodrama of laterality. It would be within a context less overtly socially engaged than the Revolutionary striving for national independence that Caroline Lee Hentz would depict most graphically the violent implications of a sibling attachment that teeters into identity annihilation. Hentz's *Ernest Linwood*, while devoid of the overt social agenda more typical to the novelist's prolific career, nevertheless affirms, in its portrayal of the romantic longings and limitations of lateral affiliation, the remarkable and complicated salience of the sibling bond to American narratives of identity and union.

CHAPTER 3

"SHE CARRIED THE ROMANCE OF SISTERLY AFFECTION TOO FAR": SIBLING LOVE AND VIOLENCE IN CAROLINE LEE HENTZ'S *ERNEST LINWOOD*

BEYOND REPRESENTING THE CAPACITY OF SIBLING ROMANCE to respond allegorically to such national crises as sectionalism and the Nullification movement, William Gilmore Simms's *The Partisan* demonstrates the merging of a courtship plot with the sibling romance tradition. The rich sentimental power of the brother–sister bond made ideal marriage mates of such pseudo-siblings as first cousins Katherine and Robert of *The Partisans*. A proxy sister like Katherine could come close to the sibling ideal, with its requisite mutuality and reciprocity, while not transgressing the incest taboo. Perhaps an even more tempting wife-choice than a sisterly first cousin was that stock sentimental figure, an adopted sister, who added to the coveted condition of sibling intimacy the benefit of a complete lack of blood relation. The adopted-sister romance made it possible for an author to combine the ultimate generic convention—romantic marriage, with the era's most supreme model of familial attachment, brother–sister love. Indeed, if market success is any measure of the efficacy of that formula, Susan Warner's phenomenally successful 1850 novel, *The Wide, Wide World* affirms the power of adopted-sister romance. When the novel's romantic hero John Humphreys could find no satisfying companionship outside of his real sister Alice, complaint he repeatedly confides to his sister, he would mold the ideal mate in their adopted sister, the novel's protagonist, Ellen Montgomery. Carefully shaping young Ellen's morality, piety, education, and reading habits, John enjoys a brotherly privilege that allowed him intimate access to his adopted sister's mind and body, including what he frequently calls his "brotherly rights" to kiss and caress his sister. In so doing, John reared his adopted sister up to be as perfectly harmonized with him as was his sister Alice, whose death literally makes room for Ellen in the Humphreys household. If Warner's beloved novel proved the sentimental capacity in sibling romance when it allows for the genre's more satisfying romantic conclusion, then a few years later the most famous antebellum Southern woman of letters would experiment with the same premise, the intensity of sibling love paving the way for a marriage bond. Caroline Lee Hentz's deployment of adopted-sister romance, though, would suggest not the supremacy of such an arrangement, but, rather, the dangers of unchecked lateral enmeshment. While Warner's evoking of the sibling romance trope in the era's most celebrated sentimental novel confirms the salience of that literary convention, even more historically significant is Hentz's subversion of the ideal, as it represents an especially fascinating challenge from a surprising source. As a prolific domestic fiction author with a well-known, conservative voice in the national and sectional politics of her day, Hentz's experimentation with the darkest consequences of the quintessential familial bond of sibling love contributes richly to the complex and destabilizing potential of this beloved cultural and literary idea.

The lasting legacy of Caroline Lee Hentz's prolific domestic fiction output in the antebellum era has certainly been its propagandistic messages, as the critical attention to the novelist has tended to focus on her fiction's vindication of slavery and of antebellum Southern domesticity.[1] Best known as the author of the most prominent anti-Tom novel, *The Planter's Northern Bride*, Hentz's defense of Southern family life and culture extends in complex ways beyond her apologia for the institution of slavery. Indeed, the family-centered defense Hentz offers as a counter to Stowe's abolitionism represents just one facet of Hentz's prolific literary responses to a social structure and culture that she saw fading from existence. While its contribution to the paternalistic defense of slavery has doomed it to a reductive legacy at best, Hentz's domestic fiction exposes complex assumptions and concerns underlying the slavery debate, sectionalism, and familial and national structures, and it holds a prominent, if fraught and forgotten, place in Southern literary history. While *The Planter's Northern Bride* presents the novelist's most direct and overt defense of slavery in her fiction, the perceptions about power, affiliation, and authority that would inform that pro-slavery novel would develop in even more compelling and complex ways in her depictions of sibling dynamics in her fiction. Over and over again in her prolific sentimental fiction output, the writer grapples with the psychological and social implications of familial attachments by imagining the dynamics between opposite-sex siblings.[2] But it would not be until she stepped away from the overt social agenda that characterized most of her literary career that Hentz would develop her most psychologically compelling portrait of enmeshed attachment in her 1856 *Ernest Linwood*.[3]

Born and raised in Massachusetts, Hentz relocated to Chapel Hill, North Carolina, shortly after her marriage, and she lived most of the remaining 30 years of her life below the Mason–Dixon line. Hentz's literary career, which flourished between 1832 until her death in 1856, usually reflected the author's deep immersion into the culture of her adopted region, as Southern settings, characters, and values would dominate her literary productions.[4] In her domestic fiction, Hentz's experiments with the sibling bond and its romantic potential spans a remarkable spectrum of opposite-sex sibling possibilities, including intensely enmeshed biological brothers and sisters, the ripening of romantic love between cousin pairs raised under the same roof as siblings, long-lost and rediscovered brother–sister pairs who narrowly avoid incest, elder brother and sister pairs who reunite after marriage and widowhood, and romantic entanglements between fraternal neighbors and friends. The intensity of sibling attachment in Hentz's fiction frequently blurs the lines of fraternal and romantic love, while maintaining the stalwart antebellum conservatism essential to the author's prominence as a respectable and best-selling Southern "scribbling woman." Whether allowing the brotherly and sisterly affection between first cousins to blossom into passion, which was certainly not taboo in the antebellum South, or exposing the passionate jealousies of a petted and beloved sister wary of her brother's impending betrothal to another woman, Hentz writes siblings with a wildly romantic and conspicuous intent that merits critical attention. Her fictional siblings at times extend and at other times expose the limitations of sibling devotion, duty, and loyalty. Taken together, they reveal a wide range of psychological potential in the sibling bond and reveal the complexities of fraternal order that the nation, and Southern patriots in particular, were grappling with in antebellum America. Even without insisting on an intentional allegory to the national divisiveness that would rise and peak during her antebellum career, Hentz's sibling romance, especially when it functions as the central model of intimacy within her novel's plot, provides a fitting and compelling lens through which to consider the anxieties of fraught familial dynamics mirrored, reflected, and dramatized on the national stage. While the bond of sibling love occupies much of this famous antebellum novelist's literary output, nowhere is it more interestingly complicated than in her 1856 *Ernest Linwood*, which was published immediately after the author's death.[5] A close examination of the costs, rewards, and implications of sibling attachments in this novel reveals the richly nuanced implication of that literary trope in the context of an authorial perspective with legendary sympathy for Southern domestic culture. Of the examples of the sibling romance genre treated in this book, Hentz's novel presents the most psychologically probing study of sibling love, and in so doing so, it evokes more elements of the American gothic tradition than any of the other novels. Situating the effects of this gothic-infused domestic novel within a history of socially engaged fiction, a gesture all the more legitimate given Hentz's reputation as a vehement defender of Southern culture, further deepens and enriches the implication of sibling affiliation in American literary history. In addition to such stock elements as mysterious lineages and hidden identities, inherited curses, and even the setting of a remote and stifling ancestral mansion, *Ernest Linwood* employs the first-person narrative point of view conventional in gothic fiction,[6] and it focuses on the dark inner turmoil of its title character, who struggles to define himself amid the strictures of a stifling family dynamic that situates him as the sole guardian and protector of his sister. Particularly evocative of the gothic is the repeated pattern of violence that manifests from this melancholy title figure's incapacity for self-consciousness, paralleled by his manic narcissism, which the narrative firmly couches in terms of his annihilating attachment to both his biological sister and his adopted sister/wife, who narrates this retrospective romance. By imagining the dark capacity for lateral love and violence to delimit the development of the self and to jeopardize dynamics between the self and society, Hentz presents a timely interrogation of the brotherly terms of affiliation that all camps of nationalism in antebellum America were appropriating, a probing that is all the more relevant given the author's conflicted loyalties as a defender of Southern domesticity and a patriotic American unionist.

Appreciating the significance of sibling love and violence in *Ernest Linwood* restores Hentz's role in disrupting or blurring such apparently distinct categories of American literary history as the American gothic, a tradition historically presumed to be socially detached and focused on the phenomenon of individual psychological development, and domestic sentimentalism, a genre historically marginalized and undervalued for its popularity and its overt resonance with the social world.[7] While firmly set within the sentimental contexts of courtship and family, feeling and sympathy, the novel's departure into such sensational episodes as near-incest and deranged murder attempts makes it as genre-disrupting as Melville's *Pierre* and Charles Brockden Brown's *Wieland*, the narratives Elizabeth Dill deems "anti-novels" for their capacity to disrupt or merge the sentimental and the sensational.[8] Such novels that defy tidy genre classification pose a particular challenge to the tradition in literary history, especially as a basis for understanding the canon, and the "resulting violence to genre stability signals a move toward a kind of writing that is too mutable to be categorized, that plays with the crossbreedings of genre" (710). Indeed, Dill's pithy master-plot summary of *Pierre* and *Wieland* can nearly apply to *Ernest Linwood*: "the bastard daughters of dead mistresses discover their paternities through erotically charged relationship with their half-brothers, and then everybody dies" (709); unlike Brown and Melville, though, Hentz would return her protagonists, literally and figuratively scarred by their participation in sensational love and violence, to the obligations of domesticity and sentimentalism, rather than relinquishing their plots to the catharsis of a tragic ending. Such destabilizing of genre and effect reflects Hentz's fraught and complicated, even at times paradoxical, positions as a native Northerner famous for defending her adopted Southern culture, a professed nationalist whose rebuttal of Stowe's version of plantation life would fuel the cause of Southern secession from the national union, and a sentimentalist deploying the sensationalistic horror of domestic violence in an exposé of lateral enmeshment in her posthumously published novel of sibling love and marital turmoil. If, as Dill suggests, "the confusion of genres is at its essence an American gesture toward a romance without a center, without a structure or hierarchy" (733), then Hentz's experiment in genre chaos makes an especially significant contribution, not only given her novel's bleak representation of lateral affiliation and its clinging to sentimental constructions of family in the wake of violence, but also given the author's extensive commitments to domesticity and her prominent, conflict-ridden engagement with the largest public debates of her time.

Hentz's Southern domestic fiction reveals her profound commitment to the hierarchical structure of the patriarchal plantation culture, but her politics are fraught with cross-purposes and conflicting implications, as may well be expected of a writer whose sympathy with her adopted South was nevertheless tempered by her native awareness of Northern biases.[9] Although it would become the symbolic manifesto of Southern domestic independence in its portrayal of the benevolent paternalism of plantation life, for instance, *The Planter's Northern Bride* presents its defense of Southern culture as a gesture of nationalism and patriotism, and not of separation and aggression, as indicated by Hentz's diplomatic preface, which states that "We believe that there are a host of noble, liberal minds, of warm, generous, candid hearts, at the North, that will bear us out in our views of Southern character, and that feel with us that our *national* honour is tarnished, when a portion of our country is held up to public disgrace and foreign insult, by those, too, whom every feeling of patriotism should lead to defend it from ignominy and shield it from dishonour."[10] Critical readings of *The Planter's Northern Bride* debate the actual extent of the nationalizing and unifying agenda the author professed, versus what appears to be the more incendiary implications of her valorized Southern heroes and vilified abolitionist characters.[11] Uncontested, though, is an important ideological premise of Hentz's fiction: a staunch devotion to Southern paternalistic hierarchy in opposition to the culture of Northern individualism. Jamie Stanesa has demonstrated how the ethic of paternalism in the "Edenic" plantation home of *The Planter's Northern Bride* serves to critique "the threat of satanic individualism to the happy Eden lodged at its center and the near anarchy resulting from the intrusion of arrogant, self-seeking individuals."[12] Also illuminating Hentz's resistance to Northern individualism, Robert Hunt examines how Hentz's fiction deploys the insulated ethic of domesticity to create a "domesticated" slavery that would appear as a "pure, undefiled response to the evils of the capitalist order," an effect she achieves specifically by "turn[ing] the spirit of the world—individual self-interest—into an alien force."[13] The notion of slavery as a domestic institution provided a model of communal order that would specifically refute the Northern focus on the self. "Providing an organizing principle for society," Elizabeth Moss explains, "slavery cemented the South into a single whole and prevented the dread disease of individualism from infecting those who lived below the Mason-Dixon Line."[14] The communal paternalism of pro-slavery arguments reinforced a strict patriarchal order, an ideological premise which, as the previous chapter noted, was instrumental in the mobilization of support for such rousing Southern causes as South Carolina's Nullification. Hentz's desperate efforts to protect the patriarchal order of the South from the threat she perceived in the individualistic interests of Northern capitalism provide an especially significant context to consider her dwelling upon the psychological consequences and implications of laterally aligned attachments. If Hentz's ideal social order was hierarchical, what does she imagine as the most extreme dangers of lateral affiliation? In *Ernest Linwood*, the most psychologically complex of her novels, sibling attachment furnishes a device for this famous defender of Southern culture to dwell upon the dangers of self-absorption and narcissism, the potential pathological outcomes of unresolved sibling enmeshment.

Hentz's posthumously published novel portrays the wrathful potential of a husband's jealousy and possessiveness, a premise that appears to reveal the marital trials of the author's own life. The violent spousal jealousy that is central to the plot of *Ernest Linwood*, though, is significantly rooted in the passionate jealousy of the title character's sister, Edith. In fact, more central to the novel than its title character is the development of its first-person narrator, Gabriella, whose romance with Ernest Linwood hinges upon the acceptance and surrender of Linwood's sister, Edith, a significant premise that I will explore following a brief plot summary. Telling her life story retrospectively, Gabriella recalls her history from her early childhood seclusion with her mother and her mother's personal servant, Peggy, both of whom die, leaving Gabriella an orphan. Adopted by the inestimable, compassionate, and commanding Mrs. Linwood and her disabled, angelic daughter, Edith, Gabriella becomes a petted dependant in an aristocratic family. After two years of Gabriella's settling into her new family situation, Ernest, the idolized son and brother, returns to his adoring mother and sister from his education abroad, to find and fall in love with his adopted sister. Despite Mrs. Linwood's warnings to Gabriella of Ernest's dark, jealous tendencies, a character trait he presumably inherited from his father, Gabriella and Ernest indeed marry. Their tumultuous marriage is marked by Ernest's violent distrust and jealousy, which culminates in his manic shooting of Gabriella and her childhood sweetheart, Richard Clyde, while they are in the midst of an embrace after discovering that they are each other's long-lost sibling (later, they realize that they are not siblings, but first-cousins). Although Gabriella and Richard miraculously survive the shooting, and Ernest, after a brief exile in Europe, returns remorseful, forgiven, and accepted back into his family, the novel ends with the somewhat dystopic realization of the unconquerable dark side of romantic passion and the irresolvable costs of familial attachment. At once domestic and gothic, the narrative casts its title character as both the romantic hero and the dark villain, both enticing and threatening the feminine narrator, whose quest for lateral belonging defines the development and crisis of her identity and her relationship to her social world.

When considered at all, *Ernest Linwood* has been treated mostly as an autobiographical revelation, with the subtitle "The Inner Life of the Author" appended upon its publication after Hentz's death. And indeed, the accounts of Hentz's own marriage support a biographical interpretation of the novel's main conflict, especially given that the couple relocated six times in three years, apparently as a result of Mr. Hentz's jealous assaults on any man who paid attention to his elegant wife.[15] In his autobiography, Hentz's son Charles recalls that his father was "very affectionate, kind... but at the same time, one of the most nervous, jealous, suspicious characters that ever lived." Noting that his mother "rarely attended any party, or social gathering, or received the polite attention of any gentleman without undergoing afterwards a stormy ordeal," Charles Hentz recollects that "from the beginning of their married life, my mother's happiness was constantly crossed & most bitterly tried by his most unreasoning and unhappy jealousy of disposition."[16] Even while Hentz's personal experiences partly account for the subject, in *Ernest Linwood* she explores with fascinating intricacy and complexity the various social and psychological implications of passion, attachment, and competition. While likely influenced by her experience of her own husband's violent attachment and her apparent submission to it, her development of these themes in her novel far surpasses a simplistic outpouring of her own tormented marital history and evolves to reflect upon the limitations and dangers of intimacies on multiple levels. Not the least important of the modes of intimacy that the novel will interrogate is the sibling bond. Not only does the novel's ostensibly central object of attachment—the romance of Ernest and Gabriella—develop between the adopted siblings, but the novel's treatment of sibling attachment also features Gabriella's dynamic with her childhood suitor/potential brother Richard Clyde and Ernest's attachment to his sister Edith, an intense enmeshment that foreshadows both Gabriella's attraction to and Ernest's capacity for violent, narcissistic passion.

The human capacity for jealousy is certainly the prominent theme and moral of this intriguing novel. The title character's violent assaults against his wife's admirers offer a compelling subject for a Freudian reading.[17] But Ernest Linwood's violent jealousy toward potential competitors only partly accounts for the novel's preoccupation with jealousy, especially given the primary role that his sister's jealousy plays not only in the development of Ernest's psyche but also, more directly, in the romance Ernest will want to protect. Understanding the novel's treatment of jealousy in the context of sibling attachment complicates the Oedipal desire that seems to motivate Ernest's passion. While Ernest's most direct and violent performance of jealousy will act upon other men, his self-effacing passion is rooted in his sibling romance, a dynamic the novel takes pains to illustrate well in advance of introducing Ernest's capacity for such violence. Expanding the critical lens to include Gabriella not as merely the *object* of desire, but as the *source* of desire, an appropriate priority given her character's prominence as the first-person narrator, magnifies the importance of the sibling love that she covets. Adding to the significance of sister Edith's role in reflecting and shaping Ernest's jealous patterns, the intense dynamic between brother and sister will influence and form

Gabriella's love ideal; indeed, Gabriella will covet and appropriate the very monogamous romance that inspires Edith's jealousy and Ernest's lack of self. Upon her first glimpse of the love Ernest returned so intensely to his sister, she would muse, "strong indeed must be the counter charm, that can rival hers."[18]

Significantly, though, the first attraction for Gabriella is not Ernest, but his sister Edith. Appealing as much for her angelic beauty as for her passionate dependence upon and attachment to her brother, Edith represents to Gabriella the ideal object of love, devotion, possession, belonging, and affiliation that the orphan pines for from the beginning of the novel. The bond between Gabriella and Edith develops for two years before the return of the brother and son, whose appearance in the novel is delayed for 15 chapters. The image the narrator shares as one burnished on her memory forever was her first sight of Edith, gliding by in her extravagant carriage: "It was that of a young girl, with very fair flaxen hair, curling in profuse ringlets on each side of her face, which was exquisitely fair, and lighted up with a soft rosiness like the dawning of morning" (37). The growing personal vanity that Gabriella confesses throughout the novel does not keep her from expecting even her own suitor, Richard Clyde, to expostulate upon the beauty of her adopted sister. "She looked so exceedingly lovely, I wondered that Richard did not burst forth in expressions of irrepressible admiration. I was never weary of gazing on her beauty. Even after an absence of a few hours, it dawned upon me with new lustre, like that of the rising day. I wondered that any one ever looked at any one else in her presence. As for myself, I felt annihilated by her dazzling fairness, as the little star is absorbed by the resplendent moon" (79). The site of romantic attachment and the direction of jealousy in this instance are significant. If any sense of competition, jealousy, or vanity surfaces in this encounter, it is not Gabriella's jealousy of Edith's superior graces in the presence of her own admirer, but her chagrin that her fair sister and main object of her admiration is underappreciated by the men around her: "Strange, all beautiful as she was she did not attract, as one would suppose, the admiration of the other sex. Perhaps there was something cold and shadowy in the ethereality of her loveliness, a want of sympathy with man's more earthly, passionate nature. It is very certain, the beauty which woman most admires often falls coldly on the gaze of man" (79).

Establishing Gabriella's identity in terms of her desire for sister Edith, the novel locates in lateral, rather than in vertical, dynamics the source of self-identification and self-replacement that motivates such potential psychological consequences as the death-drive and annihilation, firmly situating such violent potential along the lines of the lateral attachment between siblings.[19] That Gabriella is "annihilated by [the] dazzling fairness" of her adopted sister not only foreshadows but actually participates in and complicates the narrator's eventual annihilation by Edith's brother Ernest. Edith herself occupies the very center of the novel's primary jealous love triangle: Gabriella is "annihilated" not only by her attraction to Edith, but also by Edith's jealous attachment to Ernest. Edith's possessive claims on her brother make Gabriella hesitant to accept Ernest's love, lest she jeopardize the acceptance of the "dazzling" object of her passionate admiration. Gabriella realizes the extent of Edith's possessive attachment to her brother after her first encounter with the idolized Ernest. Evading the sister's interrogations about the impression her brother has made upon the adopted daughter of the family, Gabriella remarks upon Edith's attachment to her brother: "I never knew before how strong a sister's love could be, Edith. Surely you can never feel a stronger passion." Edith's impassioned soliloquy reveals the self-centric basis of her sisterly attachment:

> "Never," she cried earnestly, and coming in, she sat down on the side of the bed and unbound the ribbon from her slender waist. "The misfortune that has set me apart from my youthful companions will prevent me from indulging in the dreams of love. I know my mother does not wish me to marry, and I have never thought of the possibility of leaving her. I would not dare to give this frail frame and too tenderly indulged heart into the keeping of one who could never, never bestow the love, the boundless love, which has surrounded me from infancy, like the firmament of heaven. I have been sought in marriage more than once, it might be for reputed wealth or for imagined charms; but when I compared my would-be lovers to Ernest, they faded into such utter insignificance, I could scarcely pardon their presumption. I do not think he has ever loved himself. I do not think he has ever seen one worthy of his love. I believe it would kill me, Gabriella, to know that he loved another better than myself" (110).

Recognizing her brother's lack of self-love as a source of his fraternal devotion, Edith thus confesses to her adopted sister her expectation for her brother's unbounded and unending sacrifice and monogamous commitment to her. When the recollection of this dialogue causes the narrator to reflect, "For the first time I thought Edith selfish, and that she carried the romance of sisterly affection too far" (111), she retrospectively anticipates and recognizes the pathological interplay of self-centeredness on the one side and self-abnegation on the other that such an intense monogamy may demand.

Ernest himself acknowledges, if fleetingly, this pathology when, apologizing to his wife for one of his many violent outbursts, he admits, "The truth is, Gabriella, I have no self-esteem" (268).[20] In this rare moment of self-consciousness, Ernest reveals the important implication of his characteristic violence: the self he has sacrificed (or repressed) as a requisite of brotherly devotion, which is most darkly and dramatically manifest in his character's violent possession of his sister-wife. Juliet Mitchell theorizes the importance of sibling relationships in achieving the self-esteem necessary for relinquishing narcissism, as "the sibling experience organizes narcissism into self-esteem through accepted loss—through a mourning process for the grandiose self, the 'death' of His Majesty the Baby." Mitchell asserts that "Without this gradual and never fully established transformation of the self, the distress and disruption of the anti-social child or the maladies of madness are on the cards."[21] Ernest's madness, his manic extremes of passionate love and loathing, obsequiousness and violence, and his consistently antisocial behavior stem directly from his incapacity to develop a self that accommodates a distinctly other self in his sister, or in his adopted sister/wife.

Edith reveals her awareness of Ernest's requisite sacrifice of self at the altar of brotherhood even before her brother's return home, when she explains to Gabriella her intense love for her brother. Tellingly, Edith recognizes that her love for Ernest is a result of and contingent upon her dependence upon him and his willingness to cater to her needs. Filling the role of her dead father, Edith explained, Ernest "always seemed a protector and guardian to me. He never cared about play like other children, loving his book better than any thing else, but willing to leave even that to amuse and gratify me" (96). Edith thus casts her love for her brother as dependent upon his willingness to prioritize her happiness over his own. Significantly, in her effort to prepare her adopted sister for the arrival of the idolized son and brother of the family, Edith emphasizes the necessary self-sacrifice of this worshipped brother: "Hour after hour would Ernest hold me in his arms, and carry me about in the open air, never owning he was weary while he could give me one moment's ease" (96). Impressively, Edith's basic ability to live and to value life itself seemed to her to hinge upon her brother's devotion to her: she asserts "... how dear life was to me in spite of all my sufferings; for had I always been well, I never should have known those tender, cherishing cares which have filled my heart with so much love. It is so sweet to be petted and caressed as I have been!" Ernest's ability to self-abnegate and self-sacrifice interestingly turns the tables of antebellum expectations for hetero-monogamy, which would normally require the woman's complete self-sacrifice; the consuming effect of that inverted gender ideal is signified by the notion that other men compared to Ernest "faded into such utter insignificance" in Edith's eyes. Perhaps more compellingly, though, the psychological implication of a love defined by boundless sacrifice and possession establishes a romantic paradigm that the novel and its heroine will remorsefully accept and facilitate.

The bond between Edith and Ernest, beyond presenting a temporary obstacle to Gabriella's acceptance of Ernest's love and establishing the novel's most intense, if least overtly violent, love triangle, represented for Gabriella the monogamous passion that was suppressed and elusive in her own life. The narrator's recollection of her first evening with the reunited brother and sister reveals the impression their sibling romance made upon her:

> ... Edith occupied a low ottoman at his feet. One arm was thrown across his lap, and her eyes were lifted to his face with an expression of the most idolizing affection. And all the while he was talking, his hand passed caressingly over her fair flaxen hair, or lingered amidst its glistering ringlets. It was a beautiful picture of sisterly and fraternal love,—the fairest I had ever seen. The fairest! it was the first, the only one. I had never realized before the exceeding beauty and holiness of this tender tie. As I looked upon Edith in her graceful, endearing attitude, so expressive of dependence and love, many a sentence descriptive of a brother's tenderness floated up to the surface of memory. I remembered part of a beautiful hymn,—"Fair mansions in my Father's house/For all his children wait;/And I, your elder *brother* go,/To open wide the gate." The Saviour of mankind called himself our brother,—stamping with the seal of divinity the dear relationship. I had imagined I felt for Richard Clyde a sister's regard. No, no! Cold were my sentiments to those that beamed in Edith's upturned eyes (106).

Evocative of religious hymn and sanctified by the "seal of divinity," the reverence between siblings represents for Gabriella the ideal monogamy. Significantly, it is also her first encounter with monogamous love of any kind, as her mother was mysteriously alone and her adopted mother, Mrs. Linwood, was widowed long before Gabriella's arrival in the family. The "exceeding beauty and holiness of this tender tie" would actually serve as more than simply a model of marital consanguinity, but it would also present a significant, if temporary, barrier to the consummation of Gabriella's desire, as to marry Ernest would require her to supplant his sister. Gabriella's first response to Ernest's professed love reveals her awed acknowledgement of Edith's claim on her brother: "But Edith, dear Edith, who loves you so devotedly! She will hate me if I dare to supplant her" (189). Gabriella thus respects and reveres, but also covets, the monogamous attachment represented by this sibling, with its tantalizing capacity for the boundless familiarity and intimacy that has been suppressed and withheld from her own early life.

Deprived of knowledge about her mother's tragic history and orphaned on the cusp of womanhood, Gabriella's psychological strivings revolve around her dream of familial belonging and monogamous intimacy. Significantly, it is Ernest's return to the family unit that marks Gabriella's awakening to her own sense of alienation within the adopted family in which she had settled for two years. Retrospectively narrating the moment of Ernest's homecoming, "At first," she recollects, "forgetful of self, I sympathized in their joy." But after a while of listening to the joyous reunion from her self-imposed exile in her own room, she felt that she was "... of course forgotten in the rapture of this family reunion, thoughts of self began to steal over and chill the ardor of my sympathetic emotions" (103). Importantly, as Ernest's idol status within his own family hinges upon his abandonment of self, it is Gabriella's sense of self that disrupts her capacity for sympathizing with her adopted family. Once the thought of self invades her enjoyment of the Linwoods's reunion, it incapacitates Gabriella, if momentarily, for participation in the family, as she self-defines as a satellite to their union, or "a mote in the dazzling sunshine of their happiness." This sense of isolation, though it would be remedied by Edith's compassionate intervention, transcends for the narrator the moment of Ernest's homecoming and resonates with the mystery of her very existence: "I could not help experiencing, in all its bitterness, the isolation of my own destiny. I remembered the lamentation of the aged and solitary Indian, 'that not a drop of his blood flowed in the veins of a living being.' So it was with me. To my knowledge, I had not a living relative." Her sense of loss and lack is not alleviated by her adopted status, as the family relationships that elude her signify for her the pinnacle of human love: "Friends were kind,—some were more than kind; but oh! there are capacities for love friends can never fill. There are niches in the temple of the heart made for household gods, and if they are left vacant, no other images, though of the splendor of the Grecian statuary, can remove its desolation. *Deep calleth unto deep*, and when no answer cometh, the waves beat against the lonely strand and murmur themselves away. I tried to check all selfish, repining feelings. I tried to keep from envying Edith, but I could not. 'O that I, too, had a brother!' " (103). It is Edith's sisterly claim, more than any other familial right, which Gabriella most covets.

Gabriella's unfulfilled desire for familial belonging and possession melodramatically peaks at her discovery that her mother's isolation from the world was the result of her deception by her bigamous husband, Gabriella's father. That significant discovery about her mother's past drives Gabriella to rashly accept Ernest's love and marriage proposal, a desperate grasping at an opportunity to be passionately absorbed into and possessed by a family. The terms of Ernest's proposal fulfill the fatherless orphan's desire to belong: "I ask for nothing but your love,—your exclusive, boundless love,—a love that will be ready to sacrifice every thing but innocence and integrity for me,—that will cling to me in woe as in weal, in shame as in honor, in death as in life" (189). The jealousy and suspicion that would accompany such love, the very jealousy she witnessed as the cost of Ernest's devotion to his sister, was acceptable to Gabriella if it brought with it the intimacy that had eluded her childhood: "To be wildly, passionately loved, was my heart's secret prayer. Life itself would be a willing sacrifice to this devotion. Suspicion that stood sentinel at the door of Faith, Distrust that threw its shadow over the sunshine of truth, and Jealousy, doubting, yet adoring still, would be welcomed as household guests, if the attendants of this impassioned love. Such was the dream of my girlhood" (190).

Gabriella thus wittingly and willingly accepts the fulfillment of her wish for passionate intimacy, even after urgent warnings from Ernest's mother, who insists that he inherited his father's jealous and violent temperament, an important family history that she has kept secret from Ernest and Edith. Edith, incapable of recognizing the dark side of her brother, especially as it mirrors the jealous passion of her own inwardly absorbed self, eventually submits to the love between her brother and Gabriella, while Mrs. Linwood's consciousness of her son's Oedipal likeness to his despotic father keeps her on the fringes of the threefold intimacy that is consummated upon Gabriella's acceptance of Ernest's conditional love. In the first scene of their open courtship, Gabriella and Ernest significantly make room on their sofa for the sister who "floats near," pining, "Methinks [Gabriella] is not the only favored one." When Gabriella moves to make a seat between herself and her lover, Ernest responds by moving closer to Gabriella and purposefully situating himself in the middle of the women: "Room on the sofa, Edith, . . . and tenfold room in my heart." Having thus indicated his equal love for his sister and betrothed lover, he concludes: "This is as it should," he said, looking from one to the other with radiant countenance. "Thus would I ever bind to my heart the two loveliest, dearest, best" (215). Upon Edith's demurring reminder of their mother's dearness, Ernest responds, while "passing his arm tenderly round her waist," that his reverence for their mother sets her apart from their love. Surely the "triune band" that Ernest then coined their romantic triangle had little room for the self-consciousness of his mother's watchful presence.

Despite the proclaimed trinity of their attachment, the exclusivity that both Ernest and Edith demanded precluded such shared love. Even as Edith's jealous attachment to her brother would yield to his desire for Gabriella (barely, as on the eve of their wedding, she would tell Gabriella, "I will yield him, not to your stronger but your equal love," 234), Gabriella's sense of obligation to Edith would become an object of Ernest's jealousy. Reflecting upon the effect of her courtship with Ernest on her relationship with Edith, Gabriella recalls painfully that "the sweet unreserve of former intercourse was gone. I had come between her and her brother's heart" (226). But Gabriella's effort to include Edith on her garden walks with Ernest, as when she begs, "I cannot bear the soft reproach of her loving eye!," evokes his distrust in her exclusive love: " 'Very well,' he would answer, 'if there is nothing in your heart that pleads for a nearer communion than that which we enjoy in the presence of others, a dearer interchange of thought and feeling, let Edith, let the whole world come' " (227). Gabriella thus abandons her hope for maintaining her former intimacy with Edith in order to acquiesce to Ernest's demand for intimacy, but she recognizes the costs of that submission, as she muses, "I never imagined before that a sister's love can be *jealous*; but the same hereditary passion which was transmitted to his bosom through a father's blood, reigned in hers, though in a gentler form" (227). Gabriella's recognition of Edith's pathological jealousy reinforces the consciousness and complicity she would enact upon entering such a conditional attachment. The retrospective, first-person narrative point of view, and the conclusive sharing of such tragic lessons, affirm the agency and authority implicit in Gabriella's codependent submission.

Despite Ernest's annihilating demands on Gabriella, their marriage could never attain the sort of exclusivity of the sibling bond between Edith and Ernest. Even while Edith would be fleetingly, occasionally "supplanted" by Gabriella, her steadfast attachment to Ernest and her inaccessibility to other men would preserve her brother's reliance in her impenetrable loyalty. In contrast, Gabriella's capacity for receiving and attracting attention and her consciousness of self and others would repeatedly provoke her husband's disordered jealousy and suspicion. Even while she strives to bear submissively the burden of her commitment to this violent marriage, a submission Mrs. Linwood counsels her to accept given her willful decision to marry Ernest despite her knowledge of his personality disorder, Gabriella retains a degree of interest and willingness to invest in the social world. Modest and small though her sphere of public involvement seems, she nevertheless cannot escape the attention that will incite her husband's passionate jealousy. Even, and significantly, when the various sources of the admiration comprise such intimate identities as father, brother, paternalistic teacher, and grandfatherly physician, the mildest remark upon her beauty or hint of admiration by another man wreaks Ernest's outbursts of distrust, disgust, alienation, and outrage directed more violently at Gabriella than at the perceived rivals.[22] Ernest thus transfers to his sister-wife, Gabriella, the violence that his simultaneously self-loathing and narcissistic attachment to his sister necessarily evokes. Ernest remarkably performs the psychological merging of the narcissistic love and sibling-object love, as well as the violence that ensues from the sibling-object separating or distinguishing from the narcissistic self; as Mitchell explains, "the narcissistic love can likewise be retained so that the sibling/peer is only loved as the self and violence will erupt the moment it is conceived as marginally other."[23]

In contrast to the instability of Gabriella's attachment, Edith's inaccessibility to others allows her to retain her brother's exclusive trust and devotion, even and especially throughout the tumultuous moments of the marriage that broke up their sibling romance. Given that Edith, "all beautiful as she was she did not attract, as one would suppose, the admiration of the other sex" and Edith's own admission that she rejected potential suitors, because, compared to Ernest, "they faded into such utter insignificance," Ernest could depend upon his sister to sustain the original source of his manic enmeshment. Edith's alienation from of all but Ernest's gaze functions as the ideal image of exclusivity and devotion that Ernest would contrast to his own wife's role as the subject of "idle gossip." Articulating his outrage about hearing intimate family friends remarking, apparently mildly and amicably, upon Gabriella's attractiveness and childhood romantic conquests, Ernest insists, "There must be something wrong, Gabriella, or you would not be the subject of such remarks. Edith, all lovely as she is, passes on without exciting them" (332). Though unconscious of the pathological enmeshment that precludes Edith's participation in even such mild associations, Ernest nevertheless thus indicates his sister as the source and object of his love ideal, purely and reliably disengaged from past, potential, or imagined attachment to any but her brother, that is, at least until Edith, with Gabriella's facilitation, becomes capable of her self-realization and self-transformation, consummated in her marriage to another man, a psychological feat that will provoke the full force of Ernest's violent wrath upon sister-wife Gabriella. Ernest's horror at Gabriella's otherness, signified by her capacity to be gazed upon, manifests not only in his violence against Gabriella, but also in his reversion to his attachment to his original, unqualified sister love.

Ernest's attachment to Edith, with the suppressed violence that dynamic entails, occupies the majority of the novel, developing beyond the ostensible consummation of sibling love through his marriage to Gabriella and building up to the climactic shooting of Gabriella and her brother/suitor. In the same scene of marital turmoil that prompted

Ernest's comparison of Gabriella to his more exclusively inaccessible sister, Ernest returns to the arms of his ever-constant sister to soothe his anguish over the good-natured talk of Gabriella's girlhood romances: "As soon as our guests had departed, Ernest went up to Edith, and putting his arm round her, drew her to the harp. 'Sing for me, Edith, for my spirit is dark and troubled. You alone have power to soothe it. You are the David of the haunted Saul.' " Without seeming to notice or question the abrupt redirection of her brother's passionate confidence, Edith automatically reclaims it: "She looked up in his face suddenly, and leaned her head on his shoulder. Perhaps at that moment she felt the joy of being to him all that she had been, before he had known and loved me." For the first time in their romance, Gabriella appears to be jealous of Ernest's fickle affection, which he easily transfers back to his sister. She recalls, "He had appealed to her, in the hour of darkness. He had passed me by, as though I were not there. He sat down close to her as she played, so close that her fair ringlets swept against his cheek; and as she sang, she turned towards him with such a loving smile,—such a sweet, happy expression,—just as she used to wear!" In this moment of restored sibling devotion, Gabriella finds herself once again alienated by, rather than enfolded within, the sibling intimacy; she reflects, "I always loved to hear Edith sing; but now my spirit did not harmonize with the strains" (328). Gabriella perceives Edith as the rival she was before her marriage to Ernest, and her sense of injury is heightened by her indignation over her innocence. "What had I done," she wonders, "that he should look coldly on me, pass me with averted eye, and seek consolation from another?" At a loss for understanding how she had ignited her husband's hostilities, Gabriella exposes the trio's patterned incapacity for resolving their competing desires and attachments, the most stable factor of which is the exclusivity and constancy of Edith's devotion to her brother and his own violently self-loathing devotion.

Gabriella's jealousy of the sibling pair she once coveted transforms into repulsion, now that the turmoil of her marriage has made her more conscious of the implications and costs of the devoted love shared by the siblings. When Mrs. Linwood, whose consciousness of Ernest's disorder keeps her ever on the periphery of the siblings' rapturous interdependence, leads the alienated young wife back into the family mansion, Gabriella eschews the path that will take her past the siblings: " 'Not there,' I said, shrinking from the open door of the parlor, through which I could see Ernest, with his head leaning on both hands, while his elbows rested on the back of Edith's chair. She was still singing, and the notes of her voice, sweet as they were, like the odor of the night-flowers, had something languishing and oppressive" (329). Significantly alienated outside of the ancestral mansion whose gothic proportions ensconce the mutually static and enmeshed sibling romance, Gabriella's fear and avoidance of the specter of that attachment reinforces her otherness. Attractive and enticing as it once was to the orphaned Gabriella, the intensity of this sibling romance has lost its luster in the wake of her full consciousness of its "languishing and oppressive" tone. Edith, whose reciprocal fidelity makes her invulnerable to her brother's jealous wrath, may sustain without the threat of consciousness the harmony of this impenetrable and irreplaceable attachment. Indeed, it is the perpetuity of this sibling attachment, reciprocated and facilitated as it is by Edith, which accounts for Ernest's violent narcissism. As the acceptance of sibling difference is a crucial step in the overcoming of the narcissistic self, the absence of that psychological process has potentially catastrophic consequences. Mitchell notes, "The sibling experience organizes narcissism into self-esteem through accepted loss—through a mourning process for the grandiose self... This is the necessary acceptance that one is ordinary, which does not mean that one is not unique—just that all those other brothers and sisters are also ordinary and unique. Without this gradual and never fully established transformation of the self, the distress and disruption of the anti-social child or the maladies of madness are on the cards."[24] Ernest's patterns of reclusion, his possessiveness of his sister and wife, and the madness that leads to his repeated acts of violence, culminating in the shooting of his wife and her brother/suitor, remarkably fulfill the psychological destiny Mitchell articulates for the unresolved trauma of narcissistic sibling love (a possibility with all the more significance in the context of the pervasive logic of lateral affiliation in antebellum narratives of nation).

Indeed, although prompted by the imagined betrayal of his wife (who is herself a sister-object of Ernest's desire and loathing), it is significant that Ernest's maniacal jealousy would not climax until after his first sister eventually develops the capacity for transferring her devotion and love to another man. It is even more significant, though, that it is Gabriella's own consciousness of the violent restrictiveness of Ernest's attachment that finally facilitates Edith's relinquishment of her monogamous fidelity to her brother. It is Gabriella who discovers Edith's attraction to a young stranger during a family voyage to Niagara Falls. Ernest characteristically attempts to intervene in the blossoming romance between his sister and the young artist she encounters. Seeking to prevent his sister's romance simply by removing her from its sublime setting, his intervention is marked by the same wielding of power, if not with the violence, with which he thwarts admiring attentions to his wife:" 'Let us leave this place,' said Ernest, 'and put a stop at once to the danger we dread' " (350). And although the Linwood women, his wife included, all unquestionably submit to Ernest's authority, Gabriella enacts a powerful subversion before their departure, convincing Edith to allow herself to fall in love with the attractive stranger at the Falls. Her counsel to her sister-in-law reveals her consciousness of the sibling attachment that prevents Edith from requiting romantic love: "Do not, beloved Edith, indulge these morbid feelings. There is a love, stronger, deeper than a sister's affection. You feel it now. You forgive me for loving Ernest. You forgive him for loving me" (352). Gabriella's powerful advice will enable Edith to accept the love of the artist, whom she will eventually marry and hence surrender her hitherto impenetrable sibling fidelity, a loyalty that Gabriella recognizes as "morbid," having experienced its effect first-hand in her marriage to Ernest.

But even after she remarkably admits another man into her confidence, Edith remains free from her brother's passionate wrath, which he will ultimately quench upon his wife's realization of her most coveted dream of intimacy: he shoots Gabriella and Richard Clyde just as they discover that they are long-lost siblings. The sibling intimacy that eluded Gabriella, the boundless love and confidence between Ernest and Edith that Gabriella sought in vain through marriage, was fulfilled in the form of the more likeable suitor of her youth. Gabriella's inability to feel more than sisterly toward Richard saved her from this near incest, but it would not be until after the trials of her violently passionate romance with Ernest that she would be rewarded with, and then instantly punished for, the consummation of her dream. Before realizing her sibling relationship to Richard, her claims for sisterly affection, which she repeatedly made when rejecting his romantic gestures, were almost always qualified by her inexperience in sibling love: "I have always felt towards Richard as I imagine I would towards a brother, were I so blest as to have one" (84). Her lessons in sibling intimacy from Edith and Ernest made her doubt her sisterly feeling; reflecting upon her first encounter with their intense sibling love, she recalled, "I had imagined I felt for Richard Clyde a sister's regard. No, no! Cold were my sentiments to those that beamed in Edith's upturned eyes" (107). And, when conveying to Ernest during the early days of their acquaintance her lack of romantic interest in Richard, she confesses her insecurity about her sisterly affection, claiming, "I thought I regarded him as a brother, till now Edith has convinced me I am mistaken.... By showing me how strong and fervent a sister's love can be" (122). Indeed, while her affection for Richard seemed sisterly, and certainly she could not return his more-than-brotherly attachment, she doubted her ability to feel appropriately, especially after encountering the love between Ernest and Edith. The liminal nature of her love for Richard and her instinctively sisterly feelings prevent her incestuous acceptance of his passionate love, while she continues to doubt that the validity or adequacy of her sisterly feelings depends on her discovery of their shared paternal lineage.

Disappointed by the dangerous lack of trust and confidence in her marriage, Gabriella resumes her yearning for sibling attachment, and Richard Clyde, the provoker of Ernest's most violent jealousy, would occupy the center of that renewed striving. The novel thus continuously blurs the lines between sibling and romantic yearnings and jealousies, making Richard the object of both Gabriella's sororal desire and her husband's passionate jealousy, as well as developing his character around his central sexual desire for Gabriella. Longing to maintain intimacy with the protector of her youth, Gabriella would begin to hope that Richard Clyde would marry Edith so that "he could bind Ernest to his heart by the sacred bonds of fraternity!" (304). Upon Richard's return from his education abroad, a return which predictably triggers Ernest's rage, Gabriella pines for a connection to her rejected suitor, comparing his demeanor and love to her husband's: "Did I never contrast his sunny temper, his unselfish disposition, his happy, genial temperament, with the darkness and moodiness and despotism of Ernest? Did I never sigh that I had not given my young heart to one who would have trusted me even as he loved, and surrounded me with a golden atmosphere of confidence, calm and beautiful as an unclouded autumn sky? Did I not tremble at the thought of passing my whole life in the midst of the tropic storms, the thunders and lightnings of passions?" (367). But even in light of comparisons so unfavorable to Ernest, Gabriella's narrative reflections confess the continued intensity and exclusivity of her passion for her husband, a factor that preserves her from feeling differently than a sisterly desire for Richard. The setting of Gabriella's realization of her longed-for sibling relationship to Richard, the rustic region of their childhood companionship, reinforces the importance of this climactic union, melodramatically disrupted by Ernest's equally climactic violence.

Gabriella's unhesitating acceptance of Richard's revelation affirms her life-long yearning to claim Richard as a brother. She recalls, "Richard, the noble-hearted, gallant Richard, was my brother! My soul's desire was satisfied. How I had yearned for a brother! and to find him,—and such a brother!" (386). Her narrative reflection upon this climactic moment significantly acknowledges the void that Richard's brotherly love would fill in light of the withdrawn affection of her jealous husband. Meanwhile, at the time of their joyous discovery, Ernest had been serving a self-imposed penance of 40 days of solitude for his latest outburst, which he had aimed at his revered mother. Gabriella's discovery of her right to openly love and receive love from Richard as his sister is therefore especially timely, as she significantly recalls in her narration: "At any moment this discovery would have been welcomed with rapture. But now, when the voluntary estrangement of Ernest had thrown my warm affections back for the time into my own bosom, to pine for want of cherishing, it came like a burst of sunshine after a long and dreary darkness,—like the music of gushing waters to the feverish and thirsty pilgrim." With her heightened sense of desire, alienation, and loss, Gabriella eagerly accepted the fervent affection of Richard, who "clasped [her] to his bosom... [and] kissed [her] again and again, weeping and sobbing like a child" (385). Though climactic, the "child"-like ecstasy of brother–sister passion would be fleeting, as it would provoke Ernest's most violent act of jealousy, as he interrupts the consummating embrace between Gabriella and Richard by shooting both of them simultaneously.

Significantly, rather than furnishing the tragic conclusion of a quasi-incestuous love triangle, Ernest's ultimate act of violence against his sister-wife and her brother-suitor would serve as a catalyst for two important lateral perpetuations: it would reinforce, rather than weaken or separate, the bond of the sibling victims, both of whom survive and recover, and it would expose the morbid persistence of familial attachment, as even this most deviant act of violence will not cause Ernest's permanent exile from his family, for he will be forgiven by his mother, sister, and wife, and welcomed back into the family fold. While the latter outcome reveals the inescapably bleak pervasiveness of lateral attachment, the former re-inscribes in romantic terms that static constancy. Once Richard overcomes the horror of his taboo love and accepts his brotherly status, he devotes his life to monogamous sibling attachment. Never marrying despite having ample opportunity (he avows that he will only marry "When I can find another Gabriella"), he chooses instead to remain loyal to his primary attachment, his sister-love, and the discovery of their genetic link wins him the right to indefinitely linger as a lateral relation to Gabriella and her family (while not siblings after all, they discover that they are first-cousins, the result of a significant doubling device that has Richard's biological father steal the identity of his twin brother, Gabriella's father).

But it is Ernest's violence that consummates and reinforces the new terms of Richard and Gabriella's love. After a mutual, melodramatic recovery from their matching gunshot wounds, Gabriella recalls the basic difference between Richard's response to their newfound sibling status (namely, his awareness of his own incestuous desire) and her own emotional adaptability. "If I had loved Richard before," she reflects, "how much more did I love him now... As I had never loved him otherwise than as a brother, the revelation which had caused such a terrible revulsion in his feelings was a sacred sanction to mine. His nerves still vibrated from the shock, and he could not pronounce the word sister without a tremulousness of voice which betrayed internal agitation." While Richard suffered the shock of discovering how close he had come to committing incest, had his life's most ardent desire been fulfilled, Gabriella eagerly accepts the reward of a brother for her self-conscious martyrdom to a violent marriage attachment. Assuring Richard that she did not regret the discovery that provoked Ernest's wrath, she tells her "beloved brother," "Oh! you know not how often I have sighed for a brother's heart to lean upon, even when wedded joys were brightest,—how much more must I prize the blessing now! Surely never brother and sister had more to bind them to each other, than you and I, Richard. Suffering and sorrow, life's holiest sacraments, have hallowed and strengthened the ties of nature." That the mutual encounter with violence brings about the consummation of lateral love between Gabriella and Richard reinforces the disruptive and irresolvable paradox of their mutual identification. That is, through shared violence they fully realize the extent of their individual longings for lateral attachment: Richard with the horror of a near-incest and Gabriella with the fulfillment of the "holiest sacraments" of sorrow and suffering requisite for sanctified attachment. Lateral mutuality is thus achieved through the medium of violence and from the source of irresolvable difference.

Gabriella's insistence on the sacredness of suffering underscores the terms and conditions of lateral attachment in this narrative of sibling romance. As the adopted sister/wife of Ernest and the quasi-sister/love object of Richard, Gabriella's lateral attachments are both facilitated and circumscribed by such dichotomous dynamics as love and loathing, self and other, mutuality and difference, sexuality/sensuality and spirituality. The purchase of Richard's brotherly devotion with her husband's most violent performance, for instance, extends the paradox of attachment, loyalty, and affiliation that are contingent upon conflict and violation. After a period of exile, Ernest rejoins his unconditionally acknowledged family, and Gabriella's reconciliation with her husband signifies the extent of her dogmatic sacrifice of self to the order of lateral obligation. The unmitigated resilience of the Linwood family, rooted as it is in static patterns of violence and reconciliation, strengthens and flourishes in the face of such crisis, as signified by the presence of Edith's new husband as well as Gabriella and Ernest's daughter at the novel's conclusion. In its assertion of both the supremacy and the irrevocability of lateral affiliation, along with its bleak resignation to lateral identification and crisis, *Ernest Linwood* offers a compelling reflection upon the conditions and consequences of loyalty, especially significant for the author's own dogmatic preserving of regional social order at a time of national and sectional crisis.

If Hentz would defend "national honour" as well as Southern rights and institutions in *The Planter's Northern Bride*, her genre-disrupting representation of a sensationally violent and disordered brother, son, and husband, who finds refuge in his indissoluble family, reflects deeply upon the costs of domestic union. Whether figured in Ernest's manic possessiveness, his sister's reciprocal need for exclusive ownership of his affection, or Gabriella's coveting of the lateral belonging that first eludes her and then annihilates her sense of self, and to which she is ultimately bound, Hentz's treatment of such social identities as brother, sister, and spouse suggests the dark side of a social structure that dictates belonging in such strict terms, and at the same time it reifies the notion of obligatory participation in such a system. Hentz, despite her legacy as a stalwart defender of Southern institutions, self-identified as "a native of the North, and a dweller of the South, with affections strongly clinging to both of the beautiful divisions of our common country," as she would assert in her preface of her domestic novel *Marcus Warland; or, the Long Moss Spring. A Tale of the South* (1852).[25] As an antebellum American whose own personal and political attachments defy easy classification, Hentz's deployment of the sibling romance fittingly reflects the genre's capacity to convey lateral affiliation not as a unified and coherently positive domestic union, but as one fraught with conflicting loyalties, obligations, and consequences. The inescapability of the bond has special significance for the nation on the cusp of disunion, as the author's dark representation of a violent spouse/brother whose power cannot be avoided and who retains a position in his family represents the irrepressible power of national union, especially in the context of the language of brotherly duties and betrayals between states that was still salient since its adoption by the fictional responses to nullification two decades earlier. In many ways, Hentz's experiment with sibling romance in this least overtly propagandistic of her novels remarkably anticipates the role of sibling dynamics in the Southern gothic tradition that would emerge in the next century. In her own day, her literary experimentation affirms the representational power of sibling romance, at once evocative of a revered and familiar social convention with remarkable rhetorical power as well as metaphoric for civic infrastructures in a democratic society, a dual power that would make it an apt device for Hentz's most famous literary and social rival to present her evolving social and literary interventions.

CHAPTER 4

"A WHOLE, PERFECT THING": SIBLING BONDS AND ANTI-SLAVERY POLITICS IN HARRIET BEECHER STOWE'S *DRED*

THE STRIKING PARALLELS AND CONTRASTS BETWEEN THE CAREERS of Hentz and Stowe are legendary: both authors hailed from Massachusetts, were married to unsuccessful men, and moved to Cincinnati and joined the same literary circle in the same year, 1832. Each would proceed to become the leading literary voice of the opposing positions in the slavery debate, each woman authoring the most famous novel to represent her side of the controversy.[1] Given the compelling doubling of their literary, personal, and political identities, it is all the more fascinating and meaningful that the device of sibling romance, the appeal, conundrum, and intrigue of lateral devotion and attachment, should surface, almost simultaneously, in the fiction of these contrary writers, who themselves represent a sort of conflicted lateral relationship. Coinciding with the 1856 publication of Hentz's novel of sibling love and violence, Harriet Beecher Stowe's second abolitionist novel, *Dred*, would also seize upon the psychological and social implications of enmeshed sibling attachments, only Stowe would put the intricacies and contradictions of lateral dynamics to the service of a far more overt political agenda. If the sibling bond proved to be an apt mode for Sedgwick, Simms, and Kennedy to imagine civic kinship amid the threat to the Union during the Nullification

Crisis, it would continue to have salience for American writers grappling with conflicting categories of national, racial, and civic relatedness as the abolitionist debate gained momentum in the years leading up to the Civil War. Certainly the most divisive issue to confront the new nation, the slavery debate represented the most significant crisis of lateral civic relations in a slave-holding society, making the call to fraternal conscience more salient than ever, as captured in the abolitionist motto, "Am I Not a Man and a Brother?"[2]

More than any other antebellum author, Harriet Beecher Stowe is known for her literary contributions to abolition, and her prolific career sheds light on the relationship between literary practices and the politics of the slavery debate. Stowe's role in American literary history, though, has been a fraught one. In fact, although in the past few decades Stowe's abolitionist fiction has received more serious critical attention, it has historically been subject to overly reductive interpretations throughout most of the twentieth century, ranging from minstrel caricatures that supplanted first-hand critical readings in the first half of the century to, by the 1980s, feminist celebrations of its mother-centeredness. Given such wildly binary treatments, Stowe's antislavery literature continues to have a tenuous place in the study of American literature. While recent efforts to restore the critical importance of Stowe's fiction tend to overstate her politics,[3] there is certainly some consensus that the author's impact demands more critical attention. It is clearly time for a more thorough appreciation and understanding of Stowe's complicated relationship to American literary, cultural, and political histories. Since Stowe's politics—and her literary experimentation—would continue to evolve after her first abolitionist novel, the writer's legacy need not be limited to either, on the one hand, reducing her career to the implications of Uncle Tom's martyrdom, or, on the other, overestimating the liberal politics of that novel. Rather, a more complete understanding of Stowe's abolitionist fiction and its role in American literary history demands that we accept the limitations of *Uncle Tom's Cabin*, examine more fully the writer's other literary productions—especially her second abolitionist novel, *Dred*—and situate our understanding of those texts more carefully within their nuanced historical and political contexts.[4] Recently, critics have responded to the need to place Stowe's fiction within broader and more nuanced contexts. Cindy Weinstein and Arthur Riss have each revealed compelling links between *Uncle Tom's Cabin* and contemporary dialogues about race, slavery, and sympathy. Those multilayered, antebellum dialogues occur beyond the realms of white abolitionist fiction and domesticity that too typically limit studies of that novel.

More importantly, *Dred* is finally receiving the serious critical attention it demands, with studies appropriately situating the novel in the contexts of Stowe's complicated political and literary career.[5] The critical recovery of *Dred* confirms the importance of treating that work not only in its diminished status as Stowe's second abolitionist novel, but also as a major contribution to American literary history, and one that makes its own statement in the context of the literary, political, and cultural dialogues that it engaged. This chapter restores to that history one of the novel's most important interventions: the representation of mixed-race siblings to showcase the violation of fraternal affiliation inherent in an extended family model based in slavery. Given the centrality of the theme of family to both sides of the slavery debate in the 1850s, Stowe's revisionist approach to slavery and race in her second abolitionist novel lies in her representations of family dynamics. The sibling dynamics in *Dred* take on special significance in the context of the binary rhetorical constructions of "family" as either nuclear or extended in antislavery and proslavery arguments, respectively. After briefly summarizing that particular point of disparity in the slavery debate, I will suggest that, through her representations of multiple, opposite-sex sibling dynamics in *Dred*, Stowe attempted to complicate the binary definitions of family in antebellum America, and thereby challenge a main tenet of proslavery sentimentalist discourse. Ultimately, by adopting the domestic world of the extended family that her proslavery opponents embraced in their rhetoric, Stowe would expose the violent disruption of brother–sister bonds in families that deprived half of the paternal descendants of legitimacy and, by extension, of enfranchisement. Confronting the instability of brotherly affiliation in this light, Stowe anticipates, if tentatively, later gestures by African American novelists, who would more rigorously interrogate and re-locate the terms of lateral solidarity.

At the same time that Stowe couched her sympathetic appeals in the Northern definition of family as private and secluded from the world, proslavery writers developed their paternalistic defense of the institution around the Southern notion of family as extended and patriarchal. Just as vehemently as abolitionists like Stowe argued that slavery destroyed families, particularly through the breaking up and selling off of slave families, slavery's supporters insisted that abolitionism undermined the institution of family. As Riss has pointed out, proslavery arguments typically equate the sense of benevolence and protection the slave master provides the slave with the other patriarchal dynamics of the family, including the husband–wife and father–child dynamics, claiming that the slave, cared for and protected by his master, with whom he shares a common interest, is better off than the Northern laborer, whose relationship to his employer is merely an economic one. Stowe's mission in *Uncle Tom's Cabin*, then, was to portray families that are incompatible with the notions of family found in proslavery arguments. Specifically, the families of her first abolitionist novel were emphatically nuclear (or "hyper-biological," as Riss refers to them), with special emphasis on the mother–child bond, as in the characterization of Eliza and her son Harry.[6]

Since slavery's advocates insisted upon the notion of patriarchal benevolence and protection, *Uncle Tom's Cabin* repeatedly portrays the sale of slaves and separation of families. In pointing out that a patriarchal family where the dependents may be sold off for economic gain is a fraudulent patriarchy, Stowe exposes the false character of the Southern notion of family. As Riss observes, "Stowe posits substantive blood relations as the only determining sign of a family" (529) in order to replace the Southern notion of family with one that cannot be adopted by advocates of slavery. If Southern notions of family depend upon extended, patriarchal family to defend slavery, Stowe would argue that only biological families are genuine families. "Thus," Riss argues, "slavery is dangerous precisely because it substitutes imaginary families for real families and attempts to replace actual, substantive kinship with metaphorical and inauthentic forms of kinship" (530). For Stowe, the sham, non-biological families of slave plantations are vulnerable to being divided, and only genuine, biological families can offer adequate protection.

Proslavery writers were quick to respond to Stowe's depiction of slavery, and the sentimentalists in particular attacked the definition of family that served as Stowe's main premise in her first abolitionist novel. Indeed, even outside of the scope of her anti-Tom contributions, Hentz's fictional treatment of sibling enmeshment in *Ernest Linwood* presents an especially pronounced suspicion of nuclear family love, as I suggest in the previous chapter. In her analysis of the rhetoric of sympathy in the slavery debate, Weinstein examines the ways in which Hentz's *The Planter's Northern Bride* (1854) refutes the definitions of family found in *Uncle Tom's Cabin*. If Stowe insists in that novel that the institution of slavery threatened the biological family unit, Hentz, as Weinstein points out, responds by making biological ties unnecessary for healthy families. In her depiction of a child who develops a stronger attachment to her stepmother than her biological mother (who is portrayed in the novel as unfit for motherhood), Hentz establishes that "children don't necessarily love most their biological family, especially their birth mothers," according to Weinstein (77). For Southern defenders of slavery, undermining the notion of the natural mother–child bond serves as a particularly direct rebuttal to the biological family ideology that informs Stowe's opposition to slavery in *Uncle Tom's Cabin*. But the biological mother bond was not the only biological family presumption targeted in the anti-Tom tradition. Maria McIntosh's plantation novel, *The Lofty and The Lowly* (1853), seizes upon the supreme insularity of brother–sister love to suggest the limitations of such lateral intimacy; this famous rebuttal to Stowe portrays the betrayal of a Bostonian abolitionist brother, who abandons his sister as punishment for her marriage into a Southern, slave-holding family.[7]

As the definition of family was the most prominent premise of *Uncle Tom's Cabin*, as well as the chief point of contention from pro-slavery sentimental fiction writers, representations of family, particularly of brother–sister love, play a major role in *Dred*'s revisionist agenda. While the biological premise for family appealed to her Northern readers and neatly exposed the evils of a system that often violently separated slave families, the Southern responses to *Uncle Tom's Cabin* challenged Stowe to imagine more complex family scenarios in *Dred*. In an effort to move beyond the "hyper-biological" families of her first novel, and thereby strengthen her defense of abolitionism, Stowe adopts the sibling bond convention. Significantly, though, rather than serving to reinforce the supremacy of the nuclear family, the sibling pairs depicted in *Dred* allow Stowe to offer alternatives to nuclear family units and to pure biological bonds. In her portrayal of two sibling pairs, one fully related by blood and white, the other half-blood-related and interracial, Stowe is careful not to undermine the nuclear family; rather, she expands the possibilities of familial bonds, adding dimensions to her family-based argument against slavery that were absent from *Uncle Tom's Cabin*.[8] Even more provokingly, *Dred* deploys the sibling bond ideal to expose the illegitimacy and instability of the paternalistic, extended family paradigm that was promoted by the apologists of slavery. For, enslaved, mixed-race brothers ultimately can defend neither their white sisters nor their black sisters, and they are denied the legacy of paternal identification, a privilege essential to sustaining family lineage and fulfilling obligations of individual responsibility within any system of affiliation.

The most developed and significant character dynamics of *Dred* are the relationships between the white hero, Edward Clayton, and his sister, Anne, and between the white heroine, Nina Gordon, and her half-brother and slave, Harry. With her representations of the Gordon sibling duo, Stowe complicates the biological family assumption by acknowledging the interracial family dynamic glaringly absent from her first novel, a risky interrogation into the presumptions of American social order. Stowe further puts the sibling dynamic to the service of exposing the crisis of slave-holding plantation families by centering the novel's major conflicts around the figures of Nina's full-blooded (white) brother, Tom, and Harry's full-blooded (mixed-race) sister, Cora, characters both of whom contribute significantly to the novel's critique of a system of family lineage predicated on slavery. All descendants of a prestigious aristocratic paternal lineage, the two pairs of opposite-sex sibling couples in the Gordon family are incapacitated from full social participation, and the novel positions that dysfunction squarely along the lines of their lateral dynamics and disabilities. The complicated implications of the Gordon half- and full-siblings I will return to shortly. But it is the white Clayton sibling dynamic that most clearly resonates with the conventional domestic rhetoric about nuclear family siblings, making that pair a prototype of the sibling bond. Through her representation of the Clayton sibling pair, Stowe establishes the widely held principles of loving, intense brother–sister dynamics, and the context of that ideology serves to legitimize the attachment between the interracial sibling pair, Nina and Harry, as well as to expose the impossibility of lateral fulfillment in extended family models predicated on slavery.

The Clayton siblings are given the sort of intense, monogamous, marriage-like relationship advocated over and over in advice literature, depicted in fiction, and even reflected in the lived experiences of real-life nineteenth-century siblings.[9] Stowe introduces the bond between Anne and Edward in a chapter titled "The Clayton Family and Sister Anne." In this chapter, Anne learns that her brother has become engaged without her knowledge or approval, and she worries that his marriage choice, Nina Gordon, has a reputation as a coquette. Edward, too, much like many of the nineteenth-century men in Rotundo's study of American masculinity, has anxiety over what his betrothal will mean to his sibling relationship, and he avoids telling his sister, letting her find out from their mother. Such an emotional turmoil over a young man's marriage plans is understandable, given the proliferation of antebellum advice literature that urged brothers and sisters to model their relationships with each other after an ideal heterosexual marriage, as typified, for example, by the following words of wisdom found in one popular advice book: "the good sisters make the good wives, and the good brothers make the good husbands of the after time. If you want to know with a fair certainty what each will be in the unalterable relation and solemn responsibilities of married life, you can see it all mirrored in the life that as child and youth they led" (Aikman 186). Introducing the bond between the Clayton siblings in terms of their anxiety over Edward's engagement highlights the conflict of the close brother–sister bond that is nurtured in a tightly knit nuclear family, only to suffer loss and despair when one member of the pair marries. In fact, Anne's devotion to Edward is so complete that she decides to remain single; the narrator tells us that she "did not wish to marry—was happy enough without" (*Dred* 28).

Beyond the typical sense of loss that close siblings might experience at the news of a marriage, the crisis over Edward's engagement announcement is exacerbated because the brother violated his sibling bond when he kept his affair with Nina a secret from his sister: "At the present juncture of affairs Clayton felt himself rather awkwardly embarrassed in communicating to her an event which she would immediately feel she had a right to know before" (28). Before Clayton's return home, when the rumors about his engagement reached Anne, "she keenly felt the want of confidence, and of course was not any more charitably disposed towards the little rival for this reason" (28–29). The confrontation between the siblings reveals the extent of their attachment to each other, particularly Anne's attachment to Clayton. She asks him, "Why am I the last one to know all this? Why am I to hear it first from reports, and every way but from you? Would I have treated you so? Did I ever have anything that I did not tell you? Down to my very soul I've always told you everything!" (30). Anne's emphatic appeal to her brother's sense of intimate confidence presumes the exclusivity of their sibling attachment.

Anne's anxiety, then, has as much to do with her brother's failure to confide in her and seek her advice, as it does with losing her brother to another woman. In her references to "the want of confidence" between this sibling pair, Stowe taps into a key element of the prescriptive literature about siblings. Advice books repeatedly stress the confidence that should exist between brothers and sisters, with a language that underscores the importance of the nuclear family remaining self-contained. Aikman's *Life at Home* exemplifies this prescriptive trend in a chapter titled "Brothers and Sisters," in which he urges opposite-sex siblings to "[c]onfide in each other, and be intimate with each other" and insists that "[t]here should be such an interest shown each in the other that they will be ready mutually to speak and consult about things which would be confided to no one else" (183). In his 1858 book, *Plain Words to Young Men*, Augustus Woodbury also insists that brothers and sisters should enjoy even more confidence and intimacy with each other than with their parents: "Between brothers and sisters there is generally more confidence than between parents and children" (36).[10] Given the emphasis placed on trust and confidence in the antebellum sibling ideology, Edward's failure to approach his sister for approval and advice about his marriage choice is decidedly in violation of their sibling "marriage." The lack of confidence in the crucial subject of courtship and marriage is especially wounding to a sister, who is supposed to be her brother's moral counselor in exchange for his protection, according to the republican sibling ideology. Moreover, Edward's reason for not telling Anne about Nina—his fear that Anne will object to Nina's reputation as a coquette—is a further transgression of their sibling bond, since, as C. Dallett Hemphill has pointed out, a questionable marriage choice in antebellum America was supposed to reflect poorly on a man's sister (*Siblings*, 116).

Anne's injured response to the news of Clayton's engagement to Nina, who the narrator calls Anne's "little rival," underscores the spouselike expectations that Anne in particular held for her sibling relationship. Clayton was so afraid of his sister's reaction to his engagement that he had their mother break the news to her, but he would eventually face Anne's dismay: "the first glance that passed between Clayton and his sister, as she entered the room, on her return from the party, showed him that she was discomposed and unhappy" (29). When Edward asks his sister to imagine that she had to tell him about a fiancé he might not like, Anne's reply further reveals her monogamous devotion to her brother: " 'I can't tell,' said Anne bitterly. 'I never did love any one better than you—that's the trouble' " (30). Determined to save his "first marriage" and persuade Anne to accept Nina, Edward assures her that his love for her is irreplaceable: " 'Neither do I love anybody *better* than you, Anne. The love I have for you is a whole, perfect thing, just as it was. See if you do not find me every way as devoted. My heart was only opened to take in another love, another wholly different; and which, because it is so wholly different, never can infringe on the love I bear to you' " (30). While Edward's decision to marry would seem to disqualify him from the monogamy of sibling love, he restores his sister's faith in his devotion by carving out a separate space for his love for a wife. In contrast, Anne's incapacity for loving another man with the intensity that she loves her brother makes her a static repository for the sibling passion that would shape Edward's ability to participate in such normative social pacts as marriage. Anne's sacrifice bears a striking similarity to the Hegelian model of sibling love in which a sister supports her brother's ethical and social development while remaining incapable herself of transcending the immediate sphere of domestic attachment. While for Hegel, the functional woman would transfer that circumscribed domestic devotion to a husband, Anne's incapacity for extending her lateral attachment beyond Edward especially underscores the intensity of her sibling affiliation. Beyond Hegel, even, the double standard of sibling attachment—the presumption that a brother can (indeed, should) move beyond his sibling status while sustaining his sister's undying love—resonated with nineteenth-century sibling hegemony as it appeared in prescriptive literature and even in typical real-life dynamics between siblings. In fact, Clayton's situation as brother to one devoted woman and fiancé to another makes him very much like one of the real-life young men from Rotundo's study, who "had created a happy situation for himself. He now had two women of his own age who were committed to love and adore him, while his sister had to swallow her feelings [and] share her beloved brother" (94–95).

While it would seem that Edward's betrayals, especially his withholding of brotherly confidence, would make the Clayton pair a poor example of proper republican siblinghood, instead their conflict reveals the great extent of their passion and devotion to one another. Edward only kept his courtship with Nina a secret from his sister to protect her feelings and avoid the confrontation he knew would ensue over Nina's coquettish reputation; Anne's anxiety over her brother's questionable marriage choice grows out of her love and concern for him, and her pain over being the last to know about his affair reflects the intimacy she is accustomed to enjoying with him. Significantly, the sibling pair continues to enjoy their monogamous, marriage-like relationship after the death of Edward's fiancée, Nina. Rather than marrying either of these characters off, Stowe portrays them living and working together as political activists, continuing to enjoy through their adult lives the "unity of pursuits" that advice literature writers encouraged for sibling children. At the end of the novel, Edward settles in a township in Canada, where he moves all of the slaves from his plantation, to liberate and educate them. "Here he built for himself a beautiful residence, where he and his sister live happily together, finding their enjoyment in the improvement of those by whom they are surrounded" (543). The couple that lives "happily ever after" at the end of this novel, then, is not a traditional pair of newlyweds, but a sibling couple. Although the narrator hints vaguely that Clayton would wind up marrying one of Nina's friends, details of that plot are left open to the reader's imagination. Even the mysterious reference to Edward's apparent bride is strongly evocative of the sibling priority, as sister Anne would establish a "most intimate friendship" with Livy Ray, before introducing her to brother Edward, at which point, "The most intimate friendship exists between the three, and, of course, in such cases reports will arise; but we assure our readers we have never heard of any authentic foundation for them; so that, in this matter, we can clearly leave every one to predict a result according to their own fancies" (544–545). That Edward's marital attachment, vaguely and fleetingly suggested as it is, is predicated on his bride's intimacy with his sister performs a meaningful revision of the misguided course of his first engagement to a coquette whom his sister had neither met nor approved. Such an optimistic, if vague, possibility for the sibling pair's attachment to positively and productively impact the social world as well as the brother's marriage choice certainly contrasts sharply to the morbidly insulated and destructive "triune band" of enmeshed sibling figures—brother, sister, adopted sister/wife/sister-in-law—of Hentz's *Ernest Linwood*. *Dred* thus concludes the picture of sublime siblinghood with a careful restoring of the functional sibling prerogative to Edward and Anne's dynamic. Importantly, though, the relocation of the happy sibling pair to Canada indicates the limitations of lateral affiliation in the context of a race-based American nationalism.

Stowe establishes the ideal sibling bond paradigm through her representations of the Clayton siblings, juxtaposing that traditional brother–sister duo to the more complicated sibling dynamics involving the heroine, Nina Gordon. The Gordon family plays a central role in Stowe's revision of family, race, and slavery in *Dred*. Whereas the fatherless, weak, and fragmented families of *Uncle Tom's Cabin* were the slave families, *Dred* opens in the home of the fatherless, weak, fragmented, and dysfunctional family of a white slave-owner, Colonel Gordon. The two family members introduced in that opening chapter are interracial half-siblings: Nina, the white coquette character, and Harry, the mixed-race slave. The "legitimate" (legally recognized) Gordon family includes a pair of absent (deceased), white parents; Nina, who is left legally in charge of the family estate; Tom, Nina's estranged, violent, white brother; and Aunt Nesbit, who serves as the mistress of the family and official guardian to Nina. Beyond the acknowledged nuclear family unit, though, the Gordon family also includes Harry, and, though absent at the opening of the novel, Cora, who both share a father with Tom and Nina. The family history, including Harry's role in the family, is carefully detailed early in the novel, in a chapter titled "The Gordon Family," where we learn that Harry has been educated and brought up with Nina and Tom, a situation which deepened the resentment between the half-brothers. In his will, Colonel Gordon, the father of the three siblings, left his son, Harry, in slavery, in order "to leave him bound by an indissoluble tie" (39) to protect and serve Nina. Stowe thus sets up this revisionist novel's agenda to move beyond the strictly same-race families of *Uncle Tom's Cabin* (i.e., the "hyper-biological" families that linked the novel to Northern definitions of family, according to Riss) to imagine an interracial family history and complicated familial bonds.

Not only is the Gordon family made complicated by the centrality of a mixed-race, slave brother, but it also illustrates the ruinous effects of slavery on the "legitimate" members of white families. The explanation of the Gordon family history is framed almost entirely in the context of how owning slaves corrupted the family, causing its deterioration: Colonel Gordon, empowered by the laws of the land, leaves his own biological son in slavery; Nina, indulged by servants her entire life, is spoiled and careless, running the family estate into further debt; and Tom, having bullied around servants since his infancy, grows up to be a violent tyrant, incapable of love and sympathy, and estranged from his family. Because of the vices and vanities of the white Gordons, the Gordon family estate is run down and in debt. Furthermore, the Gordon family exhibits none of the republican family values Stowe's readers respected: the Gordon father left his own son in bondage, the Gordon daughter is (at the opening of the novel, at least) a coquette, and the white Gordon son has no sense of either filial respect or brotherly love and devotion. Significantly, the only approximation of a proper republican family dynamic is Harry's devotion to his sister, Nina, a devotion that Stowe exposes as ultimately futile, given Harry's slave status.

While Harry's role as a doting brother is problematic when we consider that he is not only Nina's brother, but also her slave, the novel capitalizes on the implication of that gesture by revealing the impossibility of mixed-race descendants to fulfill the duties of such lateral social identities as brother and husband. *Dred* performs this important intervention through the conflict between Harry and his younger, white half-brother, Tom. Upon Nina's sudden death (the conventional fate of even a reformed coquette, such as Nina, in the sentimental tradition), Tom inherits the Gordon slaves, including Harry and his wife, Lisette, but Harry immediately resists Tom's dominance. When Tom returns to the Gordon plantation to claim his inherited property, Harry attacks Tom, insisting, " 'I won't kneel to my younger brother!' " Refusing to live under his brother's tyranny for even a day, Harry absconds with his wife to the slave refuge in the swamps, under the protection and guidance of the title Black revolutionary character, Dred. Stowe, then, attempts to save her representation of Harry from the same type of criticism that was leveled against Uncle Tom, by allowing the attentive, protective republican brother at the beginning of the novel to develop into the revolutionary, independent man in the second half of the novel. More significantly, she reveals the inherent crisis of sibling duty and devotion in a family system that includes slaves, not merely as the ostensibly protected dependents that proslavery discourse made them out to be, but as lateral descendants growing into adulthood together.

Although it would be effectual, that Harry's rebellion was deferred until after Nina's death underscores the paradox of his conflicted identity as devoted slave and devoted brother. Making sense of the complicated sibling dynamic between Harry and Nina is essential to understanding Stowe's revisionist attempt to represent slavery and race in *Dred*. As Weinstein pointed out in her analysis of the pro-slavery response to *Uncle Tom's Cabin,* Stowe's strict reliance on biological/nuclear families in that novel was a premise that slavery advocates eagerly attacked. Stowe's attempt to respond to that rebuttal is reflected in the more complex familial relationships she depicts in *Dred.* In particular, imagining the relationship between a white heiress and her slave brother allows Stowe to represent "miscegenation" in a context she had carefully evaded in *Uncle Tom's Cabin*. Indeed, the centrality in *Dred* of mixed-race family lineage, an outcome endemic to slavery in the United States even while it was conscientiously hidden and ignored, was so controversial as to be unmentionable for a reviewer for *The Southern Literary Messenger*, whose repeated references to the "profanity" of the novel are surely pointing to Stowe's unabashed and unapologetic representation of mixed-race lineage.[11] Moreover, by representing the Nina and Harry dynamic in the context of the antebellum American sibling codes, Stowe attempts to legitimize a family relationship that has no lawful or social status in systems of American family and society, while at the same time exploring the implications of sibling status remaining a secret to one of the siblings. Harry's brotherly subservience to his sister, unconscious of their relation, has significant limitations, though, because it makes the character at once a "legitimate" republican brother and yet another devoted slave.

While Stowe vigorously frames Harry's commitment to Nina in the context of the brother–sister (rather than the master–slave) paradigm, the consequences of that gesture are complicated and problematic, at best. In some ways, Harry's role as a "legitimate" republican brother makes him more complex than the male characters in *Uncle Tom's Cabin*, because it reveals the conflicting identities and obligations of his circumstances. On the one hand, having been raised alongside Nina with the awareness that they were siblings, and left by their father to take care of her (and particularly to shield her from economic stresses), Harry adopted the tenets of manhood that required a man's attention and commitment to female family members, especially sisters. On the other hand, of course, Harry could never fully realize his manhood while he was a slave. His masculinity depended upon his willingness to remove himself from slavery, and from his sister/owner. Eventually, Harry's conflict is resolved with Nina's death, which allows him to seek his independence without transgressing his expected devotion to his sister. Perhaps in response to the criticism of one-dimensional Uncle Tom, Stowe portrays Harry as a "good brother," rather than merely a good slave, to Nina.

More significantly, if *Uncle Tom's Cabin* posits a "hyper-biological" notion of family that precludes family commitments between interracial relatives, then the relationship between Nina and Harry also functions to revise that claim from her first abolitionist novel. Nina, unconscious of her blood relationship to Harry, nevertheless has a stronger connection to him than she does to her full-blooded (white) brother, Tom, from whom she is mostly estranged.[12] The conflict between the white siblings is repeatedly noted with frustration by Harry, who resents the social restrictions that prevent him from openly claiming and protecting Nina as his sister. Confiding in his wife about his secret blood relation and his emotional commitment to Nina, Harry bitterly reflects upon Tom's mistreatment of Nina: "Don't you know, Lisette, that Master Tom was a dreadful boy... and he was always ugly and contrary to her?" (62). In positing Harry as a more respectable brother than Tom, the novel not only loosens the strictures of the purely biological criteria for familial identification, but it also exposes the incapacity of extended Southern family systems to sustain lateral affiliation, given its withholding of legitimacy from such good brothers as Harry. The inevitable dysfunction of that slave-holding family institution is on display when, for example, Harry is forced to look on, without the power to intervene, as his younger brother Tom intrudes upon Nina's domestic scene and forces upon her his physical claims for her affection, such as "catching her round the waist, and drawing her on his knee" and kissing her. Nina's consciousness of her brother's violation— she confesses to her servant Milly, "Do you know he took me in his arms and kissed me; and, though he is my only brother, it's perfectly dreadful to me! And I feel so worried, and so anxious!"—affirms the fissure in this dysfunctional sibling pair and, in a significant intervention in American literary history, charges a white brother, rather than a black brother, with a sexual violation against a white sister. Such lateral conflict, a deeply engrained pattern in the narrative, accounts for the broader degeneracy of the paternalist plantation family system, which leaves Nina susceptible to the violent advances of her white brother while unconscious of, or at least unable to acknowledge, the claims of affiliation of her mixed-race brother.

Nina's failure to know her true relationship to Harry stands in sharp contrast to the novel's white Claytons, who openly enjoy the mutual benefits of their sibling bond. By showcasing such contrast, Stowe exposes the far-reaching consequences of a social system that perpetuates the presence of unacknowledged siblings. The unavoidable concealment of the interracial sibling relationship profoundly impacts the development of Harry's character throughout the novel. Before Nina's death, Harry's chief frustration over his slave status is his inability to express openly his brotherly love to Nina. He complains to his wife, "the hardest of all [is] to have a sister like Miss Nina, to feel she *is* my sister, and never dare say a word of it! . . . [Tom] must have all the position, and all the respect; and then, Miss Nina often says to me, by way of apology, when she puts up with his ugliness, 'Ah! Well, you know, Harry, he is the only brother I have got in the world!' " (64). Later in the novel, when Tom makes an unexpected visit home, characteristically humiliating his sister with his vulgar behavior in front of her company, Harry listens with anger and resentment while Nina introduces her brother to her guests: "A fiery gleam, like that of a steel blade, seemed to shoot from his [Harry's] blue eyes; and each time that Nina said 'my brother,' he drew in his breath, as one who seeks to restrain himself in some violent inward emotion" (135). Tom's social prerogative as a white brother provokes both Nina's anxiety over her necessary submission to white, masculine physical violation, and Harry's suppressed, "inward" turning and "violent" emotional response. The novel thus situates proper sibling love and loyalty among the socially inappropriate mixed-race sibling pair, while exposing the violent dysfunction of white patriarchy.

While the Nina–Harry dynamic may serve to revise the "hyper-biological," racialist assumptions of *Uncle Tom's Cabin*, it nevertheless exposes the necessary limitations on racial solidarity in a family system that restricts brotherly duty to the demands of the white slave-holding family. The interracial sibling connection between Nina and Harry is not only stronger than Nina's relationship to her full brother, but it also seems to take precedence for Harry over his relationship to his mixed-race, full-blooded sister, and even over his relationship to his own wife. Harry repeatedly admits that his love for and sense of commitment to Nina is the single reason why he has not tried to escape from slavery. In a moment early in the novel—significantly, during one of Harry's diatribes against the injustice of the American government—Nina tells him "If you love me, be quiet!" Harry responds: "Love you? You have always held my heart in your hand! That has been the clasp upon my chain! If it hadn't been for you, I should have fought my way to the north by now, or I would have found a grave on the road!" (146). Harry's commitment to Nina, then, comes before his sense of protecting his wife, whose position as a slave makes her vulnerable to Tom Gordon's sexual advances, as well as his hope for a reunion with his slave sister, who was sold away from him while they were still children.

Harry's unwavering commitment to Nina reinforces the novel's emphasis on sibling attachment, while also demonstrating the conflicting interests and duties of a man caught in the paradox of slavery and brotherhood. A revealing conversation between Harry and his wife is reminiscent of a similar conversation between "Uncle Tom" and his wife, Aunt Chloe, in that the husband in each instance vehemently rejects his wife's suggestion that he turn against his owner. Just as Tom chided Chloe in response to her plea that he run away from slavery for the sake of his own family ("it goes agin me to hear one word agin Mas'r," 149), Harry quickly rejects Lisette's idea that he stop using his own earnings to save Nina's plantation and instead save his money to buy his freedom. Harry's reply to Lisette's earnest suggestion reflects his brotherly/slavish commitment to Nina: "no, I can't, Lisette. I've had the care of her all her life, and I've made it as smooth as I could for her, and I won't begin to trouble her now" (61). Even though buying his freedom papers while Nina is alive could mean gaining the position to possibly buy Lisette's freedom, as well as to seek out and help his enslaved, black sister, Cora, Harry chooses to remain dutiful to his white sister/owner. Willingly and consciously deferring his freedom to the cause of supporting Nina presents both an act of brotherly agency and one of brotherly (and husbandly) betrayal, especially given the pressing circumstances of Cora's history.

Harry's limited and restricted sense of commitment to Cora, and Cora's own precarious role as a Gordon sibling, performs a crucial intervention in the presumption of stability and paternalism in the plantation family ideal. Harry introduces the position of his mixed-blood sister while explaining to Lisette the history of his relationship to the Gordon family. To satisfy his wife's curiosity about Cora (that she had never even heard Harry mention this sister before this dialogue reflects meaningfully upon sister Cora's virtual absence in Harry's life), Harry gives a brief history of Cora's life and circumstances, including her current predicament of being a widow and mother with a large inheritance from her deceased white husband. Rather than considering methods in which he could protect his extremely vulnerable, mixed-race sister and her children from being cheated out of their inheritance and remanded to slavery, Harry returns from that diversion back to his focus on the financial problems of Nina's plantation. When Lisette asks, "Why, she [Cora] will be rich, won't she?" Harry responds simply, "Yes, if she gets it. But there's no knowing how that will be; there are fifty ways of cheating her out of it, I suppose. But now, as to Miss Nina's estate, you don't know how I feel about it. I was trusted with it, and trusted with her" (63). Eventually, Tom Gordon discovers his legal right to take possession of Cora, her children, and her inheritance. Although he makes a futile attempt to come to her aid after Nina's death and his own escape from slavery, Harry is too late to help his full-blooded sister; by then, Cora had already taken the lives of her two children to keep them from becoming Tom Gordon's slaves. Harry's brotherly loyalties appear to belong strictly to Nina, as he fails to intervene to protect his sister Cora. In this glaring conflict of brotherly interest, Stowe compellingly exposes the limitations of lateral affiliation in a system that so firmly delimits the scope of a brother's power.

Although apparently de-prioritized by her brother, Cora occupies a central role in Harry's consciousness of the injustice of his slave status. Cora's voice first enters the novel in a letter to Harry (addressed "MY DEAR BROTHER," and signed, "Your affectionate SISTER"), in which she announces Tom Gordon's seizure of her and her children and declares her intentions to kill her children before they can be remanded to slavery. Harry's response to his sister's letter reveals his consciousness of the conflicting condition of his brotherly identity:

> It is difficult to fathom the feelings of a person brought up in a position so wholly unnatural as that of Harry. The feelings which had been cultivated in him by education, and the indulgence of his nominal possessors, were those of an honorable and gentlemanly man. His position was absolutely that of the common slave, without one legal claim to anything on earth, one legal right of protection in any relation of life. What any man of strong nature would feel on hearing such tidings from a sister, Harry felt.
>
> In a moment there rose up before his mind the picture of Nina in all her happiness and buoyancy—in all the fortunate accessories in her lot. Had the vague thoughts that crowded on his mind been expressed in words, they might have been something like these:
>
> I have two sisters, daughters of one father, both beautiful, both amiable and good; but one has rank, and position, and wealth, and ease, and pleasure; the other is an outcast, unprotected, given up to the brutal violence of a vile and wicked man. She has been a good wife, and a good mother. Her husband has done all he could to save her; but the cruel hand of the law grasps her and her children, and hurls them back into the abyss from which it was his life-study to raise them. And I can do nothing! I am not even a man! And this curse is on me, and on my wife, and on my children and children's children, forever! ...

Harry's reflective soliloquy restores Cora to a more central position in his brotherly consciousness and emphasizes the lateral crisis at the heart of slavery. Here, the novel makes no mistake about the unsurpassable barrier to Harry's true brotherhood; while Nina is the main object of Harry's devotion, that priority appears to be determined by the restrictions of his slave status, and not the restrictions of his brotherly sympathy for Cora. The sphere of his brotherly influence, restricted as it is to helping Nina, is further delimited by the intrusion of Nina's full-blooded brother, Tom, whose entitlement to paternal legacy, including brotherly status to Nina, repeatedly suppresses and invalidates Harry's identity as a Gordon brother.

Reinforcing the entangled crisis of sibling affiliation in a plantation family, not only does Tom Gordon function to disrupt Harry's fraternal attachment to Nina, but he further violates Harry's brotherhood, acting out his brother-spite by disabling Harry's brother-love, in his capture of their mutual sister, Cora, and her children. In his letter asking Edward Clayton to find and assist Cora, Harry emphasizes the shared paternal lineage that especially marks the outrage of Tom's actions, which are protected by the laws of the state: "I have a sister, who, as well as myself, is the child of Tom Gordon's father." Harry's letter proceeds to explain that Cora's emancipation was declared null and void and that Tom became the legal heir of Cora's husband's estate, which included Cora and her children, who were then "in the hands of that man, with all that absolute power; and they have no appeal from him for any evil whatever" (437).

That the white Gordon brother would violently determine the fate of his half-sister underscores the novel's deployment of lateral lineage as a critique of white patriarchal order in the American south.

Tom's legal acquisition of Cora's husband's estate is explained by a history that repeats the novel's focus on the implications of lateral associations in slave-holding families. Cora's husband was the son of Colonel Gordon's sister (making Cora and her husband first-cousins). After Nina's death, and the death of the only other surviving Gordon (who was, in keeping with the novel's lateral development of character affiliation, a paternal uncle), Tom was the next surviving heir, therefore inheriting the estate of his first cousin, which included ownership of his own half-sister and her children (his nephews/nieces as well as cousins). Hardly an indictment on the general tradition of intermarrying generations of an extended Southern family, *Dred* rather exposes the implications of the unacknowledged interracial lineage of the ostensibly paternalistic extended plantation family, which robbed legal rights and status of the brothers, husbands, and marriages that formed within its auspices, while legalizing lateral betrayal, sexuality, and violence. Even Cora's own testimony at her murder trial emphasizes the irony of lateral betrayal and the hypocrisy of paternalism in her indictment of a social system that allows a man to enslave his own sister: "I was born the slave of my own father. Your old proud Virginia blood is in my veins, as it is in half of those you whip and sell. I was the lawful wife of a man of honor, who did what he could to evade your cruel laws, and set me free. My children were born to liberty; they were brought up to liberty, till my father's son entered a suit for us, and made us *slaves*. Judge and jury helped him— all your laws and your officers helped him—to take away the rights of the widow and the fatherless!" (439). Cora's speech not only indicts the legal endorsement of slave-holding, but it also underscores the insulated familial structure that contains, sustains, and condones the unacknowledged and violent legacy of the plantation family. Delivering this central argument of the novel from Cora's voice not only reinforces the lateral injustice that *Dred* repeatedly showcases through its emphasis on sibling love and violence, but it also extends agency to the most marginalized figure to result from that complicated breakdown of fraternal order, the mixed-race sister.

Rather too fleeting, indeed, the potential for Cora's representative and interventionist agency nevertheless anticipates the more thoroughly competing visions of brotherly and sisterly affiliation that would emerge by the end of the nineteenth century. With her adoption of the sibling bond trope in her second abolitionist novel, Stowe effectually complicated her own earlier representations of families in the context of slavery; in doing so, Stowe responded to critics of her literary representations of race and family from both sides of the slavery debate. More importantly, beyond serving as a crucial reminder of Stowe's responsiveness to the evolving political conversations in antebellum America, *Dred* represents an early model of the potential for the sibling romance trope to expose the very presumptions of union and solidarity that lateral affiliation typically affirmed in antebellum America, setting the stage for alternative and competing constructions of race and family that would come later in the century, with the emergence of African American literary voices. To the extent that *Dred* suggests the crisis of lateral dysfunction in a system that withholds legitimacy from siblings, Stowe anticipates a function of the sibling romance that would develop more richly in the fiction of the African American nadir, which would seize upon the nationalistic potential in lateral affiliation to expose the costs of white fraternalism and imagine revised models of unity and consanguinity.

CHAPTER 5

Reconstructing Family in the African American Nadir: The Trope of Sibling Affiliation in Works by Harper, Chesnutt, and Hopkins

IN ANTEBELLUM FICTION, the social salience of the sibling couple lies in its capacity for imagining familial affiliation as a resolution to the conflict between constructed social hierarchies and the vision of an egalitarian society. The sibling trope had special exigency in moments of national crisis, as the brother–sister affiliation and its dynamics provided a familiar model for novelists to imagine and respond to national fissure and recuperation. Peers, compatriots, partners, enjoying a shared history and lineage, and mirroring or practicing for the assigned gender roles of actual marriages, the opposite-sex sibling representation tended to reinforce the insularity and solidarity of carefully constructed and protected familial (and national) unions, which made it especially valuable to the antebellum agenda of building and protecting a national consanguinity. While their representations at times challenged or revised socially constructed categories of difference based on race, gender, and region, the hegemony of those categories was more typically critical to the rhetorical success of the device. Antebellum fiction that deployed the sibling romance to engage and resolve national conflict depended upon their readers' investment in the presumed differences and expected dynamics between a good brother and sister. For Sedgwick, Simms, and Kennedy, the codes of opposite-sex sibling love provided an apt mode for their visions of lateral union amid the crisis of Nullification; Hentz engaged the ever-pressing antebellum crisis of lateral obligation in her experiment with the psychological implications and possibilities of sibling love; and Stowe portrayed a model white sibling pair in *Dred* in order to legitimize a Black brother in the context of sibling ideology, while also demonstrating his lack of brotherly power, as well as to contrast the stagnant and dysfunctional siblings of an extended plantation family, thereby refuting the narrative of paternalistic affiliation that preponderated in proslavery discourse.

While the sibling bonds in antebellum fiction tended to echo, albeit with much nuance, the myth of national and familial consanguinity, the potential for the device of sibling romance to undermine the very narrative of union from which it emerged would most fascinatingly develop in fiction by African American writers later in the nineteenth century. Post-Reconstruction fiction by African American writers reveals the complicated and far-reaching implications of the sibling union trope. Frances E. W. Harper's *Iola Leroy* (1892), Charles Chesnutt's *The House Behind the Cedars* (1900), and Pauline Hopkins's *Contending Forces* (1900) each adopt the romantic sibling trope to imagine the possibilities for recuperation, reunion, and reconstruction. But in doing so, Harper, Chesnutt, and Hopkins would significantly revise and challenge key tenets of the romantic nuclear family and sibling bond as well as, by extension, the terms and conditions of national affiliation. When it is functional (and, as I will show, that functionality is sometimes threatened by the "contending forces" of Jim Crow America), the sibling pairs in these novels is a vehicle to the opening and broadening of—rather than the closing or insulating of—the family, including community venues and homes and multigenerational bonds. The sibling trope functions to expose and challenge the basic assumptions of the white-dominated national union. Especially compelling is the historical revision performed by the sibling solidarity of Black post-Reconstruction fiction; these sibling attachment narratives disrupt the myth of a white-led Reconstruction project and rewrite Reconstruction as an initiative of Black-centered social, community, familial reconstruction and to the rewriting of nationally enforced narratives of lineage, race, and family. In response to white-centered visions of a Reconstruction movement that would reunite North and South at the expense of the civil rights of ex-slaves, African-American-authored romances of Reconstruction adopt the sibling trope as a nucleus not of (white) national union, but of Black-centric consanguinity, solidarity, and nationalistic identity.

For too long dismissed or regarded reductively as a tradition of mimicking white literary tradition and deferring to the expectations of white audiences, the fiction to emerge from the African American Nadir—the period between the official end of Reconstruction in 1877 and the turn into the twentieth century[1]—is now recognized for its rich and progressive contributions to American literary history. Within the wide-ranging innovations of genre, theme, character, and narrative technique, a compelling commonality would characterize this first flourishing of African American fiction: revisionist intervention against white hegemony. For the novels of the Nadir, such intervention typically countered white-centered visions of Reconstruction, as they were carried out in both social realities and white-authored fiction. African American novelists would expose, mainly through their prolific representations of lynching, that the federal project of Reconstruction prioritized recuperative national politics over the support and enfranchisement of former slaves, and they would reveal the renewed power of racial hierarchy, replete with economic disempowerment and political disenfranchisement of Black Americans, virulently violent white supremacy, and the proliferation of "Jim Crow" laws.[2] White fiction writers of the day tended to treat the moment of Reconstruction romantically, nostalgically, or as utopian, privileging a concern for the national union and an end to sectional strife and situating white agency in the center of their versions of history and visions of progress. In response, black-authored novels of the post-Reconstruction era would suggest compelling revisions of history, often situating their plots within antebellum, Civil War, or Reconstruction settings, and offering counterhegemonic memories of those historic moments.

SIBLING SOLIDARITY AND DYSFUNCTION IN
RECONSTRUCTION NOVELS BY CHESNUTT AND HARPER

The shaping of such countermemories of Reconstruction is especially central to the plots of *Iola Leroy* and *The House Behind the Cedars*, which each develop significant sibling pairs in their domestic narratives. Much like the historical narratives of Revolution that emerged during the crisis of Nullification, the historical novels of Reconstruction would turn to the sibling bond to imagine the potential in a recuperative lateral affiliation. With its emphasis on *feeling* and *family*, domestic fiction contributed to the antebellum attempt to establish and protect a national identity and kinship—what Peter Coviello has recently coined the "dream of affiliation" predicated on whiteness—in the face of the growing realities of social difference and hierarchy. The family trope that had such salience for fictional representations of (white) nationalism throughout the nineteenth century would take on new significance and complexity when African American writers would adopt it to represent the costs and implications of national union and to imagine new conditions and dynamics of national, racial, and familial unity. In their family Reconstruction plots, Harper and Chesnutt would draw upon the trope of sibling affiliation to expose racial prejudice and to portray traditional and new terms of consanguinity that directly competed with predominant narratives of Reconstruction that privileged white national union over the securing of civil rights for freedpeople.

In the context of such revisionist history writing, the bond of the mixed-race sibling pair—whether represented as utopian, as in Harper's novel, or as tragically hindered by social conditions, as in Chesnutt's—replaces the romantic trope of the white Northern bride/Southern groom, a tradition Nina Silber refers to as the "reconciliation marriage,"[3] of white reconstruction fiction. While the terms of the white marital union in those plots sometimes complicated the conditions of national consanguinity, the reconciliation marriage trope nevertheless reified Reconstruction's prioritizing of national solidarity over protecting freed slaves' civil rights, and that privileging of the national bond went virtually unchallenged in white fiction. By replacing the white reconciliation marriage plot with a plot based on the struggles of sibling couples, Harper and Chesnutt suggest a critical shift in the conversation about Reconstruction. *Iola Leroy* and *The House Behind the Cedars* insist upon the discursive and representational power in the shared genealogy and social worlds of fictional, opposite-sex sibling pairs, particularly in the face of a national history predicated on a biological rationale for difference, segregation, and stratification.

Just as Chesnutt would make the sibling bond the center of his post–Civil War passing plot later in the same tumultuous decade, Harper constructed the postbellum family reunion plot of *Iola Leroy* around the coming-of-age story of the title character and her brother, Harry. *Iola Leroy*'s invoking of the sibling bond plot that was central to Harriet Beecher Stowe's popular 1856 novel *Dred* is not surprising, given that Harper's successful literary career began with her poetic responses to the famous figures of *Uncle Tom's Cabin* and to Stowe herself ("Eliza Harris," "To Harriet Beecher Stowe," and "Eva's Farewell," all published in 1854).[4] In her first novel, Harper would draw upon the family trope made famous by that icon of white abolitionist sentimentalism. But Harper's representations of Iola and Harry would make stunning revisions to *Dred*'s mixed-race and interracial sibling duos, especially in the familial and racial solidarity and the optimistic potential for progress and activism that Harper imagines in her mixed-race fictional siblings. In adopting the trope of family with an emphasized sibling nucleus, Harper suggests an extended, multigenerational Black American family that reunites and thrives independently of white support, and, most importantly, she prioritizes the reconstruction and stabilizing of that family above the project of white American nationhood.

Raised with white identities in seclusion on the plantation of their white father and white-looking, mixed-race mother (Marie), Iola and Harry grow up unaware of their mother's former slave status until the sudden death of their father subjects them and their mother to the tyranny of their father's white cousin, who finds a loophole in the parents' marriage certificate and remands Harry, Iola, and their mother to slavery. Harry, discovering the news of this family crisis while under the protection of abolitionists in his Northern school, would join a "colored regiment" of the union army in order to facilitate his search for his mother and sister, while Marie was sold one direction and Iola another, Iola ending up serving as a nurse to the union platoon that rescued her from her lecherous slave owner. Thus separating the heroine from her mother and brother, the novel follows her through her trials and efforts to reunite with her family, a reunion that would be contingent upon the success of two generations of the opposite-sex sibling bond.

Since Frances Foster Smith initiated the crucial unpacking of *Iola Leroy*'s cultural and literary interventions two decades ago, the critical conversation has mostly focused on the novel's relationship to dominant culture, particularly the politics of eugenics and racial uplift. Readers have tended either to blame Harper for "whitening" the heroine and her light-skinned marriage partner, or to dismiss the charge of eugenic alignment in light of the novel's rhetorical appeal to white sympathy or in light of Iola's and Harry's rejections of passing opportunities.[5] The significance of Harper's pronounced adoption of the sibling trope, overlooked by the dichotomous critical discussions of the novel's race politics, provides an important clue to the novel's response to cultural, literary, and historical traditions. Through its careful emphasis on multiple generations of sibling love and its diversifying of "mixed race" romance within the contexts of those affiliations, the novel pointedly disrupts the socially constructed categories of racial difference.[6]

The Reconstruction plot of *Iola Leroy* centers upon the recovery and reunion of lost siblings. In her first important milestone towards her quest to find her family (a narrative reward, perhaps, for her rejection of a marriage proposal that would have enabled her to pass into a white family), Iola discovers her mother's brother, Robert, an uncle whom she never knew. The realization of this family link depends upon Robert's persevering memory of his mother and sister, which Iola unconsciously evokes by singing a maternally passed-down hymn while nursing Robert's recovery from a battle wound. While in his injury-induced quasi-delirium, Robert's mind vacillates between imagining that Iola is his mother and his sister. Eventually coming to his senses and connecting his dreams to Iola's song, which he recalls as his mother's favorite hymn, Robert suggests the possibility that Iola is the daughter of his long-lost sister, from whom he was separated in slavery during childhood. Significantly, it is Iola's knowledge of her mother's own steadfast clinging to her memory of her brother that serves to reinforce and confirm this relation; remembering her mother's mention of her brother's tell-tale birthmark, Iola is convinced by that biological marker, which Robert reveals to her under the hair on his forehead, and by her sense of his resemblance to her own brother, Harry.[7] Having first discovered the lost brother of her mother through the significant devices of sibling affiliation, Iola would help him find his mother (Iola's unknown grandmother) before eventually finding her own brother and mother, at which point her family reunion would extend to include two generations of her mother's lost family members.

Within the contexts of sibling reunion, the novel makes important interventions and revisions of white-centered memories of Reconstruction; through both her own authorial activism and her fictional recording of the memory of socially active freedpeople, Harper provides a record of African American involvement in Reconstruction.[8] In addition to its most central positing of Black family reunion over white national reunion, it is via the conditions and methods of its envisioned family reunion that the novel rewrites racial and familial solidarity. While even the most progressive, white-authored novels of the day would position national recuperation as central to Reconstruction and white support as crucial to the project of reuniting kin divided by slavery,[9] Harper eschews white assistance in her rendering of Black family reconstruction. The government agency that would have had facilitated Iola's reunion with her family, the Freedmen's Bureau, had an ambitious scope of responsibilities, to say the least, and the complicated history of their presence in the South, their accomplishments, and the resistance to it by white supremacists is well documented.[10]

Whether credited for supporting freedpeople, blamed for not supporting them effectively, or attacked for its role in empowering them, the Freedman's Bureau in the Reconstruction-era South was so ubiquitous that its exclusion from Harper's story of a reconstructing family bears notice. The absence of governmental agencies and figures from Harper's Reconstruction story is all the more conspicuous given Harper's own famous literary reflections on US presidents and their policies and responsibilities to freedpeople in her poem, "Aunt Chloe," published in her collection *Sketches of Southern Life* (published in 1872 and again in 1891). With the glaring absence of the Freedmen's Bureau from *Iola Leroy*'s stories of former slave relatives and friends reuniting after the war, Harper situates Reconstruction among the communities, homes, and churches of its Black characters and their friends and family. Providing through her novel a powerful countermemory to the story of Reconstruction that assigns agency and responsibility (for blame or credit) to white-initiated government projects, Harper's depiction of former slaves finding each other leaves out the white support and instead portrays successful reunions under the auspices of Black communities and social networks, ranging from "colored regiments" of the military to Black churches, meetings, and homes.[11]

By imagining the Reconstruction, Harper was engaging a popular intellectual and political conversation. Propagandistic historical accounts and definitions of the Reconstruction in the 1890s were prolific, as the perception of the project as a success or failure (and the contributors to its success or failure) represented high-stakes political capital. An 1899 pamphlet, "The Colored American Republican Text Book," a "book of facts and figures, showing what the Republican Party has done for the Afro-American," tries to recruit Black Republican voters by representing Reconstruction as a successful Republican Party endeavor, crediting President McKinley for appointing African Americans to federal offices and civil service positions. Harper's fictional response to the proliferation of such propaganda removed the role of white national leaders and situated Reconstruction among the families and communities of freedpeople. Harper's exclusion of the Freedmen's Bureau from her Reconstruction story anticipates W. E. B. DuBois's critique of that agency in his *Souls of Black Folk* (1903), which, while crediting the Bureau for founding African American schools and facilitating the enfranchisement of freedpeople, nevertheless argues that it was mismanaged and corrupt, and, most interesting in light of Harper's self-reliant Black characters, that it failed "to guard its work wholly from paternalistic methods which discouraged self-reliance."[12]

Indeed, Harper's subversive rewriting of Reconstruction history anticipates DuBois's more extensive history, *Black Reconstruction in America: 1860–1880* (1935), which offers a scholarly account of African American leadership in Reconstruction—what he calls a "splendid failure"—as an alternative to white explanations of the movement. In *Black Reconstruction in America*, DuBois seeks to counter the power of white-authored historical accounts of the period, which he blamed for excluding contributions of Black Americans, distorting the circumstances of what was then known as the "Negro Problem," and exaggerating the ostensibly liberal agendas of white leaders. Harper's particular revisions correspond stunningly with the concerns DuBois would identify in his chapter "The Propaganda of History," which lists three common features of white-centered historical accounts of Reconstruction: "1. All Negroes were ignorant. . . . 2. All Negroes were lazy, dishonest, and extravagant. . . . 3. Negroes were responsible for bad government during Reconstruction."[13] Harper's own awareness of and resistance to those consequences of white history are apparent in her development of socially active and responsible, Reconstruction-serving characters committed to education, family, and community. Harper's omission of white support and her character's rejection of passing and loyalty to uplift anticipates DuBois's insistence that it was "Negro loyalty and the Negro vote alone that restored the South to the Union; established the new democracy, both for white and Black, and instituted the public schools" (733).

The histories that DuBois attacked and refuted were already appearing in full force by the time of *Iola Leroy*'s publication. Taking P. Gabrielle Foreman's cue for the novel's "histotextuality," that is, for its multilayered appeal to contemporaneous audiences as well as its significant representations of its historical setting, Harper's fictional account of Reconstruction, with its unwavering Black center, can be seen as a countertext to the type of historical accounts that DuBois criticized. The plot of *Iola Leroy* makes Black Reconstruction contingent upon the reconstruction of family, delaying the effective participation of individual Leroy family members until after they have reunited with each other, and situating the bonds of sibling "compatriots" at the center of that reunion. Iola must first find the family she lost in slavery, which begins with discovering her mother's lost brother, before she, her brother Harry, and their future spouses can effectively join Reconstructive efforts in the South. Prior to her family reunion, Iola's attempt to teach at a school for Black children in the South literally goes up in flames when vandals burn down her schoolhouse, an episode that records the terrorist violence that was historically more rampant against Black teachers than their white counterparts in the South during Reconstruction.[14] After finding her uncle, grandmother, mother, and brother, and establishing a family home with them, Iola successfully participates in Black reconstruction projects, lecturing on the duties of mothers and, eventually, returning to live and work among the freed people in the South. Iola's brother Harry also becomes a functional participant in Black Reconstruction after he has reunited with his family. Once he is "living cosily together" with his mother and sister, he begins "teaching and was a leader among the rising young men of the State. His Northern education and later experience had done much toward adapting him to the work of the new era which had dawned upon the South."[15]

By situating each of her Black characters as active agents in the project of Reconstruction, Harper revised the memory of that project—generated in white-authored novels and histories—which acknowledged white agency only, whether in celebration or denunciation of its support for the rights of freed slaves.

In her representation of Reconstruction as contingent upon the reconstruction of family and as inclusive of the socially active, reunited family members, Harper, like the writers of antebellum domestic fiction before her, positions family in the service of social agendas. Unlike the insular, private, and self-contained nuclear families of white-authored antebellum fiction, though, Harper imagines a family and community that are interdependent, often situating the reunion and construction of family in social community settings throughout the novel. The significant events in the lives of the Leroy siblings, including courtship and emotional reunions, occur outside the home, in the presence of sympathetically affiliated others. In the most meaningful of such gatherings, the reconstructed Leroys—siblings Marie and Robert and siblings Harry and Iola—attend a much-anticipated *"conversazione,"* which Iola explains to her mother as the gathering of "some of the thinkers and leaders of the race to consult on subjects of vital interest to our welfare" (243); that political context allows the family members to publicly celebrate and support each other's ideas for Black Reconstruction and, especially significant, it provides a setting for the blossoming of romances and the resulting expansion of the Leroy family.

While also centering upon a post–Civil War sibling reunion and presenting an interventionist picture of Reconstruction, the plot of Chesnutt's *The House Behind the Cedars* depicts a striking alternative to Harper's recuperative, collaborative, opposite-sex sibling couple, and its tragic Reconstruction plot contrasts the utopian project of racial uplift that Harper imagined. Corresponding to the most glaring difference that Chesnutt's fictional sibling couple elects *to* pass, rather than *not to* pass, the main characters, Rena and John Walden/Warrick, lack the familiarity, shared social world, and racial solidarity that characterize Harper's perseverant siblings. Rightly credited for exposing the sham of socially constructed racial categories as well as the virulent racism of the post-Reconstruction South, Chesnutt's first novel employs the conventions of affiliation—especially the trope of familial and sibling affiliation—to achieve his critique of national, racial, and social narratives of difference.

Chesnutt's dystopic story of the sibling quest for familial and social status opens with John's return to the home of his childhood after a decade of passing as a white lawyer, during which time he married a woman of an aristocratic Southern family, whose untimely death has left their only child motherless. Motivated by the need for a caregiver for his son, and by the desire for companionship in the lonely experience of his own passing, John persuades his mother to relinquish his only sibling, Rena, to his white world, where he will socialize her into her new white identity and give her an opportunity for social elevation, for the price of her complete severance from their mother and personal history. Having transformed Rena's social and racial identity so effectively that, after just a year of finishing school, she makes a triumphant entrance into John's social circle and wins the attachment of the most eligible bachelor, Rena's and John's passing, their reunion, and their surreptitious social rise were nearly successful.

Significantly, the catalyst for Rena's racial "outing" would be her return to her hometown to nurse her ailing mother, where her white lover discovers the racial identity that she necessarily resumed in that context. Agonizingly assuming the obligations to his own mother's family—that is, to maintain the white supremacist social order of the South—Rena's lover breaks their engagement, a trauma that convinces Rena to reclaim her maternal attachment and strive to contribute to racial uplift as a "negro school" teacher. Resisting her brother's repeated and urgent invitation to return to pass with him, resisting the sexual advances of a mixed-race school principal, and resisting the possibility of crossing paths with her white lover, who eventually decides to cast aside the social burden of racial order and rushes to reclaim his mixed-race lover, Rena eventually succumbs to the violent forces of conflicting and competing identity imperatives. Fleeing from both the predatory school principal and, comparably violating, the white lover with whom she could choose to erase her maternal heritage, Rena flees into the woods in a state of fatal delirium, thus foreclosing her perpetuation or intervention in the social project of racial identity making. Chesnutt engages the sibling pair at the center of this bleak vision of the potential for social justice or affiliation predicated on the reification of racial hierarchies. Doomed to failure because of its requisite denial of maternal and personal pasts, this sibling pair's dysfunction exposes the tragic limitations of familial and national union amid the increasingly violent project of racial segregation.

Upon the novel's opening, John's first observation of the unfamiliar woman whom he would later realize was his sister, initiates the pattern of lost affiliation and familiarity that would dominate the representation of this sibling pair and follow them until the ultimate failure of their bond. Rena's physical beauty catches her brother's attention, as his "first glance had revealed the fact that the young woman was strikingly handsome, with a stately beauty seldom encountered."[16] Attracted by her appearance, John follows her "at a measured distance," from where he could continue his assessment: "The girl's figure, he perceived, was admirably proportioned; she was evidently at the period when the angles of childhood were rounding into the promising curves of adolescence. Her abundant hair, of a dark and glossy brown, was neatly plaited and coiled above an ivory column that rose straight from a pair of gently sloping shoulders, clearly outlined beneath the light muslin frock that covered them" (7). Even Rena's voice fails to interrupt this voyeuristic reverie or to evoke a sense of brotherly familiarity; the opportunity to hear his sister speak simply furthers his detached assessment of her worth: "The sounds of her voice gave Warwick a thrill. It was soft and sweet and clear—quite in harmony with her appearance" (8).

The novel thus opens with John's homecoming after ten years of passing as white in another Southern town while necessarily avoiding his former familial connections. That John fails to immediately recognize or identify appropriately with his sister enables his gaze upon her physical appearance, movements, and "soft and sweet and clear" voice. The relational confusion that has John uncomfortably noticing his sister's "promising curves" and experiencing a "thrill" at the sound of her voice does not dissipate upon his realization of the familial connection. Rather, following her to their family home and revealing himself to their mother, he assumes an awkward physical intimacy with the sister whom just moments earlier he had mistaken for a sexy stranger:

> As she came forward, Warwick rose, put his arm around her waist, drew her toward him, and kissed her affectionately, to her evident embarrassment. She was a tall girl, but he towered above her in quite a protecting fashion .... She felt a pronounced respect from this tall gentleman who held her blushing face between his hands and looked steadily into her eyes.... He kissed her again, and then drew her down beside him on the sofa .... (19).

That Rena's blushing embarrassment at her adult brother's sudden reclaiming of brotherly rights coincides with her "pronounced respect" for his social stature foreshadows the fissured terms of this sibling couple's affiliation.

The incestuously suggestive physical intimacy between the pair, presumptuously initiated by the "towering" brother and passively and adoringly, if embarrassedly, received by his sister, has its basis in separate and conflicting dreams of sibling affiliation. Seeking to fill the void left by his wife, John has come home to take his sister from their mother's home and bring her back to pass with him into the white life he has surreptitiously established. Meanwhile, Rena "thought with a thrill how fine it would be to have such a brother as this in the town all the time" (19), an impossible fantasy of affiliation, given John's real-life association with the white community in which he passes. The schism that characterizes this sibling couple's social identities and expectations frames the plot: John would successfully convince his mother to give up Rena so that he can educate and socialize her for a life as a debutante of the white Southern aristocracy. But the experiment would end tragically when Rena's filial loyalty would send her back to her mother's sick bed, at which point her roots are melodramatically discovered by her white lover. The resulting liminality of her existence, as her brief life in white aristocracy "ruins" her for life among her Black community and the discovery of her origins exposes her to the racist ostracism of the white world, causes her mental breakdown and tragic death.

By positioning the sibling couple as the central subjects of a passing plot, *The House Behind the Cedars* employs and subverts the conventions of that bond to make radical interventions in literary genre and race theory. Chesnutt turns the sibling bond on its head by imagining a sibling couple whose separation in postslavery days painfully parallels the separation of slave family members and whose attempt to reunite and recuperate tragically backfires; in so doing, he suggests the limitations of static and constructed categories of genre, gender, race, and region. Matthew Wilson has recently argued that the novel's confrontational experimentation with such disparate, white-dominated traditions as the tragic mulatta genre and realism can be explained by the early reception of Chesnutt's short stories, whose sophisticated satirical treatment of white supremacy and subversion of "local color" narrative tradition went unnoticed by white readers.[17] Acutely aware of his white audience's expectations (Chesnutt wrote that "the literary door would be open to a Black author to the extent that he helped maintain preferred fictions of racial life,"[18]), the novelist adopted and deconstructed his audience's sympathies and assumptions. To adopt the terms Wilson calls the "locus classicus for Chesnutt scholarship,"[19] Chesnutt's "mining and infiltrating" of the sibling bond tradition is consistent with the interventions Wilson identifies in the novelist's "amalgamating" treatment of the melodramatic tragic mulatta convention and traditions of literary realism.

Not only does Chesnutt respond to and challenge the literary and cultural hegemony of his white contemporaries, but *The House Behind the Cedars* suggests bleak alternatives to the romantic utopia of Harper's fictional siblings. In addition to Harry and Iola Leroy's mutual rejection of passing opportunities that would require them to forsake their mother and grandmother, the siblings' reciprocal support for each other's work in racial uplift also contrasts starkly to the realities of Chesnutt's passing siblings. After Rena Walden is discovered by her white lover in her hometown, she rejects her brother's offer to resume her life with him as a white woman, and devotes herself instead to elevating the status of her race, accepting a teaching position at a Black school (which, by melodramatic coincidence, is located in the hometown of Rena's white lover, whose non-ideological racism caused her racial "outing"). Unlike the plot that made racial uplift endeavors dependent upon familial solidarity and support, Rena's commitment to racial uplift represents the final severing of her bond with her brother, who from that point doesn't appear again in the novel. Chesnutt's dystopic version of the sibling dynamic exposes the social circumstances—namely, the injustices of the color line—that hinder the solidarity Harper envisioned.

That both Iola Leroy and Rena want to serve the racial uplift mission by working as "negro school" teachers, and the centrality of the sibling affiliation and its optimistic potential or bleak incapacity for supporting that service, are especially compelling commonalities given the recent recovery of African American educational movements in the nineteenth-century South. Most notably, Heather Williams traces the values for self-reliance and self-determination embedded in the African American quest for education, both before and after the Civil War. Bringing to light the central roles that freedpeople played in their own education after the war, Williams points out that African Americans in the Reconstruction era "most often had no choice but to rely on one another: Southern whites rarely helped and Northern whites were scarce."[20] By making Iola's teaching career contingent upon her reconstruction of her family, Harper certainly showcases the reconstructed extended family, with a strong sibling nucleus, as crucial to the self-reliant educational movement of freedpeople. Chesnutt's thwarting of Rena's race-lifting ambitions, by contrast, dramatizes the race-based social conditions that disable and separate the brother and sister and leave Rena stranded between the competing and abnegating desires of her passing brother, white supremacist lover, predatory employer, and even her isolated, mixed-race mother.

The narrative reflection upon the failure of Rena's passing experiment emphasizes the sibling dynamic and its conflicted vision: "Warwick, who had built so well for himself, had weakened the structure of his own life by trying to share his good fortune with his sister" (183). The race-based social system that determined Warwick's material success demanded a strict individualism that precluded sibling loyalty or consanguinity of any kind. Significantly, the sibling reference would not reappear in the novel until it was evoked to describe Rena's new-found sympathy for the people of her race: "Where once she had seemed able to escape from them, they were now, it appeared, her inalienable race. Thus doubly equipped [by her Black upbringing and white education], she was able to view them at once with the mental eye of an outsider and *the sympathy of a sister*: she could see their faults and judge them charitably; she knew and appreciated their good qualities" (193–194; emphasis added). Although it would seem that the function of the sibling bond was restored in Rena's new racial "sisterhood," even that affiliation would be tragically disabling: the narrative explains that her new "sisterly" sympathy resulted from her blindness to the villainy of Jeff Wain, the mixed-race school administrator whose aggressive pursuit of Rena literally drove her off to the wilderness in delirium. Rena overlooked Wain's obvious character flaws because of the "broad manner of charity which [she] in her new-found zeal for the welfare of her people was willing to throw over all their faults. They were the victims of oppression; they were not responsible for its results" (229). The dysfunction of even that proxy sibling bond, Rena's racial sisterhood, serves to reinforce Chesnutt's exposure of the limitations of such affiliation under the conditions of white supremacy in the postbellum South.

The Contending Forces of Fraternal Loyalty and Betrayal

In *Contending Forces*, Hopkins deploys the sibling trope to expose the white-nationalist project of the Reconstruction and urges a Black-centered movement of racial uplift to combat the dangerous brotherhood of white patriots of the North and South. For Hopkins, the exigent national crisis demanding her intervention is not the sectional division of the (white) American nation, but, rather, the crisis of the costs of repairing and preserving the union of those divided sections: namely, the withholding of human rights for former slaves. The trope of sibling attachment furnishes Hopkins with a fitting and complicated metaphor for her representation of the competing and conflicting loyalties of race, family, and nation in the turbulent context of the rise of lynch law in the 1890s. Ultimately pointing to the limitations of "brotherly" sympathy and solidarity as the barrier to racial equality, Hopkins compellingly revises the historical narrative of the ostensible division between North and South and imagines the conditions of loyal filial, national, and racial solidarity.

Contending Forces tells the story of a family reunited after generations of a disunion imposed by racist violence. The novel opens with the relocation of a white, slave-holding plantation family, Charles and Grace Montfort and their two sons, Jessie and Charles, from Bermuda to a North Carolina community, where, as a result of jealousy, betrayal, and the prevalence of white supremacy, rumors quickly circulate that the beautiful and privileged Grace Montfort is of mixed race. After a lynch mob murders Charles Sr., burns down the family home, and brutalizes Grace with beatings suggestive of rape, an experience that culminates in her suicide, the Montfort sons, Jessie and Charles, are remanded to slavery. The story thus separates the descendants of the Montfort family; the novel follows Jessie into his marriage into a Black family and leaves Charles's fate a mystery until its conclusion. The family's reconstruction will depend upon the choices and paths of a pair of opposite-sex siblings, Dora and Will, the great grandchildren of the Bermudian Montforts.

As the central sibling pair of *Contending Forces*, Will and Dora Smith serve as the stable nucleus for the fascinating and intricate dynamics of affiliation that unfold around them—and even generations before them. The Smith siblings' middle names, "Jessie Montfort" and "Grace Montfort," the names of their grandfather and great-grandmother, respectively, remind the reader of their genealogical history and signify an important function of this nuclear family unit: the reconstruction and recuperation of family history. The embedding of the Montfort names into the names of the novel's central siblings reinforces the legacy of self-determination in race and union indicated by the Montfort family history. The tragic and mysterious legacy of Will and Dora's maternal grandparents' history is central to their names and their identities, and introduces the novel's complicated treatment of ancestry, racial identity, and family affiliation.

Jesse's separation from his mother, Grace, and his union with his wife, Elizabeth, mark critical shifts in the family's racial identity. The son of an elite-class Bermuda plantation owner, the young Jesse Montfort identifies as white (or, to adopt Julie Cary Nerad's expression, he is "raised and raced as white"[21]), even after the North Carolina community to which his father relocates the family questions his mother's "too much cream color in the face"[22] as a ground for the violent lynching that would result in Jesse's enslavement. Jesse's eventual rebellion and escape from slavery is motivated by a desire not to reclaim his racial identity, but to reclaim his right to self-determination. In the significant scene of his decision to escape, Jesse's self-identification is revealed in his response to a passerby who asks him "who do you belong to?" after being told that the white-seeming young Montfort was "nuthin' but a nigger"; Jesse's rebellious "I am no man's property" (77) asserts his resistance to the stigma of slavery and not directly to the racial marker of the epithet.

Jesse Montfort's first act of self-determination upon his escape from slavery would be his passing into the Black race.[23] After initially "cast[ing] his lot with the colored people of the community" (78), Jesse would continue to be pursued by his slave master, Pollock. It would not be until his marriage to the daughter of the free Black man to whom he fled for refuge and support that Jesse would be effectively "absorbed into that unfortunate race" and fully free from Pollock (78–79). Surrounding the transition of Jesse's racial identity, his familial identity has made radical shifts, as well. Formerly the brother/son of an elite-class nuclear family, Jesse Montfort spends the rest of his childhood as the slave-dependent of his father's murderer, serving the especially intimate role of personal attendant to Pollock. Following both of those imposed family affiliations (and, tellingly, read in this context, the natural, white, nuclear family parallels the master–slave affiliation in the family member/slave subject's inability to self-determine their familial roles), Jesse elects to be "adopted" into the family of his Black savior. He consummates his status as son/brother in his new family and new race by his marriage to the daughter/sister of that nuclear/racial family unit.

The legacy of familial naming in the novel disrupts and complicates traditional systems of identity related to racial, filial, and national unions, and the novel's rewriting of affiliation begins with the same-sex sibling pair, Charles and Jesse Montfort. The resolution of the mysterious separation of the Montfort brothers, separated in slavery in the retrospective opening of the novel, reveals a matrilineal, multiracial, multinational lineage. Reasserting the self-determining path of identities and affiliations, the novel resolves the Montfort mystery with a trans-Atlantic branch of the family tree. We learn in the novel's conclusion that while Jesse Montfort escaped from slavery and married into a Black American family, his brother, Charles, was rescued by a white Englishman, who brought the enslaved, white son of a Bermudian gentleman back to England and married him off to his daughter, securing for him legal action against the US government and his father's inheritance. The discovery of this family lineage by a sympathetic, liberal, white, English descendant of the Montfort family leads to the restoring of the Montfort inheritance and the remaining legal damages to the disfranchised Montfort–Smith family of Boston. More significantly, though, the restoring of the inheritance signifies the reconstruction of the transracial, transnational Montfort family, and the romantic recovery of the legal damages dramatizes an independence from the oppressive national union. The family's eventual recuperation, then, depends upon the retrospective reunion of full-blooded brothers who would end up belonging to different races and nations—a reunion accomplished three generations after their lives through the perseverant matrilineal naming of siblings.

Indeed, the Montfort brothers' restored union and its legacy achieves the novel's only instance of enduring brotherly affiliation. Despite offering its meaningful foreshadow of disloyalty within the context of female intimacy, when the narrator suggests that Dora "did not, as a rule, care much for girl friendships, holding that a close intimacy between two of the same sex was more than likely to end disastrously for one or the other" (97–98), the novel locates its key "same sex" betrayals not with the Dora–Sappho dynamic, which would endure despite male intervention,[24] but within each of the novel's main male unions, each of them interracial. The betrayal to set the tragic family plot in motion was facilitated by the intimacy and trust that the white North Carolina patriarch Anton Pollock had established with his new Bermudian neighbor, Charles Montfort. Initiating one of the novel's most subversive motifs, Pollock's secret plot to incite the white supremacist community's suspicions against Montfort was motivated by his violent lust for Montfort's wife. Generations later, sustaining the legacy of white brotherly betrayal, John Pollock Langley would maliciously covet the betrothed bride of Will Smith, his closest friend and would-be-brother (via John P.'s anticipated marriage to Will's sister, Dora).

The narrative of John P. Langley's mixed-race identity decidedly emphasizes his whiteness. Beyond the more or less obvious whitening of his character through such physical portraits as "of the Caucasian cut" (90), the history surrounding his self-selected middle name functions to highlight his white ancestry. In contrast to the careful, matrilineal preserving of Montfort familial names and their legacies, the narrator reveals that John Pollock Langley "clung to the name" Pollock because "somewhere in the dim past a woman, presumably his mother, had boasted that through her he was a direct descendant of the North Carolina Pollocks" (221–222). Significantly and subversively, it is his white ancestry that explains John P.'s deviance, including the "carefully concealed strain of sensuality in his nature" (91); his white blood is particularly coded in the scenes of his contemplating and performing his passion-motivated betrayal (e.g., "His face was pale" when he entered Sappho's bedroom determined to coerce her into becoming his concubine, 316). The "white taint" assigned to John P.'s base character—and the betrayal that it explains—performs a meaningful contradiction to the traditionally pejorative association of African ancestry. Finally, an especially unambiguous and poignant instance of white brotherly betrayal explains the tragic mystery of Sappho's past. We learn through her adopted brother, Luke Sawyer, the story of her kidnapping and rape by her father's white half-brother, who, Luke recalls, was "very warm in his expression of friendship for the family, and especially so in his assumption of relationship" (259). Like the betrayals enacted by Anson Pollock and John P. Langley, Luke's story of his father-figure's betrayal by his white brother contributes to the novel's critical project of subverting the myth of the hypersensual and threatening Black man by representing a long history of the white rapist.

Though his appearance in the novel is fleeting, Luke Sawyer's testimonial enacts another recurrent plot and character dynamic motif of critical importance to the novel. In addition to repeating the trope of disloyal, violent white brother affiliation, Luke's story about his own and Sappho's tragic histories reiterates the complicated potential of adopted sibling unions suggested by the "founding" Black-American Montfort union between Jesse and his rescuer's daughter, Elizabeth. Having also witnessed as a young child the mob murder of his family and the burning down of his home, and finding refuge in the family of free Blacks, Luke's story strongly parallels Jesse Montfort's history. In his account of his early experiences with mob violence, a memory that he shares with the Black community gathered at a meeting of the Boston chapter of the American Colored League, Luke suggests the strong bond he developed with his rescuer's daughter, whom he would rescue first from her imprisonment and forced concubinage and then from mob arson: "As a boy I worshipped her, and as a man I loved her" (260–261). Not only does Luke's public testimonial reveal the secret of Sappho's past, but it links that past meaningfully to the ongoing reign of mob terror and to the tradition of nationalist brotherly betrayal. In his significant preface to the sharing of his tragic memory, Luke insists that the conservative responses to mob violence indicated "the lack of brotherly affiliation" and demonstrated "*the contending forces that are dooming this race to despair*" (256). By assigning such title-signifying authority to the sharer of the novel's most critical plot secret within the context of a heated meeting of the American Colored League, Hopkins spotlights her assertion of racial solidarity and "brotherly affiliation" as conditions of racial uplift. In doing so, she performs an important intervention against white supremacy and participates in emergent Black nationalist movements that advocated for racial solidarity at the turn of the century.[25] A basic belief in the power of civilization and community undergirds all of the different Black nationalistic agenda, and Hopkins's insistence on "brotherly affiliation" in *Contending Forces* supports that spirit.[26] As "Brotherhood" and "sisterhood" were central paradigms for the various Black nationalism movements in the late nineteenth and early twentieth centuries, Hopkins's deployment of the nationalistic function of sibling romance reinforces racial solidarity as it appropriates and subverts the white nationalistic tradition of brotherly love.

In her sharing of the contemporaneous race and nation debates in several of the American Colored League chapters that occupy the center of the novel, Hopkins sheds light on the forces of union that motivate white nationalism at the expense of Black enfranchisement. The novel's depiction of Hon. Herbert Clapp, "a representative of the party and of the sentiment of the best white people of the country" (245), exposes the white "brotherly" loyalty that prioritized the Reconstruction of the national union and the healing of sectional division over the protection of Black Americans' civil rights. In his private political negotiations with Langley, who was serving as the self-interested and unscrupulous leader of the Boston chapter of the American Colored League, Clapp admits the white national loyalty that would suppress any meaningful militant intervention from Black activists: "Your people can't help themselves. If you rose in the South and appealed to arms you would soon be exterminated; for of course the South is our brother, and in an uprising of that sort, the National arms would necessarily be directed against the 'rioters,' as they would be termed" (234). The white politician's language of North–South brotherhood recurs in his public address at the American Colored League meeting, in which he introduces his ethos "As a white man looking upon the South as my brother, and desiring to see the welfare of that section secured along with the brother in black" (245). The slight diplomatic gesture (an ineffective one, given his audience's collective "sigh like a broken moan") of Clapp's public statement further relies on the brotherhood trope, only to reify the more privileged bond of the white national union. Intent upon national solidarity, Clapp insists that "the [race] problem is national, not sectional" and that the claims against the Black politician made by his "Southern brother" are legitimate grounds for compromise and negotiation (247). Significantly blurring the distinction between white supremacy in the South and the ostensibly liberal, white sympathy in the North, Hopkins's preface to the novel reveals her source for Clapp's public address to be "the statements and accusations made against the Negro by ex-Governor Northern of Georgia, in his memorable address before the Congregational Club at Tremont Temple, Boston, Mass., May 22, 1899" (16). Such purposeful framing of her novel's social engagement reinforces the urgency of this literary intervention in reductive narratives of nationalism and racialism.

Hopkins suggests that the powerful attraction of national unity extends to and explains even Southern, white philanthropic support for racial uplift. In its account of how Dr. Arthur Lewis, "head of a large educational institution in the South devoted to the welfare of the Negroes," gains financial support for his educational programming, the novel sarcastically attributes Southern patronage to the American romance of superiority and union:

> For the loyal white man there would be no greater joy in life than to see his poetic dream of superiority to all other governments realized in "the land of the free and the home of the brave." He knows that this can never be

while the Negro question keeps up the line of demarkation which marks the division of the North from the South. True and loyal son of his country, he would sacrifice any race, any principle, to bring about this much-desired *consummation* (my italics; 242–243).

Exposing the deep-seeded history and power of the white American love affair with national union, Hopkins compellingly intervenes in the project of national affiliation that Coviello locates as an antebellum nationalist movement that adopted "whiteness...as a premier vehicle for the nation's unifying cohesion...a kind of inborn connectedness between mutually unknown citizens."[27] Indeed, Hopkins's acerbic recognition of the "poetic dream" of the "loyal white man" points to the movement of national affiliation that Coviello identifies as the "sudden rise of whiteness as a vehicle for...nationalist intimacy" (7) in antebellum literary tradition. That affiliation of white nationhood granted cultural currency and exigency to the family plot of antebellum fiction and the "romantic reconciliation" plot of Reconstruction fiction, traditions to which Hopkins would intervene by adopting the tropes of sibling, fraternal, familial affiliation in order to expose the price of white American nationalism and to encourage new loyalties.

By restoring a sibling-based genealogy that perseveres against the odds of the "Contending Forces" of the social world, Hopkins extends the utopian potential of sibling romance to protect and recuperate identity along such shifting and unstable expanses as the temporal, the social, the racial, the biological, the historical, and even the regional or geographical, given the diasporic reconstruction of her fictional family, which began in Bermuda, was separated in the United States and reunited in England. Appropriating the lateral affiliation that tended to reify narratives of white national solidarity and supremacy, Hopkins imagines a sibling affiliation that resists the forces of both social and individual change and that harmonizes, rather than conflicts, with the exigencies of community. Hopkins thus deploys the sibling romance to resolve the very crisis that the bond itself, with its requisite loyalty, threatens to enact, that is, the crisis of the conflicting desires of mutual identity and affiliation on the one hand and the demands of change, growth, and individual identity on the other. As the most optimistic and farthest-reaching vision of the power and possibilities of lateral solidarity, the example of Hopkins's recuperative sibling narrative concludes this study of the relationship between domestic fiction and the fundamental crisis of American identity: the conflicting strivings for loyalty and independence.

The intimacy of siblings proved salient in nineteenth-century nationmaking, a project that would increasingly rely upon a race-based system of national affiliation and community. In their own representations of American identity struggles after Reconstruction, Harper, Chesnutt, and Hopkins, all major contributors to the literary movement of the Nadir, would not only adopt the family and sibling tropes that for the previous century helped American writers and readers imagine nationhood, but they would confront the complex implications and consequences of that model of national consanguinity. Taken together, Harper's utopian pairs of supportive, recuperative siblings and Chesnutt's socially circumscribed and disabled sibling couple rewrite hegemonic narratives of affiliation and difference and imagine the possibilities within the social proscriptions of race and nation, while Hopkins exposes the long history of white national brotherhood and the limitations of the "brotherly affiliation" taken for granted by the national narrative. Breaking from traditions of nation and history (or, family and genealogy), Hopkins proposes, perhaps, the most progressive and subversive shift away from conventional consanguinity, which both anticipates the revisionist histories and literary interventions of the Harlem Renaissance and demands a critical reconsideration in the context of familial and national narratives of affiliation and kinship.

Epilogue: Sibling Romance in/and the Canon; Or, the Ambiguities

> He who is sisterless, is as a bachelor before his time. For much that goes to make up the deliciousness of a wife, already lies in the sister.
>
> —Herman Melville, *Pierre; Or, the Ambiguities*[1]
>
> Perhaps an even more relevant Mitchell "text" might be her early effort, now destroyed, called " 'Ropa Carmagin." In it, a young white aristocrat called "Europa," living in a crumbling plantation house, falls in love with a mulatto man who is probably her half-brother. It was as if Mitchell had started to write *Absalom, Absalom!* in 1927 and was stopped by her husband's dislike of the story. *Gone with the Wind* seems altogether tamer. Still, it was inevitable that someone tell that southern story about the black brother and white sister who wanted to become lovers: it was the unarticulated nightmare of the South.
>
> —Diane Roberts, *Faulkner and Southern Womanhood*[2]

THE RECONSTRUCTION NOVELS OF HARPER, Chesnutt, and Hopkins expose the limitations of a national affiliation predicated on such constructed and arbitrary factors as race. Throughout their novels, mysterious identities abound, obscuring familial and racial ties. The consequences of that confusion are particularly dramatized in sibling dynamics, which function either to realign power toward the utopian dream of racial solidarity, or to expose the utter instability of race-based hierarchies. When he depicts John Warwick's taboo gaze at his sister's maturing physique, a momentary transgression caused by the absence of sibling identification, Chesnutt both draws upon the sibling romance popularized by nineteenth-century domestic fiction and anticipates the literary trope of interracial sibling incest that would develop in later eras of American literature, making *The House Behind the Cedars* a crucial link between the sentimental tradition of sibling romance and the treatment of sibling incest in modernism and beyond. The roles that gender and genre would play in that lineage are reflected in the mysterious history surrounding the "other" fictional work that Margaret Mitchell would attempt to publish in 1936. Following a brief discussion of the intriguing story of Mitchell's lost novella, I close with a brief consideration of how the sibling romance tradition in antebellum and postbellum US literature, which this book has explored through the mostly noncanonical founders of that tradition, impacts our understanding of such celebrated authors as Faulkner, Hawthorne, Melville, and Poe.

Mitchell's popular status, and the suppression of a work that may have aligned her with contemporaries deemed more serious and worthy of critical attention, typifies the binary critical tradition that has rigorously devalued sentimentalism and female authorship; that in her subversive, unpublished work this sentimental author would delve into the most taboo extension of sibling romance—interracial incest—further blurs static critical categories, with the trope of brother–sister attachment being at the heart of such possibilities. For those implications, Mitchell's " 'Ropa Carmagin" offers a tantalizing symbol for the complicated legacy of the sentimental tradition and its relationship to the construction of race, gender, and nation in American literary history. Never published, Mitchell apparently penned her story of miscegenation and sibling incest a decade before she would share it with Macmillan publishers, along with her much lengthier *Gone with the Wind*. Explanations of the novella's fate range from the publisher declining it for its diminutive size, to Mitchell's husband first discouraging its creation and later burning the manuscript. Multiple accounts of the story establish its compelling premise of interracial, incestuous romance, delivered with a fusion of dystopian realism and Southern gothic. Based upon second-hand recollections, biographers' interpretations, and presumptions of male-authored sources for Mitchell's story, the only consensus seems to be the "Faulkneresque" quality of Mitchell's mysterious novella.[3] The most hotly debated suggestion from the various accounts, not surprisingly, is that the story dabbles in miscegenation, and that contested history surely reveals more about tenacious cultural anxieties over white femininity than anything else; one biographer seems downright indignant about the implication that Mitchell had a "latent fascination with black men," protesting that the author's "obsessions" did not include "this category of folk."[4] In 1936, Macmillan editor Harold Latham, despite rejecting " 'Ropa Carmagin" on account of its brevity, reassured the young author that the sophisticated style of her novella proves that she "can handle more than one type of material and character."[5] The type of material from Mitchell that would instead appear in print in the same year as

Faulkner's *Absalom, Absalom!* would evoke the double-edged reception so typical of sentimental fiction.

Although *Gone with the Wind* was a phenomenal success in the literary marketplace, literary critics from all political camps and regions would lambast its female-centeredness, apparent lack of political consciousness, sentimentality, and nostalgia for the old South. The critical reviews of its own era emphasized the author's gender as precluding the possibility of her novel's trustworthy reflection upon social and political realities, and their efforts to control the way readers would interpret the novel revealed their angst over its capacity to shape popular understandings about the South at a moment when the stakes for such representational power were especially high.[6] As her critics were wringing their hands over the terrific market success of what they strenuously insisted to be a debased literary effort—a sentimental production—the author whose instant fame was wrapped up in this conflation of popularity with critical and artistic failure would abandon the literary gesture that would more overtly align her with the progressive literary movement of her own era and region. More interestingly, the silencing of Mitchell's alternative literary initiative, whether self-imposed, insisted upon by others, or both, signals the pervasiveness of a linear literary history that insists upon such rigid distinctions as romantic and realistic, feminine and masculine, popular and critically acclaimed. Even recent efforts to restore a sense of seriousness and legitimacy to the critical reception of *Gone with the Wind* do so by disassociating the novel with the sentimental tradition; it would seem that placing Mitchell among her more important Southern counterparts hinges upon extricating her most famous work from its gendered literary context.[7]

Margaret Mitchell's suppressed and burned story, according to the readers' accounts, develops a plot uncannily similar to Faulkner's narrative of the tragic romance between Judith Sutpen and her mixed-race half-brother and lover, Charles Bon. Almost more crucial than the veracity of any of the accounts of the plot, the nearly century-long struggle to suppress it, or at least to qualify and reconcile its place in the imagination of a white woman writer of Southern romance, speaks volumes of the long-standing anxieties about the role of the female author and of "woman's fiction" in American literary history, not to mention more deeply seeded anxieties about the implications of an uncontrollable and unknowable history of mixed-race lineage on such colossal social missions as family, race, gender, and nation. If Mitchell's legacy as author of the twentieth century's most beloved sentimental rendering of the old South seems at odds with her authorship of a repressed tale of such enormous social taboos as interracial love and sibling incest—taboos that Faulkner would treat in *Absalom, Absalom!* with much acclaim and attention by academic literary critics—that is only because of the failure of literary history to adequately account for the impact of sentimentalism and the domestic tradition.[8] As the most popular genre of the nineteenth century, the domestic novel exists not marginally, but at the very center of American literary tradition, and perhaps no sentimental figure to come out of this family-focused genre more fittingly signifies that lineage than the trope of sibling attachment.

In significant ways, sibling romance mediates the gap that has historically separated sentimental and domestic fiction from the rest of the US literary canon. While the classical authority on doubling and sibling incest traces the genealogy of Faulkner's treatment of those themes to Edgar Allan Poe, Mark Twain, and Henry James, if the nineteenth century is the source of that history, then the domestic tradition certainly serves as its most essential root.[9] Surely, no more compelling origin for the modernist treatment of the withholding of white paternal inheritance as a premise for interracial sibling incest can be found than the romantic brotherly attachment the mixed-race hero of Stowe's *Dred* maintains for his half-sister, who, because of such powerful social dictums as patriarchal family order, white nationalism, and genteel womanhood, can never know that her doting slave is her own brother. When Stowe thus suggests the potential for lateral affiliation to both reify the romance of affectionate solidarity and dramatically undercut such stalwart institutions as white, aristocratic family lineage, and when she imagines a mixed-race slave whose violence and rebellion against his white brother-owner follows the death of the white sister to whom he had pledged a secret, unrequited brotherly commitment, she certainly anticipates the paradoxically cohesive and disruptive capacity for sibling romance in the context of white-centered nationhood, a capacity that later, canonical American authors, from Faulkner to Morrison, would extend and complicate.

In a more recent critical landmark in Faulkner studies, Karl Zender dwells on the political implications of *Absalom, Absalom!*, a gesture that intervenes in the classical insistence that the great modernist literature was necessarily detached from social and political contexts and motives. A key to Zender's move to place Faulkner in context is his revisionist attention to the special significance of sibling incest, as opposed to parent–child incest. While traditional Faulkner readers, following the lead of psychoanalytic theorists more generally, insisted that there was no distinct significance of sibling love and incest, that the sister was simply a mother substitute in the Oedipal triangle, Zender argues for the distinct understanding of lateral affiliation and psychology as essential to appreciating the cultural and social implications of Faulkner's focus on incest. For Zender, Faulkner's politics are traceable specifically through the increasingly complicated representations of sibling incest in his fiction. Especially suggestive of the impact of the "sibling romance" tradition is his claim for the affirming and romanticizing capacity of sibling incest (following Percy Shelley), in stark contrast to the inescapably violent and tyrannical consequences of father–daughter incest.[10] While Faulkner's choice of aristocratic sibling incest specifically upends the poor white trash trope of sibling incest that typified twentieth-century ideas of the South, the ultimate failure and tragedy of this romanticized sibling incest reveals the striking limitations of sibling love, which Faulkner's Southern predecessors Caroline Lee Hentz and John Pendleton Kennedy anticipated a century earlier. Tracing that lineage to the mostly nationalizing, or nation-engaging, domestic tradition points to an essential lesson for its impact on literary history: sibling attachment is political, social, cultural, and not strictly an isolated or detached psychological phenomenon. Situating the trope of sibling romance that emerged from domestic fiction as a key influence in US literary history reinforces the relevance of cultural and historical contexts to understanding sibling love and incest across genres and eras.

Occupying a place of intriguing liminality in this lineage, Herman Melville's 1852 *Pierre; or, the Ambiguities*, straddles genres as either sentimental or a satire of sentimentalism, belongs both within and on the fringes of the canon, and simultaneously contributes to the sibling incest tradition in American literature while participating in the sentimentalized sibling romance trope that this book has explored. Before devolving into the incest tragedy that would allow it interestingly to both echo the early American seduction novel and anticipate the modernist treatment of incest,[11] *Pierre* establishes as its premise the supremacy of the ideal brother–sister bond. It casts the title character's attachment to his mother in fraternal terms, and links his eventual betrayal of his domineering mother to his newly acquired bond to his lost and unacknowledged sister, whom he will pretend to marry in order to surreptitiously bring her into the family fold. Reinforcing the narrator's insistence that the love between a brother and sister represents the most ideal relationship, a familiar notion to Melville's antebellum audience, the plot would supplant a longed-for sister for Pierre's mother as well as for his betrothed wife.

While one critical reading suggests that the novel "inaugurated a tradition of sibling writing,"[12] clearly, in *Pierre*, Melville was tapping into a narrative trend that the domestic fiction of his day had already popularized. *Pierre*'s relationship to sibling romance captures at once the immediate impact of the popular literary convention that Melville seized upon, while its provocative reminder of the proximity of that beloved notion to a most rigid taboo gestures significantly to the inwardly gazing and chaotic capacity of the apparently safe and socially condoned, romantic idea of brother–sister love. While perhaps that gesture was premature by at least a half-century for American audiences, Melville's subversive evoking of the sentimental brother–sister narrative resoundingly speaks to the influence of domestic fiction's sibling romance. Moreover, the competing critical understandings of Pierre as either a satirical jab at the sentimental fiction that dominated the literary marketplace during the time of his career, or as a desperate, failed effort to participate in the spectacularly successful sentimental genre, suggests the fraught status of sibling love in and out of the canon, especially when at stake is the potential association of a revered, male literary legend with the debased history of the female-dominated literary marketplace of the nineteenth century.[13] Finally, the recent appreciation for *Pierre* as an experiment in genre-busting makes it a fitting testimony for the impact of the sibling romance in American literature. As Elizabeth Dill suggests in her reading of the text as an "anti-novel" that disrupts the apparently coherent distinctions between the novels of seduction and novels of family, the "incest romance proposes a haltingly forthright union between the sensational (sex) and the sentimental (family), a union that draws on the interrelatedness and ensuing volatility of these two genres."[14] Whether regarded as a failed sentimental novel in his own day, or as a progressive and misunderstood satire of sentimentalism throughout the twentieth century, Melville's provocative merging of the seduction and the romantic traditions drew upon the domestic trope most salient to both of those apparently distinct traditions.

A sure sign of the impact of the recent movement to recover domestic fiction's legacy is the renewed interest in Hawthorne's second novel, particularly in the context of its relevance to contemporaneous social issues. In recent decades, critical interpretations of *The House of the Seven Gables* have grappled with the novel's conservative ending, romantic aesthetics, and engagement with contemporaneous social upheavals, with much emphasis on the domestic elements and referents of the novel.[15] But that reinvigorated critical conversation has paid little attention to the novel's most relevant and central family dynamic: the relationship between siblings Clifford and Hepzibah Pyncheon. The romantic union between Phoebe and Holgrave in the novel's conclusion has provoked the most debate as to whether Holgrave's submission to a stable home life reveals Hawthorne's conservative angst about the rapid changes he was witnessing as a result of the Jacksonian free market, or whether Phoebe's power over Holgrave offer positive affirmation of a mediating female presence that "contains the lawless forces of this new order within the boundaries of love and the family."[16] However, the pair with more narrative development and attention certainly warrants more critical attention. The separation between Clifford and Hepzibah, their long-awaited reunion, the conflict of Hepzibah's unrequited sisterly adoration, and the pair's adventures together as they confront, flee, and overcome the past that haunts them, make up the novel's main narrative, and the conclusion, while featuring Holgrave and Phoebe's betrothal, also highlights the successful retirement of the persevering sibling couple.

If Hepzibah's ardent attachment to her brother evokes the antebellum language of sibling love, then Clifford's repulsion from his sister and his failure to reciprocate her boundless love and devotion to him present a sharp contrast to the cultural ideology and literary trope of mutual sibling attachment; Hawthorne resolves that main conflict through the novel's notoriously conservative ending, which restores the recuperated sibling pair to domestic comfort and stability. The narrator attributes Hepzibah's heroic qualities, which "never could have characterized her in what are called happier circumstances,"[17] to her sisterly sorrow, as she spends her adult life pining for her absent brother. The exclusivity of Hepzibah's love for Clifford echoes the codes for sibling love as well as the adoption of that familial dynamic in sibling romance novels: "In her own behalf, she had asked nothing of Providence, but the opportunity of devoting herself to this brother, whom she had so loved,—so admired for what he was, or might have been,—and to whom she had kept her faith, alone of all the world, wholly, unfalteringly, at every instant, and throughout life." Fully embodying the role of a self-sacrificing sister, Hepzibah would rejoice at the notion that her prodigal brother would be "thrown on her sympathy, as it seemed, not merely for the bread of his physical existence, but for everything that should keep him morally alive." Striving to serve as her brother's sole source of moral and physical comfort, the aging, spinster sister would try "to wrap Clifford up in her great, warm love, and make it all the world to him, so that he should retain no torturing sense of the coldness and dreariness without!"[18]

But Hepzibah would be disappointed in her sisterly dream, and she would have to defer to another woman, Phoebe, to fulfill her brother's needs. While Hawthorne sets the stage for a traditionally romantic and beautiful reunion of brother and sister, he disrupts that ideal family plot by portraying Hepzibah's dramatic shortcomings in the eyes of her sensually oriented brother as well as Clifford's failure to return his sister's unconditional love. The novel's emphasis on such corporeal factors of Clifford's repulsion as the unpleasant sound of his sister's voice, which "had, in the course of her sorrowful lifetime, contracted a croak," reinforces the failed romance of this sibling love. The narrator's elaborate suggestion that such a croak is symptomatic of "a settled melancholy" akin to mourning reinforces the implication of the dying away of this sibling romance. Further deepening the failed romance of the reunion scene is Hepzibah's fleeting inclination to reach for the harpsichord to comfort her brother, the consequences of which the narrator anticipates with bemused horror, "Poor Clifford! Poor Hepzibah! Poor harpsichord! All three would have been miserable together."[19] That abandoned gesture, with its "threatening calamity," contrasts strikingly with Hentz's scene of sibling bliss in which Edith Linwood's angelic voice serenades her prodigal brother.

The utmost disruption in the romantic reunion of brother and sister lies in Clifford's disgust over his sister's physical appearance, which the narrator significantly notes has worsened partly out of "resentment against the world for his sake." Despite the fact that her ugliness signifies her physical sacrifice at the altar of sister love, her brother, as an "instinctive lover of the Beautiful," could not bear to look at her, an aversion that signifies the ultimate fissure in sibling love. The narrator explains Clifford's failure to reciprocate his sister's love upon their reunion as a result of his self-indulging, "Sybarite" nature. The narrator's expectation of Hepzibah to know and accept that her brother's nature was "always selfish in its essence" and that she must "give it leave to be so, and heap [her] heroic and disinterested love upon it so much the more, without a recompense" (109) offers a clear, if unsettling, rationale for the lack of mutuality between these siblings. Despite the absence of a brother's proper reciprocation, in this suggestion for the sister's natural yielding to her brother's needs and interests, Hawthorne's vision of the Pyncheons' dynamic is not far from the "equilibrium" Hegel theorized for ideal opposite-sex siblinghood, in which a sister, naturally lacking a developed consciousness, serves the larger needs of her brother's active psyche. But the appeal and comfort of familial security would eventually overcome Clifford's selfishness as well as his fantasy of abandoning domestic conventions for a nomadic, wandering lifestyle, a dream that he communicates in the chapter "The Flight of Two Owls," much to his sister's alarm. Indeed, while the critical attention to the novel's ending typically notices Holgrave's conversion to conventional domesticity via his marriage to Phoebe, the novel just as significantly retires its other wandering male, Clifford, into a stable home with the monogamous female companionship of sister Hepzibah. Giving up his vision of a home-free existence, in the end Clifford submits to a traditionally domestic lifestyle with his sister, and their cozy conclusion parallels, but is surely not secondary to, the marriage-ending of the novel's romantic couple. Together, the two pairs reinforce the novel's return, whether with an ironic or crowd-pleasing treatment, to a conventional social order.

If Melville's deploying of the sibling trope blurred the lines between the sensational and the sentimental, and if Hawthorne imagined a perversely antithetical brother response to ideal sister devotion, only to restore conventional sibling domesticity in the end, their antebellum counterpart to bring the culture of sibling love most fully into a gothic relief was Edgar Allan Poe. While the disordered brand of attachment and loathing between Roderick and Madeleine Usher has been the subject of no end of psychoanalytic treatment, that enduring conversation has paid remarkably little attention to either the sibling-specific psychological implications of the morbid brother and sister pair or the rich relevance of opposite-sex sibling love in cultural and US literary history. In an important exception to that omission, Leila S. May has suggested that the gothic short story seized upon the metaphoric potential of the family, "reduced to its most basic unit: the sibling dyad."[20] For May, the entombment and escape of sister Madeleine exposes the untenable paradox of the nuclear family's roles as both the facilitator of masculine public participation and a morally pure and unsullied retreat from the public sphere, a refuge contingent upon the sexual purity of women, particularly sisters. In this reading, Madeleine's entombment represents the repression of female desire, and her rising from the tomb signifies the collapse of the literal and metaphoric "house of Usher." May articulates the value of reading Poe's gothic rendering of the psychological phenomenon of dread specifically within the context of antebellum society's investment in the family as a stabilizing institution. The short story's profound evoking of horror is predicated on its exposure of the dark implications of the elevated social institution, "wherein the fundamental building block of the Victorian family—the 'ideal' brother–sister relation—once revealed for what it is and taken to its logical extreme, must necessarily (and horribly) self-destruct" (391).

Beyond its relevance to Victorian family ideology broadly, its universally significant portrait of lateral identification and narcissism, and even its intriguing comparison to Poe's own sibling-like marriage to his first cousin, Virginia, whom he called "Sis,"[21] though, the richest significance of Madeleine and Roderick's sibling dynamic lies in its historical implications. The Ushers' enmeshment, violence, and self-destruction engage domestic social conventions and consequences that particularly resonated with the antebellum American experience. After all, in 1839, Poe could hardly have chosen a more effective premise to evoke horror in the minds of his nineteenth-century readers than the perversion of the sentimental ideal for brother–sister love. And the effect of that gothic treatment of a cherished social ideal, which the popular domestic tradition made ubiquitous, would have all the more allegorical power as a response to the profound crises of lateral affiliation that beset the nation in the midst of sectional divisions, in the unsettling aftermath of the Nullification crisis, and in the face of the contradictions of a slave-holding patriarchal society espousing democratic ideals. Even Poe's own conservative ideas about slavery, race, and family cannot neutralize the tantalizing complexity of the brother–sister attachment in his most celebrated short story, fittingly rendered in Madeleine and Roderick's capacity to capture the conflicting impulses of attachment, need, longing, belonging, and mutuality on the one hand, and individuation, independence, separation, and violence on the other. Both for its perverse evoking of the romance of sibling love as a social custom and literary trope, and for its powerful anticipation of the metaphoric power of that elevated family bond in the context of the nation's crisis, Poe's story and its canonical status suggest the rhetorical and cultural salience of the tradition of sibling romance that emerged in the so-called margins of US literary history.

NOTES

INTRODUCTION

1. Richard Murray points out that Thayer's public exhibition of the major paintings of his family at the same time in 1890 serves as a public testimony to his attachment to his children as "his source of spiritual strength" after his wife's death. Richard Murray, "Abbott Thayer's 'Stevenson Memorial,' " *American Art* 13.2 (1999): 2–25, 10. Murray also suggests that, by adopting varied subjects and contexts, Thayer could repeatedly affirm his devotion to his children, while obscuring that direct interpretation (14).
2. See Kristin Schwain, *Signs of Grace: Religion and American Art in the Gilded Age* (Cornell University Press, 2008), 121.
3. Elizabeth Lee makes a compelling case for Thayer's social consciousness, and especially his concern over the nation's declining morality. Elizabeth Lee, "Therapeutic Beauty: Abbott Thayer, Antimodernism, and the Fear of Disease," *American Art* 18.3 (2004): 32–51.
4. The recovery of the significance of the family to American literary history may be traced to a number of crucial interventions, most famously to Jane Tompkins, *Sensational Designs* (New York: Oxford University Press), which famously refuted the notion that sentimental literature "feminized" and degraded American culture. More recent and influential contributions to the restoring of the role that fictions of family and sentimentalism play in the shape of American cultural and literary history include Kirstin Boudreau, *Sympathy in American Literature* (Gainesville: University Press of Florida, 2002); Cindy Weinstein, *Family, Kinship, and Sympathy in Nineteenth-Century American Literature* (New York: Cambridge University Press, 2004); and Elizabeth Barnes, *States of Sympathy: Seduction and Democracy in the American Novel* (New York: Columbia University Press, 1997). Conversations of family and sentimental literature have shed light on the significance of affiliation, allegiance, and kinship in the context of national divisiveness. Elizabeth Duquette's *Loyal Subjects: Bonds of Nation, Race, and Allegiance in Nineteenth-Century America* (New Brunswick: Rutgers University Press, 2010) particularly situates the concept of loyalty as a distinct and meaningful discursive construct within the context of the Civil War, and Amy Murell Taylor, *The Divided Family in Civil War America* (Chapel Hill: The University of North Carolina Press, 2005) examines the "divided family" as both

a historical reality during the war era and a literary motif, with particular attention to the trope of courtship and marriage as an allegory for the Union.
5. The significance of siblings has had more attention in British literary studies than in American. See Valerie Sanders, *The Brother–Sister Culture in Nineteenth-Century Literature, from Austen to Woolf* (New York: Palgrave, 2004) and Leila S. May, *Disorderly Sisters: Sibling Relations and Sororal Resistance in Nineteenth-Century British Literature* (Lewisburg: Bucknell University Press, 2001). Elsewhere, May's attention to an American example situates the brother–sister dynamic of that short story in the context of euro-centric traditions and cultural movements, which, she argues, shaped American literature and culture, as well. Leila S. May, " 'Sympathies of a scarcely intelligible nature': the Brother–Sister Bond in Poe's 'Fall of the House of Usher' " *Studies in Short Fiction* 30 (1993): 387–396. While these contributions suggest that the nineteenth-century intrigue for sibling love occupied literary imaginations on both sides of the Atlantic, the significance of fictional representations of siblings to the tumultuous history of nineteenth-century America, especially the role of national identity making to that history, has gone mostly unnoticed. In an intriguing exception, Denis Flannery theorizes same-sex sibling representations in examples of American writing from the nineteenth-century to the contemporary period, with a focus on the capacity for lateral dynamics to articulate queer desire; Flannery's attention to homoerotic implications of sibling love throughout the American canon complements my more historically focused study of the presence of opposite-sex sibling romance in the nineteenth century. Denis Flannery, *On Sibling Love, Queer Attachment, and American Writing* (Burlington, VT: Ashgate, 2007).
6. Michael Shapiro historicizes and contextualizes the contemporary neoconservative project of "redeeming an imagined past and colonizing the present and future" via the dissemination of values surrounding the "traditional" American family. *Moral Ambiguity: National Culture and the Politics of the Family* (Minneapolis: University of Minnesota Press, 2001), 1.
7. Recently, the subject of siblings in American history has attracted more serious and extensive critical attention. In her recent study of real-life brothers and sisters in American history, Annette Atkins examines examples of sibling dynamics in a variety of antebellum American families, mostly through personal letters, to demonstrate the significance of that relationship to American family life during that time period. Annette Atkins, *We Grew Up Together: Brothers and Sisters in Nineteenth-Century America* (Urbana: Illinois University Press, 2001). In a more comprehensive study of American siblings in the nineteenth century, C. Dallett Hemphill contributes a timely overview of the cultural emphasis on sibling dynamics in American history. C. Dallett Hemphill, *Siblings: Brothers and Sisters in American History* (New York: Oxford University Press, 2011).
8. For key interdisciplinary examples of studies that explore the paradigm of family with nation, see, in addition to the works cited in my first note,

George B. Forgie, *Patricide in the House Divided: A Psychological Interpretation of Lincoln and His Age* (New York: Norton, 1981); Elizabeth Duquette, *Loyal Subjects*, and Nancy Cott, *Public Vows: A History of Marriage and the Nation* (Cambridge: Harvard University Press, 2000).

9. Taylor's examination of the trope of the divided family as an allegory for the divided nation focuses on novels that exhibit what she notes to be the "existing literary association of the Union with a marriage" (125); her examples showcase the tradition of Civil War novels that adopt marriage as a metaphor for the relationship between the North and South (see especially 123–153). Taylor's chapter on siblings divided by the war focuses mostly on real-life experiences and letters between siblings and on the tradition of "fratricide" discourse. Karen A. Keely considers the "reconciliation marriage" between a Northern groom and Southern bride to be the dominant allegory for the national union in postbellum literature. Karen A. Keely, "Marriage Plots and National Reunion: The Trope of Romantic Reconciliation in Postbellum Literature," *Mississippi Quarterly* 51.4 (Fall 1998): 621–648. Also, Duquette examines how reunion romances "disseminate loyalty on the national scale by demonstrating the domestic felicity of coerced consent and propose that companionate unions predicated on loyalty would stabilize rebellious tendencies and harmonize political families" (62). Chapter 5 will add sibling romance to the conversation of familial allegories of national recuperation after Reconstruction.

10. Peter Coviello, *Intimacy in America: Dreams of Affiliation in Antebellum Literature* (Minneapolis: University of Minnesota Press, 2005). The capacity for the sibling romance trope to support the project of affiliation that Coviello examines particularly surfaces in the last chapter of this study, which demonstrates the ways in which postbellum African American fiction would deploy the solidarity of brother–sister union to expose the limitations of white-centric narratives of affiliation.

11. See especially Atkins's study, which reveals the importance and strength of sibling ties in such socializing processes.

12. Hemphill, *Siblings*, 7.

13. While the focus of this book is opposite-sex sibling bonds, for an important study of the implications of difference in sisterly dynamics in fiction, see *Sororophobia: Difference among Women in Literature and Culture* (New York: Oxford University Press, 1992).

14. Here I want to distinguish my use of the term "sibling love" from sibling incest. While the concepts certainly overlap—sentimental sibling representations surely can be read incestuously, and at times my analysis will address incestuous overtones of sentimental love. Likewise, many of the subjects of sibling incest blur the lines between the lasciviousness of incest and the sentimentalism of romance. Elizabeth Dill focuses on sibling incest as a vehicle to understand the literary lineage of such apparently distinct traditions as the sensational and the sentimental. Elizabeth Dill, "That Damned Mob of Scribbling Siblings: The American Romance as Anti-novel in *The Power of*

Sympathy and *Pierre*," *American Literature* 80.4 (December 2008): 707–738. While the implications of sibling incest, especially as it is manifest in psychological dynamics, will sometimes surface in the analytical work of this study, my use of "sibling love" basically refers to an affiliation that does not manifest in overt sexuality, and my study focuses mostly on opposite-sex sibling pairs in nineteenth-century American fiction.

15. Gillian Brown traces Locke's influence on American culture in the history of children's literature, which disseminated the famous Lockean philosophies of consent and of children's ability to reason. Gillian Brown, *Consent of the Governed: The Lockean Legacy in Early American Culture* (Cambridge: Harvard University Press, 2001).

16. Jay Fleigelman's classic study has established this philosophical history and its implications in American discourse history. Jay Fleigelman, *Prodigals and Pilgrims: The American Revolution against Patriarchal Authority, 1750–1800* (New York: Cambridge University Press, 1982), 12–21. Also, see Elizabeth Barnes's explication of the Lockean underpinnings of Thomas Paine's antipatriarchal discourse in *Common Sense*. Barnes, 26–31.

17. For more on Hegel's relevance to sibling representations in nineteenth-century literature, see May's *Disorderly Sisters*, especially 32–41.

18. Miriam Leonard traces what she calls "psychoanalysis's backward gaze to Hegel" (135), pointing out that of the philosophers who interrogated the connection between psychoanalysis and Hegelianism, Derrida intervened most productively, especially in the conceptualization of sexual difference. Miriam Leonard, *Athens in Paris: Ancient Greece and the Political in Post-War French Thought* (Oxford: Oxford University Press, 2005). For another brilliant intervention in the Oedipal legacy in the twentieth-century Anglo and Germanic imagination, see Jill Scott, *Electra after Freud: Myth and Culture* (Ithaca: Cornell University Press, 2005). It is beyond the scope of this project to interrogate or debate Hegel's theories of the dialectic and their impact on gender identity theory, as I mainly invoke Hegel here to demonstrate the salience and relevance of the sibling dialectic to the tradition of sibling representations in nineteenth-century siblings. That said, the remainder of this book will engage in a close analysis of literary representations of siblings and their implications surrounding issues of gender and social difference, revealing the rich and varied engagement with these debates in nineteenth-century American fiction.

19. David V. Ciavatta intervenes in long-standing assumptions about the importance of the marriage bond to Hegelian philosophy (and, by extension, modern psychology) with his insistence that "the logic of the marriage bond, as Hegel ... articulates is, is actually closer to the prepersonal logic of sibling relations (and of parent/child relations) than it seems." David V. Civiatta, *Spirit, the Family, and the Unconscious in Hegel's Philosophy* (New York: SUNY Press, 2009), 170.

20. Judith Butler points out that "The Hegelian legacy of Antigone interpretation appears to assume the separability of kinship and the state, even as it posits an essential relation between them." Judith Butler, *Antigone's Claim: Kinship between Life and Death* (New York: Columbia University

Press, 2000), 5. For new psychoanalytic and feminist pragmatism, recognizing the legacy of this logic, and redefining the implications of Antigone within the contexts of contemporary crises (*à la* Butler) has become a central tool for reorganizing and blurring the lines between kinship and the state, and understanding the liminal spaces of figures on the margins of historically normalized culture.

21. Hegel's reading of Antigone, a definitive interpretive performance for his philosophy of human psychological development, appears abruptly with a statement that, along with its meaningful footnote, would come to symbolize the gender distinctions that premise his philosophy of the ethical life: "The loss of a brother is thus irreparable to the sister, and her duty toward him is the highest." The simple and straightforward literary reference he would append as a footnote to this assertion—"Cp. Antigone. 1, 910."—sheds light on the classical source for the Hegelian model of gendered psychological and civic development, at the same time that it reifies the definitive interpretation of the tragic Sophoclean heroine that celebrates her supposed filial and spiritual submission. G. W. F. Hegel, *The Phenomenology of Mind* (New York: Harper Torchbooks, 1967), 477.

22. Kelly Oliver argues that the brother-sister dialectic central to Hegel's philosophy on ethical order undermines the premise of his philosophy of self-consciousness, which, as she points out, insists that mutual recognition is contingent upon desire. Kelly Oliver, *Witnessing: Beyond Recognition* (Minneapolis: University of Minnesota Press, 2001).

23. As George Steiner demonstrates, "Between c. 1790 and c. 1905, it was widely held by European poets, philosophers, and scholars, that Sophocles's *Antigone* was not only that finest of Greek tragedies, but a work of art nearer to perfection than any other produced by the human spirit" (1). George, Steiner, George, *Antigones* (Oxford: Clarendon Press, 1984). See also May's invocation of Steiner in her contextualization of sibling representations in nineteenth-century British literature (*Disorderly Sisters*, 37).

24. See Caroline Winterer, "Classicism and Women's Education in America: 1840–1900," *American Quarterly* 53.1 (2001): 70–93.

25. The ideology that discouraged women from political activity is well established, beginning with the landmark essay by Barbara Welter, "The Cult of True Womanhood," *American Quarterly* 18.2, Part 1 (Summer, 1966), 151–174. For foundational studies on gender spheres, see Nancy Cott, *The Bonds of Womanhood: "Woman's Sphere" in New England 1780–1835* (New Haven: Yale University Press, 1977) and Linda Kerber, *Women of the Republic: Intellect and Ideology in Revolutionary America* (Chapel Hill: University of North Carolina Press, 1980). For examples of the vast amount of literature that challenges the notion of separate spheres, see Cathy Davidson and Jessamyn Hatcher, eds., *No More Separate Spheres* (Durham: Duke University Press, 2002); Linda Kerber et al., "Beyond Roles, beyond Spheres: Thinking about Gender in the Early Republic," *The William and Mary Quarterly* 46.3 (1989): 565–585, and Laura McCall and Donald Yacavone, eds., *A Shared Experience: Men, Women, and the History of Gender* (New York: New York University Press, 1998). While recently scholars have sought to

debunk the history of separate spheres, nineteenth-century discourse nevertheless reveals a strict, if nuanced and contested, proscription against female agency in the public sphere. This book's exploration of the nationalizing capacity of the sibling romance, a trope that appears in mostly domestic fiction, takes as its premise the politicizing potential in domesticity. In that way, it aligns with Amy Kaplan's suggestion that antebellum women's novels "of domesticity and female subjectivity [are] inseparable from narratives of empire and nation building" ("Manifest Domesticity," *American Literature* 70.3 (Sep. 1998): 581–606, 584.

26. R. D. Hinshelwood and Gary Winship take as their classic Greek example of the sibling paradigm Orestes and Electra, a pair that, according to their argument, symbolizes not only the extreme form of sibling devotion, but also, in Aeschylus's rendering of their dynamic, the anarchist potential in democratic experiments. Given the matricidal union of Orestes and Electra, it is noteworthy that during the nineteenth century, an era characterized by unquestioning acceptance of the democratic ideal, would favor the Antigone model of sisterly loyalty. R. D. Hinshelwood, and Gary Winship, "Orestes and Democracy," in *Sibling Relationships*, edited by Prophecy Coles (New York: Karnac, 2006).

27. Mary Kelley, in *Learning to Stand and Speak*, recognizes that, in *Woman in the Nineteenth Century*, Fuller "contested common definitions of masculinity and femininity. She severed the common link between femininity and dependence. And she called for opportunities that enabled women to develop their potential, not only as wives and mothers whose lives were defined by domesticity but also as individuals, each of whom had particular inclinations, desires, and talents." Mary Kelly, *Learning to Stand and Speak: Women, Education, and Public Life in America's Republic* (Chapel Hill: University of North Carolina Press, 2006), 222.

28. In this famous epistolary exchange, Abigail Adams urges her husband to "remember the ladies and be more generous and favorable to them than your ancestors. Do not put such unlimited power into the hands of the husbands.... Why, then, not put it out of the power of the vicious and the lawless to use us with cruelty and indignity with impunity?" to which John Adams's responds: "Depend upon it, we know better than to repeal our masculine systems. Although they are in full force, you know they are little more than theory. We dare not exert our power in its full latitude. We are obliged to go fair and softly, and, in practice, you know we are the subjects. We have only the name of masters, and rather than give up this, which would completely subject us to the despotism of the petticoat, I hope General Washington and all our brave heroes would fight." Abigail Adams and John Adams, *The Book of Abigail and John: Selected Letter of the Adams Family, 1762–1784*, edited by L. H. Butterfield, et al. (Boston: Northeastern University Press, 2002), 121, 123.

29. Of the vast history of literary criticism on the incestuous theme in Poe's "The Fall of the House of Usher," May ("Sympathies of a Scarcely Intelligible

NOTES

Nature") focuses the most squarely on the cultural implications of the Ushers as a sibling pair. May argues that Poe's short story is "prophetic in its anticipation of a vision of the collapse of a society built on the seemingly secure foundations of a family." May's reading of the significance of the collapse of the incestuous mansion especially aligns with my own study of the potential for sibling romance to complicate the role that female sacrifice necessarily plays in the presumption of family structure: "As in texts as diverse as *Antigone, Frankenstein,* and *Wuthering Heights,* it is significantly the sister who must be sacrificed—here literally entombed, buried alive deep within the tomb of the familial edifice—and it is her breaking free from that entombment that provokes the collapse of the entire structure" (May, 391).

30. Juliet Mitchell (2000) notes that "Siblings are the great omission in psychoanalytic observation and theory," and she redresses that omission by reclaiming the role of sibling enmeshment as a primary source of the death drive. Juliet Mitchell, *Siblings: Sex and Violence* (Cambridge: Polity Press, 2003), 23. Also, Prophecy Coles asserts that "the Oedipus complex, as the fulcrum of our psychic development, is an oversimplification," and she postulates whether "we fear the power of sibling relationships." Prophecy Coles, *The Importance of Sibling Relationships in Psychoanalysis* (London: Karnac, 2003), 2. Despite the fundamental difference in their conclusions (that is, Coles objects to the death-drive as a necessary element of the human psyche), both psychoanalysts turn to literary representation to complement, and at times, fill in the holes left by the dearth of sources in clinical literature. Another major contributor to the new turn toward lateral psychoanalysis is Jill Scott, whose recovery of the impact of Electra to modernist literature suggests a compelling alternative to the Oedipal master narrative. Jill Scott, *Electra after Freud: Myth and Culture* (Ithaca: Cornell University Press, 2005).

31. Hemphill points to Mitchell's work in sibling psychology as an example of how contemporary theory tends to extrapolate the Freudian premise of sibling rivalry. Mitchell's reading of the role that lateral enmeshment may play in the motivation of the death drive, and the ensuing catastrophe of an absent self-consciousness, have particular relevance to my analysis of Hentz's story of lateral jealousy and violence, a voice that we must factor into the discursive and representational history surrounding American identity and affiliation. Whether read as supportive of or competitive with identity development, shifting the critical focus from the traditionally vertical alignment to lateral dynamics is a fruitful method of diversifying our understanding of the development of the human psyche and the culture's response to it.

CHAPTER 1

1. William A. Alcott, *Familiar Letters to Young Men on Various Subjects* (Buffalo: Derby, 1850), 266.
2. Steven Mintz notes that "Nineteenth-century middle-class culture idealized the bond between sisters and brothers as purer and more innocent than any

other social relationships, untouched by sexuality and selfishness." Steven Mintz, *Huck's Raft: A History of American Childhood* (Cambridge: Belknap Press, 2004), 86.

3. In his study of American manhood, Rotundo points out that the brother–sister pair in the nineteenth century was nurtured to be a "trial run at marriage." E. Anthony Rotundo, *American Manhood: Transformations in Masculinity from the Revolution to the Modern Era* (New York: Harper, 1993), 96.

4. Steven Mintz, *A Prison of Expectations: The Family in Victorian Culture* (New York: New York University Press, 1985), 150–151.

5. See Gillian Brown, *Consent of the Governed: The Lockean Legacy in Early American Culture* (Cambridge: Harvard University Press, 2001).

6. Rev. John Angell James, *Family Monitor; A Help to Domestic Happiness* (Boston: Crocker and Brewster, 1830), 148–149.

7. In *Siblings*, Hemphill draws upon the example of Sedgwick's attachment to her brothers: C. Dallett Hemphill, *Siblings: Brothers and Sisters in American History* (New York: Oxford University Press, 2011), see especially 108, 116, 129, and 172–173.

8. James, 149.

9. William Aikman, *Life at Home; or, The Family and Its Members* (New York: Wells, 1870), 183.

10. Augustus Woodbury, *Plain Words to Young Men* (Concord, NH: E. C. Eastman, 1858), 36.

11. James, 151.

12. Ibid., 151.

13. Richard Broadhead, "Sparing the Rod: Discipline and Fiction in Antebellum America," *Representations* 21 (1988): 67–96. Broadhead asserts the "disciplinary intimacy" of children's literature, particularly of periodical literature, in which editors seek to shape child readers through the process of textual selection as well as explanatory insertions.

14. Lorinda Cohoon, *Serialized Citizenships: Periodicals, Books, and American Boys 1840–1911* (Landham, MD: Scarecrow Press, 2006) emphasizes the role that periodicals played in shaping model citizens.

15. For more on the sense of community in *St. Nicholas*, see Suzanne Rahn, "St. Nicholas and Its Friends: The Magazine–Child Relationship" in *St. Nicholas and Mary Maples Dodge: The Legacy of a Children's Magazine*, edited by Susan Gannon (Jefferson, NC: McFarland, 2004). Also, Greta Little points out the ways in which nineteenth-century American children's periodicals encouraged aspiring writers. In an especially valuable internet project, Pat Pflieger brings to life what she terms the "online community of the nineteenth-century" with an overview of readers' correspondence that includes embedded links to full-text primary source examples from *Robert Merry's Museum* ("An Online Community of the Nineteenth Century," http://www.merrycoz.org/papers/online/online.htm).

16. Hemphill explicates examples of this emphasis on sibling grief in children's literature, too; see *Siblings*, 132–133.

NOTES   167

17. See Gordon R. Kelly, *Children's Periodicals* (Westport: Greenwood Press, 1984), 508–509.
18. See James Marten, *The Children's Civil War* (Chapel Hill: The University of North Carolina Press, 1998), 31–32.
19. For a discussion of the metaphor and actual history of the divided family during the Civil War, see Amy Murrell Taylor, *The Divided Family in Civil War America* (Chapel Hill: The University of North Carolina Press, 2005). While Taylor's chapter on "Brothers and Sisters" (63–91) sheds light on the history of sibling divisiveness and solidarity during the Civil War, her attention to the fictional representations of the divided family metaphor mostly centers upon the allegorical treatment of the Union as a marriage (see 123–153).
20. Elizabeth Young contends that in Alcott's Civil War fiction, "a reciprocal metaphor connects gender and nation: the national conflict symbolizes individual struggles against gender norms, while such internal civil wars allegorically reconstruct the warring nation"; Elizabeth Young, "A Wound of One's Own: Louisa May Alcott's Civil War Fiction," *American Quarterly* 48.3 (1996): 439–474, 441.
21. Notwithstanding its stature as a classic work of domestic fiction, *Little Women* appears here as a text that contributes to context, rather than as one of the primary works in this study. While it certainly showcases sibling love generally (see Hemphill's discussion of this in *Siblings*, 141), it does not develop the focused plot of opposite-sex sibling love that I identify as key to the "sibling romance" novel. Laurie's brother-like relationship to the March sisters and his eventual marriage to Amy make his role in the plot comparable to that in the sibling romance novels, if marginally. More pertinent to the scope of this project is the ways in which Alcott's novel evokes and reinforces the efficacy of sibling literary representations.
22. Alcott's success was largely associated with the children's periodicals market. Besides contributing to *Our Young Folks*, she served as the editor for *Merry's Museum* from 1868 to 1870, and eventually became a high-profile (and high-earning) contributor to the most prominent children's magazines, *St. Nicholas*, in 1874. For a discussion of Alcott's relationship with the famous editor of *St. Nicholas*, see Daniel Shealy, "Work Well Done: Louisa May Alcott and Mary Maples Dodge," in *St. Nicholas and Mary Maples Dodge: The Legacy of a Children's Magazine, 1873–1905*, edited by Susan Gannon, et al. (Jefferson, NC: McFarland, 2004): 171–191.
23. See R. Gordon Kelly's *Children's Periodicals of the United States* (Westport: Greenwood Press, 1984), 331.
24. A review of *Battles at Home* notes Alcott's praise as affirmation of the novel's merit: "We began to read this story with a more than ordinary degree of interest, for the reason that it had been warmly praised by Miss Alcott, of whom it may be said that, if the ability to write a good book comprehends the ability to recognize a good one by another, her judgment ought to be beyond appeal" (*The Literary World*, volumes 1–2, original from Harvard University digitized on Google Books, July 2007).

25. See Hemphill, *Siblings*, 149.
26. Suzanne Rahn establishes Dodge's editorial philosophy with special emphasis on the magazine's relationship to its readers. See the following three contributions by Rahn in *St. Nicholas and Mary Maples Dodge: The Legacy of a Children's Magazine,* edited by Susan Gannon et al.: "*St. Nicholas* and Its Friends: The Magazine-Child Relationship" (93–111); "Young Eyewitnesses to History" (111–119); and "In the Century's First Springtime: Albert Bigelow Paine and the *St. Nicholas* League" (119–143).
27. The full text of Dodge's letter to Roswell Smith is included in *St. Nicholas and Mary Maples Dodge: The Legacy of a Children's Magazine,* edited by Susan R. Gannon et al.
28. These academic differences between boys and girls were particularly coded into gender representations in children's literature of the day. A *St. Nicholas* short story titled "How Cousin Marion Helped" (Vol. 24.2, May 1897) suggests how a pre-adolescent girl may restore harmony with her twin brother by allowing him to excel her in math performance. Pat Pflieger explains how readers engaged in vocal debates over the presumed intellectual superiority of men. Pat Pflieger, "A Visit to Merry's Museum; Or, Social Values in a Nineteenth-Century American Periodical for Children" (Doctoral Dissertation: University of Minnesota, 1987); see especially Chapter II for a compelling analysis of the "algebra war" among readers of *Merry's Museum*.
29. For a discussion of Dodge's interventions in hero-worship via her editorial practices in *St. Nicholas*, see Susan R. Gannon, "Heroism Reconsidered: Negotiating Autonomy in *St. Nicholas Magazine* (1873–1914)" in *Culturing the Child, 1690–1914: Essays in Memory of Mitzi Myers,* edited by Donelle Ruwe (Lanham, MD: The Children's Literature Association and The Scarecrow Press, 2005): 179–198.
30. "Children's Literature: What 'St. Nicholas' Has Done for Boys and Girls," in *Overland Monthly and Out West Magazine* 16.96 (Dec. 1890), 668.
31. Anna Barbauld (1743–1825) was a famous British children's author. "Peter Parley" was the pseudonym for Samuel Goodrich (1793–1860), prolific children's author best known for historical and biographical writing, and also as the editor of the children's periodicals *Parley's Magazine* and, later, *Merry's Museum* (see Kelly, *Children's Periodicals of the United States*, 345–355). Here, Dodge appears to be criticizing the older models of children's literature that have lost favor and relevance with the children of her own day in the latter decades of the century.
32. Dodge's reference to " 'good-y' talk" alludes to the famous 1765 "The History of Little Goody Two-Shoes" by British children's author John Newberry.

Chapter 2

1. Sedgwick's earlier novel *Hope Leslie* (1827) and James Fenimore Cooper's *The Last of the Mohicans* (1826) and *The Spy* (1821) appropriated and Americanized Scott's historical fiction tradition.

2. For classic critical attention to Scott's influence on American fiction, see Lawrence Buell, *New England Literary Culture, from Revolution through Renaissance* (New York: Cambridge University Press, 1986) and George Dekker, *The American Historical Romance* (Cambridge: Cambridge University Press, 1987).
3. For recent work on Scott's own relationship to national history, see Katie Trumpener's *Bardic Nationalism: The Romantic Novel and the British Empire* (Princeton: Princeton University Press, 1997).
4. Disrupting the historical tendency to read nationalism as a static and stable construct in the nineteenth century, Robert S. Levine has highlighted key literary interventions in white American nationalism, exposing the limitations of historical perspectives that too strictly define the relationship between race and nation, North and South, regionalism and sectionalism. See Robert S. Levine, *Dislocating Race and Nation: Episodes in Nineteenth-Century American Literary Nationalism* (Chapel Hill: University of North Carolina Press, 2008).
5. Richard E. Ellis, *The Union at Risk: Jacksonian Democracy, States' Rights, and the Nullification Crisis* (New York: Oxford University Press, 1987), 12.
6. Ellis explains three positions on the nature of the federal union: nullifiers, nationalists, and traditional states' rights advocates (10–12). Signifying the complexity of the debate is Jackson's complex position as both an advocate of states' rights and a determined protector of the Union (Ellis, 13–40).
7. William Freehling, *Prelude to Civil War: The Nullification Controversy in South Carolina, 1818–1836* (New York: Oxford University Press, 1992). Freehling explains the "Great Reaction" to Nullification in the years just following its political resolution, when South Carolina planters increased their vigilant defense of slavery and enforced test oaths to secure Unionist's loyalty to the state (301–339). Clearly, while the compromise of 1833 resolved the Nullification issue in legislative terms, the cultural anxiety over conflicting allegiances was heightened as a result of the controversy.
8. "The Debate in the Senate of the United States," *The North American Review* 31.69 (Oct, 1830): 533.
9. Quoted in William Freehling, *The Nullification Era: A Documentary Record* (New York: Oxford University Press, 1992) 54.
10. Ibid., 127.
11. Ibid., 173.
12. See James Brewer Stewart, " 'A Great Talking and Eating Machine': Patriarchy, Mobilization and the Dynamics of Nullification in South Carolina," *Civil War History* 27.3 (1981): 197–220. Stewart points out that the leaders of the Nullification movement were conscious of "the fundamental importance of family relationships in structuring South Carolina's politics and social arrangements" (200).
13. In addition to Stewart, other studies that have established the paternalistic culture of slavery include Reginald Horsman, *Race and Manifest Destiny: The Origins of American Racial Anglo-Saxonism* (Cambridge: Harvard University Press, 1981); Eugene Genovese, *Roll, Jordan, Roll: The World the Slaves Made*

(New York: Pantheon Books, 1974); and Herbert Gutman, *The Black Family in Slavery and in Freedom* (New York: Pantheon Books, 1976).

14. Stewart, 204.
15. Several scholars have noted the nationalistic strain running through much of Sedgwick's writing. In her introduction to Sedgwick's short story, "Cacoethes Scribendi" in *Provisions: A Reader from 19th-Century American Women* (Bloomington: Indiana University Press, 1986: 41–49), Judith Fetterley explains that Sedgwick "grew up in an atmosphere pervaded by politics and informed by a commitment to translating political beliefs into public acts" and that her works "reflect her profound belief in the American democratic experiment and her deep commitment to devoting her talents, as her father did before her, to the service of her country" (41, 44). For a rich discussion of Sedgwick's nationalism in her personal and authorial contexts, see Mary Kelly, "Negotiating a Self: The Autobiography and Journals of Catharine Maria Sedgwick," *New England Quarterly* 66 (Sept, 1993): 366–398. Also, scholars have paid particular attention to the role of national politics in *Hope Leslie*: see Maria Karafilis, "Catharine Maria Sedgwick's *Hope* Leslie: The Crisis between Political Action and US Literary Nationalism in the New Republic," *American Transcendental Quarterly* 12 (Dec, 1998): 327–344; T. Gregory Garvey, Gregory. "Risking Reprisal: Catherine Sedgwick's *Hope Leslie* and the Legitimation of Public Action by Women," *American Transcendental Quarterly* 8 (Dec, 1994): 287–298; Susan Harris, "The Limits of Authority: Catharine Maria Sedgwick and the Politics of Resistance," in *Catharine Maria Sedgwick: Critical Perspectives,* edited by Lucinda Damon-Bach and Victoria Clements (Boston: Northeastern University Press, 2003: 272–285).
16. While Sedgwick's nationalism has been a predominant premise of most critical discussions, Philip Gould makes an interesting corrective in his reading of the novelist's transnational engagement in *The Linwoods*, which, he asserts, promotes a "spirit of the enlightened cosmopolitan ... urging her readers to think national and transatlantic terms simultaneously" (258). See Philip Gould, "Catharine Sedgwick's Cosmopolitan Nation," *New England Quarterly* 78 (2005): 232–258.
17. Catharine Maria Sedgwick, *The Linwoods; or, "Sixty Years Since" in America,* edited by Maria Karafilis (Hanover: University Press of New England, 2002), xv.
18. Quoted in Sedgwick, xii.
19. See VanDette, "It Should Be a Family Thing: Family, Nation, and Republicanism in Catharine Maria Sedgwick's *A New-England Tale* and *The Linwoods,*" *ATQ* (March 2005): 51–74.
20. See Jay Fliegelman, *Prodigals and Pilgrims: The American Revolution against Patriarchal Authority, 1750–1800* (New York: Cambridge University Press, 1982), 57–58.
21. See C. Dallett Hemphill, *Siblings: Brothers and Sisters in American History* (New York: Oxford University Press, 2011), 108. Also, in her autobiography

Sedgwick admits that her older brother, Robert, was especially important to her: "I looked... upon my favorite brother as my preserver. He was more than any other my protector and companion. Charles was as near my own age, but he was younger, and a feeling of dependence—of most loving dependence—on Robert began then, which lasted through his life." Catharine Maria Sedgwick, *The Power of Her Sympathy: The Autobiography and Journal of Catherine Maria Sedgwick*, edited by Mary Kelley (Boston: Massachusetts Historical Society, 1993), 72. Not only were Sedgwick's brothers protective in the sense prescribed by the domestic advice literature, but they were also, according to Sedgwick, loving and supportive, and they directly impacted her literary career. As Mary Kelley notes in her introduction to Sedgwick's *The Power of Her Sympathy*, Sedgwick's brothers "encouraged the initially reluctant author, applauded the novels and stories, and negotiated with the publishers" (29). The close bonds between brothers and sisters in *The Linwoods* echo Sedgwick's own sentiments from her autobiography, where she says, "I can conceive of no truer image of the purity and happiness of the equal loves of Heaven than that which unites brothers and sisters" (89).

22. *Southern Literary Messenger*, 1.5 (May 1835), 522. Kennedy's biographer notes that his reputation was just as acclaimed in northern presses as it was in the South, pointing out that the *New England Magazine,* the *Knickerbocker,* and the *American Quarterly Review* all received *Horse-Shoe Robinson* warmly and ranked Kennedy with James Fenimore Cooper. See Charles H. Bohner, *John Pendleton Kennedy: Gentleman from Baltimore* (Baltimore: Johns Hopkins University Press, 1961), 97.

23. Charles H. Brichford makes this interpretive claim in a rare example of critical treatment of *Horse-Shoe Robinson*. According to Brichford, especially when it is compared alongside Simms's *The Partisan*, Kennedy's novel presents a "surprisingly non-partisan and realistic portrayal of the Revolution." Charles H. Brichford, "That National Story: Conflicting Versions and Conflicting Visions of the Revolution in Kennedy's *Horse-Shoe Robinson* and Simms's *The Partisan*," *Southern Literary Journal* 21.1 (Fall 1988): 64–85, 64. On the other hand, Bohner points to the failure of the novel to achieve trans-Atlantic success as an indicator of its American nationalism.

24. Bohner, 93.

25. For a discussion on the flexibility of gender roles in brother–sister dynamics, see Hemphill, 74–77.

26. For a classic reading of this effect of incest, see Peter L. Thorslev, Jr. "Incest as Romantic Symbol," *Comparative Literature Studies* 2.1 (1965): 41–58. Thorslev interprets Percy Shelley's portrayal of incest as signifying a "sense of the past as being parasitic upon the future; of fathers, authorities; institutions, and traditions having outlived their usefulness, but being unwilling to grow old gracefully and wither away and even attempting grotesquely to renew their youth by devouring their youth or reproducing upon them" (49).

27. Bohner notes that "As the country drifted toward disruption and civil war, Kennedy, like the chorus in a Sophoclean tragedy, warned but was powerless to change. He thought that 'the conception and estimate of a *gentleman*' had been entirely obliterated from the popular mind" (227).
28. While Simms would attain some political success, eventually being elected to the South Carolina House of Representatives in 1844, his notoriety mostly came from his prolific and popular fiction output. James Perrin Warren notes that "More important than his political ambition is Simms's position as the leading man of letters in the antebellum South," and that he achieves status as a "figure of cultural authority." James Perrin Warren, *Culture of Eloquence: Oratory and Reform in Antebellum America* (University Park: The Pennsylvania State University Press, 1999), 141.
29. J. Quitman Moore, "William Gilmore Simms," *DeBow's Review* 29.6 (Dec. 1860): 702–712, 708.
30. For a detailed account of the development of Simms's political views, see Jon L. Wakelyn, *The Politics of a Literary Man: William Gilmore Simms* (Westport: Greenwood Press, 1973).
31. Quoted in Wakelyn, 26.
32. C. Hugh Holman points out that *The Partisan* reflects Simms's investment in both "movements for a national and for a distinctively Southern literature between 1830 and 1860" (445). Simms, like most antebellum writers, believed that sectionalism/regionalism supported the larger body of national literature. C. Hugh Holman, "William Gilmore Simms' Picture of the Revolution as Civil Conflict," *The Journal of Southern History* 15.4 (Nov. 1949), 441–462.
33. The crisis of Walton's oath of loyalty to the British anticipates what Elizabeth Duquette has established as the cultural encoding of coercive loyalty during and after the Civil War, signified by the emergence of "test oaths" that would require Confederates to swear their loyalty to the nation and by such historically enduring texts as the Pledge of Allegiance. See Elizabeth Duquette, *Loyal Subjects: Bonds of Nation, Race, and Allegiance in Nineteenth-Century America* (New Brunswick: Rutgers University Press, 2010). Freehling locates the test oath controversy during the Nullification crisis, and especially during the backlash period following the compromise, when Southern Unionists were compelled to testify their loyalty to the South; see 263, 268–270, 171, 309–322. The novel's emphasis on this Revolutionary character's repudiation of his oath of loyalty further reveals Simms's rhetorical sensitivity to the complicated nuances of loyalty and nationalism in the Nullification-era South.

Chapter 3

1. For a good discussion of the domestic social agenda of Hentz's literary works, see Elizabeth Moss, *Domestic Novelists in the Old South: Defenders of Southern Culture* (Baton Rouge: Louisiana State University Press, 1992).

2. Besides *Ernest Linwood*, another compelling site of sibling romance, while outside the scope of the close psychoanalytical reading in this chapter, is her collection of short stories and novellas, *The Banished Son* (1856). The title novella as well as several of the collected stories feature a recurring narrative of sisterly/brotherly romance in the shape of cousins or adopted sibling pairs.
3. Moss restores critical recognition of Hentz's prolific propagandist fiction career, pointing out that *Ernest Linwood* was a rare example of a Hentz novel that is noticeably devoid of overt pro-South agenda.
4. See Jamie Stanesa, "Caroline Lee Whiting Hentz" (Profile), *Legacy* 13.2 (1996): 130–139, 130–131.
5. See Rhoda Coleman Ellison, "Caroline Lee Hentz's Alabama Diary, 1836," 254, n. 2, for this history. Also, the history of the novel's posthumous publication and its immediate reception is recorded in Mary Eileen Kennedy, *A Criticism of the Novels of Mrs. Caroline Lee Hentz* (Dissertation, The Catholic University of America: 1923). According to Kennedy, Hentz's publisher, John P. Jewett & Company, announced in the Boston *Evening Transcript* the author's untimely death of pneumonia in Marianna, Florida, which they say they learned about on the day they commenced the publication of "her new and beautiful, and alas, little did we think it, her *last* literary effort": "Ernest Linwood will be to us, and to the hundreds of thousands of admirers of this gifted and lamented authoress, as the '*last notes of the dying swan.*' Her closing chapter, like the Requiem of Mozart, seems almost prophetic of her own speedy dissolution." The *Transcript* reported that sales of the novel reached 5,000 in one week (15–16).
6. Also, as Stanesa has suggested, this experimental first-person narrative technique serves as a "precursor to the mature *bildungsroman* of the period as well as the psychological realism of Henry James" (Profile, 136).
7. In an early recovery of the legacy of female contributors to the gothic, Kay Mussel suggests the overlapping conventions of women's "gothic" and "romantic" novels, but she nevertheless reasserts the notion that the gothic plot is less interested in love and romance than in "vicarious danger," and she contrasts that convention to the "more domestic" women's fiction, such as popular romance novels. Kay Mussel, *Women's Gothic and Romantic Fiction: A Reference Guide* (Westport, CT: Greenwood Press, 1981), xi, x; Leslie Fielder, in *Love and Death in the American Novel* (New York: Stein and Day, 1982), contended that the American version of the genre in the nineteenth century prioritized an inward focus on the human psyche, in contrast to the presumably more historically and socially engaged British tradition of gothic. Toni Morrison's famous intervention in that conversation (*Playing in the Dark: Whiteness and the Literary Imagination* (Cambridge: Harvard University Press, 1992) insists upon the historically situated racializing implications of American gothic fiction. Also, Cathy Davidson, in *Revolution and the Word: The Rise of the Novel in America* (New York: Oxford University Press, 1986), established the capacity for the early American gothic to expose and criticize individualism, and Teresa A. Goddu illuminates "the gothic's

intimate relation to the romance," and the infiltration of the American literary canon by the "popular, the disturbing, and the haunting of history"; Teresa A. Goddu, *Gothic America: Narrative, History, and Nation* (New York: Columbia University Press, 1997), 8. By suggesting the psychological significance of sibling love in *Ernest Linwood* in the context of historical narratives of crisis and nation, I want to acknowledge the historical and social relevance of Hentz's experimentation with gothic gesturing in a novel of domestic love and violence.

8. Elizabeth Dill, "That Damned Mob of Scribbling Siblings: The American Romance as Anti-Novel in The Power of Sympathy and Pierre," *American Literature* 80.4 (December 2008): 707–737.

9. This conflict likely caused intellectual and personal as well as pragmatic anxieties for Hentz. Not only did she probably retain some sympathy with attitudes about race, family, and nation that were typical in the North, but also her success in the literary marketplace provided crucial financial support for her family, and that success was contingent upon the continued approval by her Northern publishers.

10. Caroline Lee Hentz, *The Planter's Northern Bride* (Chapel Hill: University of North Carolina Press, 1970), 4.

11. For a reading of *The Planter's Northern Bride* as a nationalistic gesture that aligns with Stowe's literary domesticity in idealizing American womanhood above sectional difference, see Carme Manuel Cuenca, "An Angel in the Plantation: The Economics of Slavery and the Politics of Literary Domesticity in Caroline Lee Hentz's *The Planter's Northern Bride*," *Mississippi Quarterly* 51.1 (1997): 87–104. In a competing reading, Elizabeth Moss, situating the novel as a foundational text in the tradition of Southern domesticity, locates the publication of *The Planter's Northern Bride* as a turning point in Hentz's growing sectionalism; she argues that "Whereas in previous novels Hentz had portrayed Northerners with some degree of consistency, emphasizing the common humanity of residents above and below the Mason-Dixon Line, in *The Planter's Northern Bride* she depicted Yankees as largely reprehensible" (110).

12. Jamie Stanesa, "Caroline Hentz's Rereading of Southern Paternalism; Or, Pastoral Naturalism in *The Planter's Northern Bride*," *Southern Studies* 3.4 (1992): 221–252, 234. Also, in her *Legacy* Profile of Hentz, Stanesa observes more generally that, "Writing from within the ethic of paternalism rather than against it, Hentz often rejected bourgeois notions of individualism as selfish and immoral and upheld instead Southern notions of the pastoral garden of chattel, revising them to encompass a greater sense of the rights and responsibilities of women within it" (134).

13. Robert Hunt, "A Domesticated Slavery; Political Economy in Caroline Hentz's Fiction," *The Southern Quarterly* 34.4 (1996): 24–35, 26, 27.

14. Moss, 117.

15. See Rhoda Coleman Ellison, "Mrs. Hentz and the Green-Eyed Monster," *American Literature* 22 (1951): 345–350. Ellison makes a strong case for the

validity of the autobiographical connections in *Ernest Linwood*. In an especially compelling example, the scene in the novel in which Gabriella receives a secret note from a strange man at the opera closely resembles an episode in Hentz's own life, which provoked the real-life jealous rage of Hentz's husband, according to their son's memoirs.
16. Charles A. Hentz, *A Southern Practice: The Diary and Autobiography of Charles A. Hentz. M. D.*, edited by Steven M. Stowe (Charlottesville: University Press of Virginia, 2000), 406.
17. See Dawn Keetley, "A Husband's Jealousy: Antebellum Murder Trials and Caroline Lee Hentz's *Ernest Linwood*," *Legacy: A Journal of American Women Writers* 19 (2002): 26–34. Keetley invokes the Freudian concept of melancholia to explain Ernest Linwood's unfulfilled desire for masculine intimacy. In another exception to the dearth of contemporary critical attention to *Ernest Linwood*, Elizabeth Barnes focuses on the embedded narrative of Gabriella's mother's seduction story, showcasing how this novel contributes to an important tradition in literary history that Barnes calls "mother-texts." See Elizabeth Barnes, *States of Sympathy: Seduction and Democracy in the American Novel* (New York: Columbia University Press, 1997), 101–114.
18. Caroline Lee Hentz, *Ernest Linwood* (Boston: John P. Jewett & Co, 1856), 122.
19. Recent innovations in psychoanalysis support this possibility for lateral dynamics as a source of the repression of the self. In her revisionist treatment of hysteria, for instance, Juliet Mitchell traces the fear of annihilation to the occurrence of a sibling birth, which sets the stage for a formative trauma: "the realization that one is not unique, that some stands exactly in the place as oneself, and that though one has found a friend, this loss of uniqueness is, at least temporarily, equivalent to annihilation." Juliet Mitchell, *Siblings: Sex and Violence* (Cambridge: Polity Press, 2003), 43.
20. Ernest's sense of his jealous and violent behavior as a disorder is comparable to Hentz's husband's self-diagnosis; according to Charles Hentz, his father, he "sometimes, especially in the later years of life, spoke of his infirmity, and spoke of it as a disease" (406).
21. Mitchell, 205.
22. Gabriella's attractiveness and Ernest's violent possessiveness resoundingly echo the portrayal of the Hentz's marriage by their son, Charles, who says that his mother "was possessed of the most lovely, sunny dispositions that ever existed—Was charming in person & conversation, and was always a centre of attraction, wherever she went, and the attention that she drew inevitably, always excited my poor, dear father's jealous temperament to frenzy" (406).
23. Ibid., 206.
24. Ibid., 205.
25. Caroline Lee Hentz, *Marcus Warland; or, The Long Moss Spring, a Tale of the South* (Philadelphia: A. Hart, Carey, & Hart, 1852), 7.

Chapter 4

1. Katherine Adams connects Hentz and Stowe in her chapter, "Harriet Beecher Stowe, Caroline Lee Hentz, Herman Melville, and American Racialist Exceptionalism" in *A Companion to American Fiction 1780–1865,* edited by S. Samuels (Oxford: Blackwell Publishing Ltd, 2007). Also, see Amy Elizabeth Cummins, *A Common School: Models of Instruction in the United States Common School Movement and the 1850s Literature of Harriet Beecher Stowe, Caroline Lee Hentz, Fanny Fern, and Mary Jane Holmes* (PhD Dissertation, University of Kansas, 2004).
2. Beyond this well-known motto, an idea credited to Josiah Wedgewood (c. 1787) and most famously evoked in the broadsides of anti-slavery poet and activist John Greenleaf Whittier in the 1830s, the appeal to brotherhood was one of the most prevalent devices of abolitionist discourse. In 1843, Rev. Steven S. Foster famously evoked the concept Christian brotherhood in his controversial abolitionist manifesto against American clergy, *The Brotherhood of Thieves, or, A True Picture of the American Church and Clergy.* On the concept of "brotherhood" as a vital "fighting word" for the development of Black-centered abolitionist discourse, see Timothy Shortell, "The Rhetoric of Black Abolitionism," *Social Science History* 28.1 (spring 2004): 75–109.
3. Cindy Weinstein contributes a much-needed analysis of the contrasting sentimentalism in *Uncle Tom's Cabin* and its pro-slavery responses, but assertions about the "progressive politics of [Stowe's] abolitionism" and the "progressive force" of *Uncle Tom's Cabin's* sympathetic appeals (67) somewhat overstate Stowe's liberalism, even within nineteenth-century contexts. Cindy Weinsten, *Family, Kinship, and Sympathy in Nineteenth-Century American Literature* (New York: Cambridge University Press, 2004).
4. In addition to Weinstein, on the importance of reading Stowe within her historical context, see Susan Ryan, "Charity Begins at Home: Stowe's Antislavery Novels and the Forms of Benevolent Citizenship," *American Literature* 72 (2000): 751–782, maintains the importance of historical context for understanding Stowe.
5. Acknowledging that "Stowe's moral and racial politics should be historicized more thoroughly" (751), Ryan interprets the interracial politics of *Dred* through the linkage between national citizenship and benevolence in antebellum America. And, in another important effort to free the novel from beneath the shadow of *Uncle Tom's Cabin,* Gail K. Smith exposes the politics of reading and interpretation, which is a theme that moves beyond, while couched in, abolitionism. Gail K. Smith, "Reading with the Other: Hermeneutics and the Politics of Difference in Stowe's Dred," *American Literature: A Journal of Literary History, Criticism, and Bibliography* 69.2 (1997): 289–313.
6. The significance of the mother figures in *Uncle Tom's Cabin* has been well established, most prominently by Jane Tompkins, *Sensational Designs: The Cultural Work of American Fiction 1790–1860* (New York: Oxford University Press, 1985) and by Elizabeth Ammons, "Stowe's Dream of the

Mother-Savior: *Uncle Tom's Cabin* and American Women Writers Before the 1920s" in *New Essays on Uncle Tom's Cabin*, edited by Eric J. Sundquist (Cambridge: Cambridge University Press, 1986). Other studies that explore the rhetorical significance of motherhood and family themes throughout the novel include the following: Myra Jehlen, "The Family Militant: Domesticity Versus Slavery in *Uncle Tom's Cabin*," *Criticism* XXXI.4 (Fall 1989): 383–400; Carle E. Krog, "Women, Slaves, and Family in *Uncle Tom's Cabin*: Symbolic Battleground in Antebellum America," *Midwest Quarterly* 31.2 (Winter 1990): 252–269; S. Bradley Shaw, "The Pliable Rhetoric of Domesticity" and Susan L. Roberson, "Matriarchy and the Rhetoric of Domesticity," both in *The Stowe Debate: Rhetorical Strategies in Uncle Tom's Cabin*, edited by Mason Lowance, Jr., Ellen E. Westbrook, and R. C. De Prospo (Amherst: University of Massachusetts Press, 1994).

7. Moss examines McIntosh's *The Lofty and the Lowly* as an attempt to preserve Southern domesticity. Elizabeth Moss, *Domestic Novelists in the Old South: Defenders of Southern Culture* (Baton Rouge: Louisiana State University Press, 1992), 92–98. Jordan-Lake revisits the novel as a product and agent of Southern patriarchy. Joy Jordan-Lake, *Whitewashing Uncle Tom's Cabin: Nineteenth-Century Women Novelists Respond to Stowe* (Nashville: Vanderbilt University Press, 2005), 120, 139.

8. The sibling bond is the most developed and sustained, but not the sole method Stowe used to break away from the biological model of family in *Dred*. The novel's conclusion offers two striking alternatives to the extended families of the plantation tradition. After suffering the loss of her 12 biological children, all of whom were either sold away from her or murdered, former slave Milly lives out her old age taking care of homeless children, who she refers to as her "family": "I calls 'em all mine; so I's got good many chil'en now" (547). The other non-biological family that concludes the novel is headed by a fugitive slave character, Tiff, who absconded to New England and made a home with the two white children of his abusive, alcoholic owner. Susan Ryan interprets these two final family images in the context of "benevolent citizenship" in antebellum America, but the closing family scenes also reflect the novel's attempt to move beyond the biological prerequisite for family that made Stowe's earlier abolitionist arguments vulnerable to attack by proslavery writers.

9. C. Dallett Hemphill, *Siblings: Brothers and Sisters in American History* (New York: Oxford University Press, 2011) is the definitive new source of this cultural history. See also E. Anthony Rotundo, *American Manhood: Transformations in Masculinity from the Revolution to the Modern Era* (New York: Harper, 1993); and Steven Mintz, *A Prison of Expectations: The Family in Victorian Culture* (New York: New York University Press, 1985).

10. See Chapter 1 for more extensive excerpts and analysis of these domestic advice examples.

11. "Mrs. Stowe and Dred," *Southern Literary Messenger* (October 1858): 284–286.

12. Nina's ardent attachment to Harry despite being unconscious that he is her brother may be explained by Clifton Cherpack's concept of the *cri du sang* or *force du sang*, which acknowledges the convention in sentimental and gothic traditions of "an instinctive knowledge of consanguinity which informs literary characters who may never have seen each other that they are linked by ties of blood": *The Call of Blood in French Classical Tragedy* (Baltimore: John Hopkins University Press, 1958), 3.

CHAPTER 5

1. See Rayford W. Logan, *The Negro in American Life and Thought: the Nadir, 1877–1901* (New York: Dial Press, 1954) and Carla L. Peterson, "Commemorative Ceremonies and Invented Traditions: History, Memory, and Modernity in the 'New Negro' Novel of the Nadir," in *Post-Bellum, Pre-Harlem: African American Literature and Culture, 1877–1919*, edited by Barbara McCaskill and Caroline Gebhard (New York: New York University Press, 2006).
2. For an extensive discussion of literary representations of lynching by African American authors of the period, see M. Giulia Fabi, "Reconstructing the Race: The Novel After Slavery," in *Cambridge Companion to the African American Novel*, edited by Maryemma Graham (Cambridge: Cambridge University Press, 2004): 34–49.
3. Nina Silber, *The Romance of Reunion: Northerners and the South, 1865–1900* (Chapel Hill: University of North Carolina Press, 1997). Also, see Karen A. Keely, "Marriage Plots and National Reunion: The Trope of Romantic Reconciliation in Postbellum Literature." *Mississippi Quarterly* 51 (Fall 1998): 621–648, 621).
4. In suggesting the intertextual comparison between Harper's use of the sibling trope and Stowe's *Dred*, I am acknowledging Harper's complicated revisionist responses to the abolitionist writer, and not suggesting that Harper's works, in Frances Foster's famous words of indictment of this critical history, "should be read as attempts—weak and inadequate, but, given their situation, rather heroic—to imitate the literary productions of Euro-Americans" [Frances Smith Foster, introduction to *Minnie's Sacrifice, Sowing and Reaping, Trial and Triumph: Three Rediscovered Novels by Frances E. W. Harper*, edited by Frances Smith Foster (Boston: Beacon Press, 1994), xxiii]. For more on Harper's relationship to white female abolitionists, see Alice Rutkowski, "Leaving the Good Mother: Frances E. W. Harper, Lydia Maria Child, and the Literary Politics of Reconstruction," *Legacy: A Journal of American Women Writers* 25 (January 2008): 83–104.
5. Teresa Zackodnik argues that both Harper's *Iola Leroy* and Hopkins's *Contending Forces* were "signifying, rather than reifying," the tragic mulatta trope. Teresa Zackodnik, "Little Romances and Mulatta Heroines: Passing for a 'True Woman' in Frances Harper's *Iola Leroy* and Pauline Hopkins's *Contending Forces*," *Nineteenth-Century Feminisms* 2 (Spring/Summer 2000):

103–124. Also, see M. Giulia Fabi, Patricia Bizzell, Hazel Carby, Barbara Christian, and Ann duCille.
6. Foreman credits the novel with rewriting history via "histotextuality," which she describes as "a strategy marginalized writers use to incorporate historical allusions that both contextualize and radicalize their work by countering the putatively innocuous generic codes they seem to have endorsed". Foreman P. Gabrielle, " 'Reading Aright': White Slavery, Black Referents, and the Strategy of Histotextuality in *Iola Leroy*," *The Yale Journal of Criticism* 10.2 (1997): 327–354, 328.
7. Harper's portrayal of Robert and Marie's tenacious memories of each other resonates with the real history of sibling attachments in slavery and the trauma of separated siblings. See Hemphill, C. Dallett, *Siblings: Brothers and Sisters in American History* (New York: Oxford University Press, 2011): 186–196.
8. Robert H. Abzug, "The Black Family during Reconstruction," in *Key Issues in the Afro-American Experience,* edited by Nathan I. Huggins et al. (New York: Harcourt Brace Jovanovich, 1971): 26–41. Abzug restores the history of the freedmen's effort to establish normal family life in freedom, and exposes how their attempts for stability were undermined by white violence and economic subjugation. Also, correspondence documentary projects that have contributed significantly to the recovery of African Americans' roles in Reconstruction are featured in Berlin and Rowland, eds. *Families and Freedom: A Documentary History of African-American Kinship in the Civil War Era.* More recently, Eric Foner, *Forever Free: The Story of Emancipation and Reconstruction* (New York: Alfred A. Knopf, 2005), revises the story of Reconstruction to feature the real participation of African Americans, and Heather Williams, *Self-Taught: African American Education in Slavery and Freedom* (Chapel Hill: University of North Carolina Press, 2005), documents the history of African American educational leaders before and after the Civil War.
9. Karsten H. Piep, "Liberal Visions of Reconstruction: Lydia Maria Child's *A Romance of the Republic* and George Washington Cable's *The Grandissimes,*" *Studies in American Fiction* 31.2 (Autumn 2003): 165–190. Piep points out that even in the "Liberal visions of reconstruction" of George Washington Cable's *The Grandissimes,* "Blacks... neither affect nor contribute to historical progress" (183). Caroline L. Karcher also explains that even Albion Tourgee's most progressive of white-authored efforts to imagine a Black-centered Reconstruction plot eventually "reorients... toward addressing the issue of national reunification in lieu of Black self-determination" (*Bricks without Straw*: Albion W. Tourgee's 'Black Reconstruction.' " *REAL: The Yearbook of Research in English and American Literature* 22 (2006): 241–258, 241, 255).
10. See Paul A. Cimbala, *Under the Guardianship of the Nation: The Freedmen's Bureau and the Reconstruction of Georgia, 1865–1870* (Athens: University of Georgia Press, 2003); Eric Foner, *Forever Free: The Story of Emancipation*

and Reconstruction (New York: Random House, 2005); and Williams, *Self-Taught*.
11. For a reading that examines how Harper deployed the gothic tradition to rewrite Reconstruction, see Justin D. Edwards, *Gothic Passages: Racial Ambiguity and the American Gothic* (Iowa City: University of Iowa Press, 2002), 53–71.
12. W. E. B. DuBois, *The Souls of Black Folk* (New York: Norton, 1999), 30.
13. W. E. B. DuBois, *Black Reconstruction in America, 1860–1880* (New York: Free Press, 1998), 711–712.
14. Williams, 24.
15. Frances E. W. Harper, *Iola Leroy; or, Shadows Uplifted* (Boston: Beacon Press, 1987), 201. Further references to *Iola Leroy* are to this edition and will be cited parenthetically in the text.
16. Charles Chesnutt, *The House Behind the Cedars* (Athens: The University of Georgia Press, 1988), 7. Further references to *The House Behind the Cedars* will be cited parenthetically in the text.
17. Matthew Wilson, *Whiteness in the Novels of Charles Chesnutt* (Jackson: University Press of Mississippi, 2004), 60–61.
18. Quoted in Wilson, 67.
19. Ibid., 67.
20. Williams, 80.
21. See Julie Cary Nerad, "Slippery Language and False Dilemmas: The Passing Novels of Child, Howells, and Harper," *American Literature* 75.4 (December 2003): 813–841.
22. Pauline Hopkins, *Contending Forces: A Romance Illustrative of Negro Life North and South* (New York: Oxford University Press, 1988,), 41. Further references to *Contending Forces* will be cited parenthetically in the text.
23. Nerad's important intervention in the study of passing novels examines the tradition of "unintentional passers" that "reveals how race functions in the United States to maintain socioeconomic inequalities by controlling an individual's sense of identity and her place within family, community, and nation" (814). My suggestion that Jesse "passes" for Black and thus shifts the racial identity of the Montfort family draws similarly upon the critical understanding of "passing" (whether deliberate or not) from one constructed racial identity to another as a disruption of the notion of biologically constructed racial identity.
24. The sisterly bond between Dora and Sappho, enduring the threats of male violence, emergent within and linked to the surrounding community of women, and consummated by Dora's naming of her first-born after her close friend, remarkably fulfills the African American "womanist aesthetic," which Lovalerie King locates in Alice Walker and dates back to Zora Neale Hurston. Lovalerie King, "Womanism from Zora Neale Hurston to Alice Walker," in *The Cambridge Companion to the African American Novel*, edited by Maryemma Graham (Cambridge, UK: Cambridge University Press, 2004):

NOTES 181

233–252. Hopkins's participation in the womanist aesthetic suggests an even earlier history for this tradition.

25. See Carol Allen, *Black Women Intellectuals: Strategies of Nation, Family, and Neighborhood in the Works of Pauline Hopkins, Jessie Fauset, and Marita Bonner* (New York: Garland Publishing, Inc., 1998). Allen explains Hopkins's burgeoning Black nationalism at the turn of the century, tracing polemical and fictional texts by Hopkins that contribute to various nationalist camps, including both extra-continental expatriation and a separate Black state within the United States (30–33). A classic source for that history is Essien Udosen Essien-Udom, *America Black Nationalism: A Search for Identity in America* (Chicago: University of Chicago Press, 1995; first edition, 1962). A more contemporary account that examines the history of public discourse shaping Black nationalism is Melanye Price, *Dreaming Blackness: Black Nationalism and African American Public Opinion* (New York: New York University Press, 2009).

26. A classic source for that history is Essien Udosen Essien-Udom, *America Black Nationalism.* . Hopkins's emphasis on "brotherly affiliation" aligns remarkably with Price's definition of the Black nationalist, particularly in the attention the novelist gives to a separate, self-determining Black community, as well as its focus on the Diaspora in its multi-continental setting of the Montfort family history.

27. Peter Coviello, *Intimacy in America: Dreams of Affiliation in Antebellum Literature* (Minneapolis: University of Minnesota Press, 2005), 27.

Epilogue

1. Herman Melville, *Pierre: or, The Ambiguities* (New York: Penguin, 1996), 7.
2. Diane Roberts, *Faulkner and Southern Womanhood* (Athens: University of Georgia Press, 1995), 95.
3. For various accounts of the novella and its history, see Anne Edwards, *Road to Tara: The Life of Margaret Mitchell* (New Haven: Ticknor & Fields, 1983), 129–130; Joel Williamson, "How Black Was Rhett Butler," in *The Evolution of Southern Culture*, edited by Numan V. Bartley (Athens: University of Georgia Press, 1988), 103–105; Roberts, *Faulkner and Southern Womanhood*, 95; and Darden Asbury Pyron, *Southern Daughter: The Life of Margaret Mitchell* (New York: Oxford University Press), 215–217; Finis Farr, *Margaret Mitchell of Atlanta: The Author of Gone with the Wind* (New York: William Morrow & Company, 1965), 77 and 103.
4. Pyron, 216.
5. Quoted in Farr, 103.
6. For an excellent study of the novel's reception, see Amanda Adams, " 'Painfully Southern': Gone with the Wind, the Agrarians, and the Battle for the New South," *Southern Literary Journal* XL.1 (Fall 2007): 58–75.

7. While offering a timely suggestion for revisiting the novel's legacy within its contemporary literary and political contexts, Adams distances the novel from the sentimental tradition.
8. For important studies that recover the presence of domestic fiction in the modernist and contemporary eras, respectively, see Susan Edmunds, *Grotesque Relations: Modernist Domestic Fiction and the U.S. Welfare State* (New York: Oxford University Press, 2008) and Kristin J. Jacobson, *Neodomestic American Fiction* (Columbus: The Ohio State University Press, 2011).
9. John T. Irwin, *Doubling and Incest/Repetition and Revenge: A Speculative Reading of Faulkner* (Baltimore: The John Hopkins University Press, 1975), 11–21.
10. Karl Zender, "Faulkner and the Politics of Incest," *American Literature* 70.4 (December 1998): 739–765, 741–742.
11. For the connection between *Pierre* and the early American seduction novel, see Elizabeth Dill, "That Damned Mob of Scribbling Siblings: The American Romance as Anti-novel in *The Power of Sympathy* and *Pierre*," *American Literature* 80.4 (December 2008): 707–738.
12. Denis Flannery, *On Sibling Love, Queer Attachment, and American Writing* (Burlington, VT: Ashgate, 2007), 11.
13. See Gillian Silverman, "Textual Sentimentalism: Incest and Authorship in Melville's *Pierre*," *American Literature* 74.2 (June 2002): 345–372. Silverman challenges the traditional reading of Pierre as a parody of sentimentalism, pointing out not only Melville's correspondence about the novel and its initial reception, but also the conventional employment of self-directed mockery in the sentimental tradition (348–350).
14. Dill, 708.
15. For examples of recent attention to the novel in the context of domesticity and gender, see Keiko Arai, "Phoebe is No Pyncheon: Class, Gender, and Nation in *The House of the Seven Gables*," *Nathaniel Hawthorne Review* 34.1–2 (Spring-Fall 2008): 40–62; Holly Jackson, "The Transformation of American Family Property in *The House of the Seven Gables*," *ESQ: A Journal of the American Renaissance* 47.3 (Summer 2011): 227–260; Robert S. Levine, "Genealogical Fictions: Race in *The House of the Seven Gables* and *Pierre*," in *Hawthorne and Melville: Writing a Relationship*, edited by Jana L. Argersinger and Leland S. Person (Athens: University of Georgia Press, 2008): 227–247; and Roberta Weldon, *Hawthorne, Gender, and Death: Christianity and Its Discontents* (New York: Palgrave Macmillan, 2008).
16. Theresa Goddu, "The Circulation of Women in *The House of the Seven Gables*," *Studies in the Novel* 23.1 (Spring 1991): 119–127, 125. For an overview of the criticism of the novel's ending, see Michael T. Gilmore, *American Romanticism and the Marketplace* (Chicago: The University of Chicago Press, 1985), 96. Also, Gallagher points out that some twentieth-century readings of the novel's ending interpret it as an ironic commentary upon Phoebe and Holgrave's union (12–13, n. 23).

17. Nathaniel Hawthorne, *The House of the Seven Gables* (New York: W. W. Norton & Co., 1967), 133.
18. Ibid., 133, 134.
19. Ibid., 134, 135.
20. Leila S. May, " 'Sympathies of a Scarcely Intelligible Nature': The Brother-Sister Bond in Poe's 'The Fall of the House of Usher,' " *Studies in Short Fiction* 30.3 (Summer 1993): 387–397, 391.
21. May notes this biographical context, 391, n. 10.

WORKS CITED

Adams, Abigail and John Adams. *The Book of Abigail and John: Selected Letters of the Adams Family, 1762–1784.* Ed. L. H. Butterfield, et al. Boston: Northeastern University Press, 2002.

Abzug, Robert H. "The Black Family during Reconstruction," in *Key Issues in the Afro-American Experience.* Ed. Nathan I. Huggins et al. New York: Harcourt Brace Jovanovich, 1971: 26–41.

Adams, Katherine. "Harriet Beecher Stowe, Caroline Lee Hentz, Herman Melville, and American Racialist Exceptionalism," in *A Companion to American Fiction 1780–1865.* Ed. S. Samuels. Oxford: Blackwell Publishing Ltd, 2007.

———. *Owning Up: Privacy, Property, and Belonging in U.S. Women's Life Writing.* New York: Oxford University Press, 2009.

Aikman, William. *Life at Home; or, The Family and Its Members.* New York: Wells, 1870.

Alcott, Louisa May. *Little Women.* New York: Penguin, 1989.

———. "Netty's Hospital," *Our Young Folks,* 1865: 267–277.

Alcott, William A. *Familiar Letters to Young Men on Various Subjects.* Buffalo: Derby, 1850.

———. *The Young Man's Guide,* 10th ed. Boston: Perkins, 1836.

Allen, Carol. *Black Women Intellectuals: Strategies of Nation, Family, and Neighborhood in the Works of Pauline Hopkins, Jessie Fauset, and Marita Bonner.* New York: Garland Publishing, Inc., 1998.

Ammons, Elizabeth. "Stowe's Dream of the Mother-Savior: *Uncle Tom's Cabin* and American Women Writers before the 1920s," in *New Essays on Uncle Tom's Cabin.* Ed. Eric J. Sundquist. Cambridge: Cambridge University Press, 1986.

Arai, Keiko. "Phoebe Is No Pyncheon: Class, Gender, and Nation in *The House of the Seven Gables,*" *Nathaniel Hawthorne Review* 34.1–2 (Spring-Fall 2008): 40–62.

Atkins, Annette. *We Grew Up Together: Brothers and Sisters in Nineteenth-Century America.* Urbana: Illinois University Press, 2001.

Barnes, Elizabeth. *States of Sympathy: Seduction and Democracy in the American Novel.* New York: Columbia University Press, 1997.

Baym, Nina. *Woman's Fiction: A Guide to Novels by and about Women in America, 1820–1870.* 2nd ed. Urbana: University of Illinois Press, 1993.

Berlin, Ira, Steven F. Miller, and Leslie S. Rowland. "Afro-American Families in the Transition from Slavery to Freedom," *Radical History Review* 42 (1988): 89–121.

Berlin, Ira and Leslie S. Rowland, eds. *Families and Freedom: A Documentary History of African-American Kinship in the Civil War Era.* New York: New Press, 1997.

Bizzell, Patricia. " 'Stolen Literacies' in *Iola Leroy*" in *Popular Literacy: Studies in Cultural Practices and Poetics.* Ed. John Trimbur. Pittsburgh: University of Pittsburgh Press, 2001.

Bohner, Charles H. *John Pendleton Kennedy: Gentleman from Baltimore.* Baltimore: Johns Hopkins University Press, 1961.

Boudreau, Kristin. *Sympathy in American Literature.* Gainesville: University Press of Florida, 2002.

Brichford, Charles H. "That National Story: Conflicting Versions and Conflicting Visions of the Revolution in Kennedy's *Horse-Shoe Robinson* and Simms's *The Partisan*," *Southern Literary Journal* 21.1 (Fall 1988): 64–85.

Broadhead, Richard. "Sparing the Rod: Discipline and Fiction in Antebellum America," *Representations* 21 (1988): 67–96.

Brown, Gillian. *Consent of the Governed: The Lockean Legacy in Early American Culture.* Cambridge: Harvard University Press, 2001.

Butler, Judith. *Antigone's Claim: Kinship between Life and Death.* New York: Columbia University Press, 2000.

Butterfield, L. H., Marc Friedlaender, and, Mary-Jo Kline, eds. *The Book of Abigail and John: Selected Letters of the Adams Family, 1762–1784.* Northeastern University Press, 2002 (originally published by Harvard University Press, 1975).

Carby, Hazel. *Reconstructing Womanhood: The Emergence of the Afro-American Woman Novelist.* New York: Oxford University Press, 1987.

Cherpack, Clifton. *The Call of Blood in French Classical Tragedy.* Baltimore: John Hopkins University Press, 1958.

Chesnutt, Charles. *The House Behind the Cedars.* Athens: The University of Georgia Press, 1988.

"A Child's Dream of a Star," *Robert Merry's Museum*, 1867: 166–169.

"Child's Grief," *The Youth's Companion*, April 2, 1846: 190–191.

"Children's Literature: What 'St. Nicholas' Has Done for Boys and Girls," in *Overland Monthly and Out West Magazine* 16.96 (December 1890): 667–670.

Christian, Barbara, *Black Woman Novelists: The Development of a Tradition.* Westport, Conn: Greenwood Press, 1980.

Cimbala, Paul A. *Under the Guardianship of the Nation: The Freedmen's Bureau and the Reconstruction of Georgia, 1865–1870.* Athens: University of Georgia Press, 2003.

Civiatta, David V. *Spirit, the Family, and the Unconscious in Hegel's Philosophy.* New York: SUNY Press, 2009.

Cohoon, Lorinda. *Serialized Citizenships: Periodicals, Books, and American Boys, 1840–1911.* Landham, MD: Scarecrow Press, 2006.

Coles, Prophecy. *The Importance of Sibling Relationships in Psychoanalysis.* London: Karnac, 2003.

Cott, Nancy. *The Bonds of Womanhood: "Woman's Sphere" in New England 1780–1835.* New Haven: Yale University Press, 1977.

———. *Public Vows: A History of Marriage and the Nation.* Cambridge: Harvard University Press, 2000.

Coviello, Peter. *Intimacy in America: Dreams of Affiliation in Antebellum Literature.* Minneapolis: University of Minnesota Press, 2005.

Cuenca, Carme Manuel. "An Angel in the Plantation: The Economics of Slavery and the Politics of Literary Domesticity in Caroline Lee Hentz's *The Planter's Northern Bride*," *Mississippi Quarterly* 51.1 (1997): 87–104.

Cummins, Amy Elizabeth. *A Common School: Models of Instruction in the United States Common School Movement and the 1850s Literature of Harriet Beecher Stowe, Caroline Lee Hentz, Fanny Fern, and Mary Jane Holmes.* Dissertation Abstracts International, Section A: The Humanities and Social Sciences, 2005 March; 65 (9): 3384 University of Kansas, 2004.

Darling, Mary Greenleaf. *Battles at Home.* Boston: Lee and Shepard Publishers, 1877.

"The Debate in the Senate of the United States," *The North American Review* 31.69, October, 1830: 462–568.

Davidson, Cathy and Jessamyn Hatcher, eds. *No More Separate Spheres: A New Wave American Studies Reader.* Durham: Duke University Press, 2002.

———. *Revolution and the Word: The Rise of the Novel in America.* New York: Oxford University Press, 1986.

Dill, Elizabeth. "That Damned Mob of Scribbling Siblings: The American Romance as Anti-novel in *The Power of Sympathy* and *Pierre*," *American Literature* 80.4 (December 2008): 707–738.

Dodge, Mary Maples. *Donald and Dorothy.* New York: The Century Co, 1893.

DuBois, W. E. B. *Black Reconstruction in America, 1860–1880.* New York: Free Press, 1998.

———. *The Souls of Black Folk.* New York: Norton, 1999.

duCille, Ann. *The Coupling Convention: Sex, Text, and Tradition in Black Women's Fiction.* New York: Oxford University Press, 1993.

Duquette, Elizabeth. *Loyal Subjects: Bonds of Nation, Race, and Allegiance in Nineteenth-Century America.* New Brunswick: Rutgers University Press, 2010.

Edmunds, Susan. *Grotesque Relations: Modernist Domestic Fiction and the U.S. Welfare State.* New York: Oxford University Press, 2008.

Edwards, Justin D. *Gothic Passages: Racial Ambiguity and the American Gothic.* Iowa City: University of Iowa Press, 2002.

Ellis, Richard E. *The Union at Risk: Jacksonian Democracy, States' Rights, and the Nullification Crisis.* New York: Oxford University Press, 1987.

Ellison, Rhoda Coleman. "Caroline Lee Hentz's Alabama Diary, 1836," *The Alabama Review* (1951): 254–269.

———. "Mrs. Hentz and the Green-Eyed Monster," *American Literature* 22. (1951): 345–350.

Essien-Udom, Essien Udosen. *Black Nationalism: A Search for Identity in America.* Chicago: University of Chicago Press, 1995 (first edition, 1962).

Fabi, M. Giulia. "Reconstructing Literary Genealogies: Frances E. W. Harper's and William Dean Howells's Race Novels," in *Soft Canons: American Women Writers and Masculine Tradition.* Ed. Karen L. Kilcup. Iowa City: University of Iowa Press, 1999: 48–66.

———. "Reconstructing the Race: The Novel after Slavery," in *Cambridge Companion to the African American Novel.* Ed. Maryemma Graham. Cambridge: Cambridge University Press, 2004:34–49.

Fetterley, Judith. "Introduction to "Cacoethes Scribendi"," in *Provisions: A Reader from 19th-Century American Women.* Bloomington: Indiana University Press, 1986. 41–49.

Fielder, Leslie. *Love and Death in the American Novel.* New York: Stein and Day, 1982.

Flannery, Denis. *On Sibling Love, Queer Attachment, and American Writing.* Burlington, VT: Ashgate, 2007.

Fliegelman, Jay. *Prodigals and Pilgrims: The American Revolution against Patriarchal Authority, 1750–1800.* New York: Cambridge University Press, 1982.

Foner, Eric. *Forever Free: The Story of Emancipation and Reconstruction.* New York: Alfred A. Knopf, 2005.

Forgie, George B. *Patricide in the House Divided: A Psychological Interpretation of Lincoln and His Age.* New York: Norton, 1981.

Foreman, P. Gabrielle. "'Reading Aright': White Slavery, Black Referents, and The Strategy of Histotextuality in *Iola Leroy*," *The Yale Journal of Criticism* 10.2 (1997): 327–354.

Foster, Frances Smith. Introduction to *Minnie's Sacrifice, Sowing and Reaping, Trial and Triumph: Three Rediscovered Novels by Frances E. W. Harper.* Ed. Frances Smith Foster. Boston: Beacon Press, 1994.

Freehling, William. *Prelude to Civil War: The Nullification Controversy in South Carolina, 1818–1836.* New York: Oxford University Press, 1992.

Fuller, Margaret. *Woman in the Nineteenth Century.* New York: Greely & McElrath, 1845.

Gannon, Susan R. "Heroism Reconsidered: Negotiating Autonomy in *St. Nicholas Magazine* (1873–1914)," in *Culturing the Child, 1690–1914: Essays in Memory of Mitzi Myers.* Ed. Donelle Ruwe. Lanham, MD: The Children's Literature Association and The Scarecrow Press, 2005: 179–198.

Garvey, T. Gregory. "Risking Reprisal: Catherine Sedgwick's *Hope Leslie* and the Legitimation of Public Action by Women," *American Transcendental Quarterly* 8 (December 1994): 287–298.

Goddu, Teresa A. *Gothic America: Narrative, History, and Nation.* New York: Columbia University Press, 1997.

Gould, Philip. "Catharine Sedgwick's Cosmopolitan Nation," *New England Quarterly* 78 (2005): 232–258.

Harper, Frances E. W. *Iola Leroy; or, Shadows Uplifted.* Boston: Beacon Press, 1987.
Harris, Susan K. *19th-Century American Women's Novels: Interpretive Strategies.* New York: Cambridge University Press, 1990.
———. "The Limits of Authority: Catharine Maria Sedgwick and the Politics of Resistance," in *Catharine Maria Sedgwick: Critical Perspectives.* Ed. Lucinda Damon-Bach and Victoria Clements (Boston: Northeastern University Press, 2003): 272–285.
Hawthorne, Nathaniel. *The House of the Seven Gables.* New York: W. W. Norton & Co., 1967.
Hegel. G. W. F. *The Phenomenology of Mind.* New York: Harper Torchbooks, 1967.
Hemphill, C. Dallett. *Bowing to Necessities: A History of Manners in America 1620–1860.* New York: Oxford University Press, 1999.
———. *Siblings: Brothers and Sisters in American History.* New York: Oxford University Press, 2011.
Hentz, Caroline Lee. *Ernest Linwood.* Boston: John P. Jewett & Co, 1856.
———. *Marcus Warland; or, The Long Moss Spring, a Tale of the South.* Philadelphia: A. Hart, Carey, & Hart, 1852.
———. *The Planter's Northern Bride.* Chapel Hill: University of North Carolina Press, 1970 (1854).
Hentz, Charles A. *A Southern Practice: The Diary and Autobiography of Charles A. Hentz, M.D.* Ed. Steven M. Stowe. Charlottesville: University Press of Virginia, 2000.
Hinshelwood, R. D. and Gary Winship. "Orestes and Democracy," in *Sibling Relationships,* Ed. Prophecy Coles. New York: Karnac, 2006.
Holman, C. Hugh. "William Gilmore Simms' Picture of the Revolution as Civil Conflict," *The Journal of Southern History* 15.4 (November 1949), 441–462.
Hopkins, Pauline. *Daughter of the Revolution: The Major Non-Fiction Works of Pauline Hopkins.* New Brunswick: Rutgers University Press, 2007.
Hopkins, Pauline. *Contending Forces: A Romance Illustrative of Negro Life North and South.* New York: Oxford University Press, 1988.
Horsman, Reginald. *Race and Manifest Destiny: The Origins of American Racial Anglo-Saxonism.* Cambridge: Harvard University Press, 1981.
Howard, Oliver. "Good Sometimes," *Our Young Folks,* 1872: 296–297.
Hunt, Robert. "A Domesticated Slavery; Political Economy in Caroline Hentz's Fiction," *The Southern Quarterly* 34.4 (1996): 24–35.
Garvey, T. Gregory. "Risking Reprisal: Catharine Sedgwick's *Hope Leslie* and the Legitimation of Public Action by Women," *American Transcendental Quarterly* 8 (1994): 287–298.
Genovese, Eugene. *Roll, Jordan, Roll: The World the Slaves Made.* New York: Pantheon Books, 1974.
Gutman, Herbert. *The Black Family in Slavery and in Freedom.* New York: Pantheon Books, 1976.

Irwin, John T. *Doubling and Incest/Repetition and Revenge: A Speculative Reading of Faulkner.* Baltimore: The Johns Hopkins University Press, 1975.
Jacobson, Kristin J. *Neodomestic American Fiction.* Columbus: The Ohio State University Press, 2011.
Jackson, Holly. "The Transformation of American Family Property in *The House of the Seven Gables*," *ESQ: A Journal of the American Renaissance* 47.3 (Summer 2011): 227–260.
James, Rev. John Angell. *Family Monitor; A Help to Domestic Happiness.* Boston: Crocker and Brewster, 1830.
Jehlen, Myra. "The Family Militant: Domesticity versus Slavery in *Uncle Tom's Cabin*," *Criticism* XXXI.4 (Fall 1989): 383–400.
Jordan-Lake, Joy. *Whitewashing Uncle Tom's Cabin: Nineteenth-Century Women Novelists Respond to Stowe.* Nashville: Vanderbilt University Press, 2005.
Kaplan, Amy. "Manifest Domesticity," *American Literature* 70.3 (September 1998): 581–606.
Karafilis, Mary. "Catharine Maria Sedgwick's *Hope Leslie*: The Crisis between Political Action and US Literary Nationalism in the New Republic," *American Transcendental Quarterly* 12 (December 1998): 327–344.
Karcher, Caroline. "*Bricks without Straw*: Albion W. Tourgee's 'Black Reconstruction,'" *REAL: The Yearbook of Research in English and American Literature* 22 (2006): 241–258.
Keely, Karen A. "Marriage Plots and National Reunion: The Trope of Romantic Reconciliation in Postbellum Literature," *Mississippi Quarterly* 51.4 (Fall 1998): 621–648.
Keetley, Dawn. "A Husband's Jealousy: Antebellum Murder Trials and Caroline Lee Hentz's *Ernest Linwood*," *Legacy: A Journal of American Women Writers* 19 (2002): 26–34.
Kelley, Mary. *Learning to Stand and Speak: Women, Education, and Public Life in America's Republic.* Chapel Hill: University of North Carolina Press, 2006.
———. "Negotiating a Self: The Autobiography and Journals of Catherine Maria Sedgwick," *New England Quarterly* 66 (September 1993): 366–398.
———. *Private Woman, Public Stage: Literary Domesticity in Nineteenth-Century America.* New York: Oxford University Press, 1984.
Kelly, R. Gordon. *Children's Periodicals of the United States.* Westport: Greenwood Press, 1984.
———. *Mother Was a Lady: Self and Society in Selected American Children's Periodicals, 1865–1890.* Westport, CT: Greenwood Press, 1974.
Kennedy, John Pendleton. *Horse-Shoe Robinson: A Tale of the Tory Ascendency.* New York: George P. Putnam, 1852 (1835).
Kennedy, Mary Eileen. *A Criticism of the Novels of Mrs. Caroline Lee Hentz.* Dissertation, The Catholic University of America (1923).
Kerber, Linda. *Women of the Republic: Intellect and Ideology in Revolutionary America.* Chapel Hill: University of North Carolina Press, 1980.
———, et al. "Beyond Roles, beyond Spheres: Thinking about Gender in the Early Republic," *The William and Mary Quarterly* 46.3, 1989: 565–585.

King, Lovalerie. "Womanism from Zora Neale Hurston to Alice Walker," in *The Cambridge Companion to the African American Novel.* Ed. Maryemma Graham. Cambridge, UK: Cambridge University Press, 2004: 233–252.

Krog, Carl E. "Women, Slaves, and Family in *Uncle Tom's Cabin*: Symbolic Battleground in Antebellum America," *Midwest Quarterly* 31.2 (Winter 1990): 252–269.

Leavett, Sarah Abigail. *From Catharine Beecher to Martha Stewart: A Cultural History of Domestic Advice.* Greensboro: University of North Carolina Press, 2002.

Lee, Elizabeth. "Therapeutic Beauty: Abbott Thayer, Antimodernism, and the Fear of Disease," *American Art* 18.3 (2004): 32–51.

Leonard, Miriam. *Athens in Paris: Ancient Greece and the Political in Post-War French Thought.* Oxford: Oxford University Press, 2005.

Levine, Robert S. *Dislocating Race and Nation: Episodes in Nineteenth-Century American Literary Nationalism.* Chapel Hill: University of North Carolina Press, 2008.

———. "Genealogical Fictions: Race in *The House of the Seven Gables* and *Pierre*," in *Hawthorne and Melville: Writing a Relationship.* Ed. Jana L. Argersinger and Leland S. Person. Athens: University of Georgia Press, 2008: 227–247.

Little, Greta. "The Care and Nurture of Aspiring Writers: Young Contributors *Our Young Folks* and *St. Nicholas*," *Children's Literature Association Quarterly* 17.4 (1992): 19–23.

Locke, John. *Some Thoughts Concerning Education.* Ed. John W. Yolton and Jean S. Yolton. New York: Oxford University Press, 1989.

Logan, Rayford W. *The Negro in American Life and Thought: The Nadir, 1877–1901.* New York: Dial Press, 1954.

Marten, James. *The Children's Civil War.* Chapel Hill: The University of North Carolina Press, 1998.

May, Leila S. *Disorderly Sisters: Sibling Relations and Sororal Resistance in Nineteenth-Century British Literature.* Lewisburg: Bucknell University Press, 2001.

———, "'Sympathies of a Scarcely Intelligible Nature': The Brother-Sister Bond in Poe's Fall of the House of Usher," *Studies in Short Fiction* 30 (1993): 387–396.

McCall, Laura and Donald Yacavone. *A Shared Experience: Men, Women, and the History of Gender.* New York: New York University Press, 1998.

Melville, Herman. *Pierre: or, The Ambiguities.* New York: Penguin, 1996.

Mintz, Steven. *A Prison of Expectations: The Family in Victorian Culture.* New York: New York University Press, 1985.

———, *Huck's Raft: A History of American Childhood.* Cambridge: Belknap Press, 2004.

Mitchell, Juliet. *Siblings: Sex and Violence.* Cambridge: Polity Press, 2003.

Mitchie, Helena. *Sorophobia: Differences among Women in Literature and Culture.* New York: Oxford University Press, 1992.

Moore, J. Quitman. "William Gilmore Simms," *DeBow's Review*. 29.6 (December 1860): 702–712.

Morrison, Toni. *Playing in the Dark: Whiteness and the Literary Imagination*. Cambridge: Harvard University Press, 1992.

Moss, Elizabeth, *Domestic Novelists in the Old South: Defenders of Southern Culture*. Baton Rouge: Louisiana State University Press, 1992.

Murray, Richard. "Abbott Thayer's 'Stevenson Memorial.'" *American Art* 13.2 (1999): 2–25.

Mussell, Kay. *Women's Gothic and Romantic Fiction: A Reference Guide*. Westport, Conn.: Greenwood Press, 1981.

Nerad, Julie Cary. "Slippery Language and False Dilemmas: The Passing Novels of Child, Howells, and Harper," *American Literature* 75.4 (December 2003): 813–841.

Oliver, Kelly. *Witnessing: Beyond Recognition*. Minneapolis: University of Minnesota Press, 2001.

O'Sullivan, John L. "The Democratic Principle," *The United States Magazine and Democratic Review* I, October. 1837:1–15.

Parille, Ken. "'What Our Boys Are Reading': Lydia Sigourney, Francis Forrester, and Boyhood Literacy in Nineteenth-Century America," *Children's Literature Association Quarterly* 33.1 (2008): 4–25.

Peterson, Carla L. "Commemorative Ceremonies and Invented Traditions: History, Memory, and Modernity in the 'New Negro' Novel of the Nadir" in *Post-Bellum, Pre-Harlem: African American Literature and Culture, 1877–1919*. Ed. Barbara McCaskill and Caroline Gebhard. New York: New York University Press, 2006: 34–56.

Pflieger, Pat. "An Online Community of the Nineteenth Century," http://www.merrycoz.org/papers/online/online.htm

———. "A Visit to Merry's Museum; Or, Social Values in a Nineteenth-Century American Periodical for Children" (Doctoral Dissertation: University of Minnesota, 1987).

Phillips, Michelle H. "Along the 'Paragraphic Wires': Child-Adult Mediation in *St. Nicholas Magazine*," *Children's Literature* 37 (2009): 84–113.

Phillips, Rev. S. *The Christian Home*. Detroit: H.C. Johnson, 1865.

Piep, Karsten H. "Liberal Visions of Reconstruction: Lydia Maria Child's *A Romance of the Republic* and George Washington Cable's *The Grandissimes*," *Studies in American Fiction* 31.2 (Autumn 2003): 165–190.

Pryce, Melanye. *Dreaming Blackness: Black Nationalism and African American Public Opinion*. New York: New York University Press, 2009.

Rahn, Suzanne. "St. Nicholas and Its Friends: The Magazine-Child Relationship" in *St. Nicholas and Mary Maples Dodge: The Legacy of a Children's Magazine*. Ed. Susan Gannon. Jefferson, NC: McFarland, 2004.

Roberson, Susan L. "Matriarchy and the Rhetoric of Domesticity," in *The Stowe Debate: Rhetorical Strategies in Uncle Tom's Cabin*. Ed. Mason Lowance, Jr., Ellen E. Westbrook, and R. C. De Prospo. Amherst: University of Massachusetts Press, 1994.

Roberts, Diane. *Faulkner and Southern Womanhood.* Athens: University of Georgia Press, 1995.
Rotundo, E. Anthony. *American Manhood: Transformations in Masculinity from the Revolution to the Modern Era.* New York: Harper, 1993.
Rutkowski, Alice. "Leaving the Good Mother: Frances E. W. Harper, Lydia Maria Child, and the Literary Politics of Reconstruction," *Legacy: A Journal of American Women Writers* 25.1 (January 2008): 83–104.
Ryan, Susan. "Charity Begins at Home: Stowe's Antislavery Novels and the Forms of Benevolent Citizenship," *American Literature* 72 (2000): 751–782.
Sanders, Valerie. *The Brother-Sister Culture in Nineteenth-Century Literature, from Austen to Woolf.* New York: Palgrave, 2004.
Schwain, Kristin. *Signs of Grace: Religion and American Art in the Gilded Age.* Cornell University Press, 2008.
Scott, Jill. *Electra after Freud: Myth and Culture.* Ithaca: Cornell University Press, 2005.
Sedgwick, Catharine Maria. *Means and Ends, or Self-Training.* Boston: Marsh, Capen, Lyon, & Webb, 1839.
———. *The Linwoods; or, "Sixty Years Since" in America.* Ed. Maria Karafilis. Hanover: University Press of New England, 2002.
———. *The Power of Her Sympathy: The Autobiography and Journal of Catherine Maria Sedgwick.* Ed. Mary Kelley. Boston: Massachusetts Historical Society, 1993.
Shapiro, Michael. *Moral Ambiguity: National Culture and the Politics of the Family.* Minneapolis: University of Minnesota Press, 2001.
Shaw, S. Bradley. "The Pliable Rhetoric of Domesticity" in *The Stowe Debate: Rhetorical Strategies in Uncle Tom's Cabin,* Ed. Mason Lowance, Jr., Ellen E. Westbrook, and R. C. De Prospo. Amherst: University of Massachusetts Press, 1994.
Shealey, Daniel. "Work Well Done: Louisa May Alcott and Mary Maples Dodge," in *St. Nicholas and Mary Maples Dodge: The Legacy of a Children's Magazine, 1873–1905,* Ed. Susan Gannon, et al. Jefferson, NC: McFarland, 2004: 171–191.
Shortell, Timothy. "The Rhetoric of Black Abolitionism," *Social Science History* 28.1 (Spring 2004): 75–109.
Silber, Nina. *The Romance of Reunion: Northerners and the South, 1865–1900.* Chapel Hill: University of North Carolina Press, 1997.
Silverman, Gillian. "Textual Sentimentalism: Incest and Authorship in Melville's *Pierre,*" *American Literature* 74.2 (June 2002): 345–372.
Simms, William Gilmore. *The Partisan: A Romance of the Revolution.* New York: AMS Press, 1968 (1835).
Smith, Gail K. ""Reading with the Other: Hermeneutics and the Politics of Difference in Stowe's Dred," *American Literature: A Journal of Literary History, Criticism, and Bibliography* 69.2 (1997): 289–313.
Southern literary messenger; devoted to every department of literature and the fine arts. May 1835. Volume 1, Issue 9.

Stanesa, Jamie. "Caroline Lee Whiting Hentz" (*Legacy* Profile). *Legacy* 13.2 (1996): 130–139.

———. "Caroline Hentz's Rereading of Southern Paternalism; Or, Pastoral Naturalism in *The Planter's Northern Bride*," *Southern Studies* 3.4 (1992): 221–252.

Steiner, George. *Antigones*. Oxford: Clarendon Press, 1984.

Stewart, James Brewer. "'A Great Talking and Eating Machine': Patriarchy, Mobilization and the Dynamics of Nullification in South Carolina," *Civil War History* 27.3 (1981): 197–220.

"Mrs. Stowe and Dred," *Southern Literary Messenger* (October 1858): 284–286.

Stowe, Harriet Beecher. *Dred: A Tale of the Great Dismal Swamp*. Ed. Robert S. Levine. New York: Penguin, 2000.

Taylor, Amy Murrell. *The Divided Family in Civil War America*. Chapel Hill: The University of North Carolina Press, 2005.

Thorslev, Peter L. Jr. "Incest as Romantic Symbol," *Comparative Literature Studies*, 2.1 (1965): 41–58.

"Thoughts on Sunday Schools," *Southern Literary Messenger* 4.4 (1838): 224–227.

Tompkins, Jane. *Sensational Designs: The Cultural Work of American Fiction 1790–1860*. New York: Oxford University Press, 1985.

Trumpener, Katie. *Bardic Nationalism: The Romantic Novel and the British Empire*. Princeton: Princeton University Press, 1997.

VanDette, Emily E. "It Should Be a Family Thing: Family, Nation, and Republicanism in Catharine Maria Sedgwick's *A New-England Tale* and *The Linwoods*," *ATQ* (March 2005): 51–74.

Wakelyn, Jon L. *The Politics of a Literary Man: William Gilmore Simms*. Westport, Conn: Greenwood Press, 1973.

Warren, James Perrin. *Culture of Eloquence: Oratory and Reform in Antebellum America*. University Park: The Pennsylvania State University Press, 1999.

Weinstein, Cindy. *Family, Kinship, and Sympathy in Nineteenth-Century American Literature*. New York: Cambridge University Press, 2004.

Weldon, Roberta. *Hawthorne, Gender, and Death: Christianity and Its Discontents*. New York: Palgrave Macmillan, 2008.

Welter, Barbara. "The Cult of True Womanhood," *American Quarterly* 18.2, Part 1 (Summer 1966): 151–174.

Williams, Heather. *Self-Taught: African American Education in Slavery and Freedom*. Chapel Hill: University of North Carolina Press, 2005.

Wilson, Matthew. *Whiteness in the Novels of Charles Chesnutt*. Jackson: University Press of Mississippi, 2004.

Winterer, Caroline. "Classicism and Women's Education in America: 1840–1900," *American Quarterly* 53.1 (2001): 70–93.

Woodbury, Augustus. *Plain Words to Young Men*. Concord, NH: E. C. Eastman, 1858.

Young, Elizabeth. "A Wound of One's Own: Louisa May Alcott's Civil War Fiction," *American Quarterly* 48.3 (1996): 439–474.

Zackodnik, Teresa. "Little Romances and Mulatta Heroines: Passing for a 'True Woman' in Frances Harper's *Iola Leroy* and Pauline Hopkins's *Contending Forces.*" *Nineteenth-Century Feminisms* 2 (Spring/Summer 2000): 103–124.

Zender K. "Faulkner and the Politics of Incest," *American Literature: A Journal of Literary History, Criticism, and Bibliography* 70.4 (December 1998): 739–765.

Index

Notes: Locators followed by 'n' refer to note numbers

A

abolitionism, 29, 109–12, 176n2
  see also slavery
Absalom, Absalom! (Faulkner, 1936),
  151–3
Adams, Abigail, 12, 164n28
Adams, John, 12
adopted-sister romance, 85–6
advice literature, 5, 14, 23–4,
  115–17
  sibling relationships in, 19,
  24–32
African American Nadir, 129, 147
  see also Reconstruction
Aikman, William, 115
Alcott, Louisa May, 37–8, 167n21,
  167n22, 167n24
Alcott, William, 23, 30–1, 45
Aldrich, Thomas Bailey, 38
American Colored League,
  144–5
Antigone (Sophocles), 8–11, 13,
  162n20, 163n21, 163n23
anti-paternalism, 7–8, 23, 83
  see also paternalism

B

The Banished Son (Hentz, 1856),
  173n2
Barbauld, Anna, 168n31
Battles at Home (Darling, 1870),
  38–42, 167n24

black nationalism, 15, 21, 144,
  181n25, 181n26
  see also nationalism
Black post-Reconstruction Fiction, *see*
  Contending Forces; Iola Leroy; The
  House Behind the Cedars
Black Reconstruction in America
  (DuBois, 1935), 133
Bohner, Charles H., 66
brother-sister relationships, *see*
  opposite sex sibling
  relationships
"Brother and Sister" (Thayer, 1889),
  1–3
Brown, Charles Brockden, 89
Brown, Gillian, 7
Burke's Weekly for Boys and Girls
  (periodical), 35

C

Chesnutt, Charles, 15, 21, 130,
  135–40, 147
  see also The House Behind the Cedars
childhood mortality, 33–6
children's literature, 5, 14, 32–46,
  166n13, 167n22
Civil War, 15, 53, 75
  in children's literature, 37–8
Clay, Henry, 52
confidence between siblings, 5, 12,
  29–31, 71, 80, 101, 115
Contending Forces (Hopkins, 1900),
  21, 128, 140–7

Cornwallis, Charles, 66, 68
Coviello, Peter, 4, 21, 129

D
Darling, Mary Greenleaf, 38–42
Dill, Elizabeth, 89, 154
Dodge, Mary Maples, 42–6
domestic advice literature, *see* advice literature
domesticity, 27–8, 110, 157, 163n25
   in children's literature, 36–7, 39
   Hentz and, 14, 20, 86, 88–90, 174n11
Donald and Dorothy (Dodge, 1893), 42–6
Don Giovanni (Mozart, 1787), 80
Drayton, William, 53
Dred (Stowe, 1856), 20, 109–26, 128
   as abolitionist novel, 109–10, 176n5
   contrasted with *Ernest Linwood*, 117–18
   influence of on *Iola Leroy*, 130
   mixed-race sibling relationships in, 118–25
   representations of family in, 111, 113–26, 177n8
   sibling incest in, 152
DuBois, W. E. B., 133–4
Dupin, Amantine, 12

E
egalitarianism, 8, 23
Electra, 164n24
emancipation, 29
   see also slavery
enfranchisement of women, 12–13, 26
Ernest Linwood (Hentz, 1856), 10, 83, 87–107, 173n3
   as autobiography, 91–2, 174n16, 175n22
   contrasted with *Dred*, 117–18
   genre classification of, 88
   posthumous publication of, 173n5
   relative obscurity of, 17, 175n17
   sibling relationships in, 14, 20, 87–8, 92–6, 98–107, 112
Euripides, 13

F
familial naming, 142
family as nation metaphor, 3–4, 7–8, 15–16, 37, 54–5, 57–8, 82–3, 127–8, 161n9, 167n20
family, representations of
   as central theme in domestic fiction, 3
   in *Dred*, 111, 113–26, 128, 177n8
   "hyper-biological," 112–13, 118, 120, 122
   non-biological, 112, 177n8
   Northern *vs.* Southern definitions, 111–12
   in political discourse, 54–5
   slavery and, 119–24, 126
Faulkner, William, 16, 150, 151–3
female submission, 67, 99
feminine passivity, 9–11, 70n25
feminism, 11–13, 28
   see also women's rights
filial loyalty, 4
   in children's literature, 23
   contrasted with sibling relations, 6–7, 19
   in *Dred*, 119
   in *The House Behind the Cedars*, 138
   in Revolutionary War fiction, 11, 51–6, 59–60, 62–3, 67, 76–8, 80, 82
   see also parent-child relationships
Foreman, Gabrielle P., 134
Freedmen's Bureau, 132–3
Freeman/Mumbet, Elizabeth, 55
Fuller, Margaret, 11–13, 28

G
gender differentiation, 5–6, 8–10, 12–13, 65
genre classification, 88–9

INDEX

Gilded Age, 2
Godwin, William, 12
Gone with the Wind (Mitchell, 1936), 150
Goodrich, Samuel, 168n31
gothic fiction, 16, 88, 107, 157, 173n7

H

Hamilton, James, Jr, 53
Harlem Renaissance, 147
Harper, Frances E. W., 21, 128–35, 147, 178n4
  see also Iola Leroy
Hawthorne, Nathaniel, 16, 150, 154–7
Hegel, Georg Wilhelm Friedrich, 8–10, 12–13, 31, 63–4, 116, 156, 163n22
  Antigone and, 163n21
  marriage and, 162n19
  psychoanalytical theory and, 162n18
Hemphill, C. Dallett, 5–6, 24, 116, 160n7, 165n31, 166n7
Hentz, Caroline Lee, 83, 86–92, 106–7, 174n9
  contrasted with Hawthorne, 156
  contrasted with Stowe, 109
  as defender of Southern culture, 14, 20, 86–7, 88–90, 106–7, 174n11, 174n12
  Ernest Linwood as autobiography, 91–2, 174n16, 175n22
  Faulkner and, 153
  representations of family and, 112
  see also Ernest Linwood; The Planter's Northern Bride
histiotextuality, 179n6
Hopkins, Pauline, 15, 21, 128, 140–7
  black nationalism of, 181n25, 181n26
  see also Contending Forces

Horse-Shoe Robinson (Kennedy, 1835), 11, 17, 51–2, 66–73, 82–3
  realism of, 170n23
The House Behind the Cedars (Chesnutt, 1900), 15, 21, 130, 135–40, 149
House of the Seven Gables (Hawthorne, 1851), 154–7
"hyper-biological" families, 112–13, 118, 120, 122

I

incest, 10, 73, 149–54, 161n14, 164n29, 171n26
individualism, 6, 8, 18, 20, 66, 139
  Northern, 90, 174n12
Iola Leroy (Harper, 1892), 21, 128–35, 138–9

J

Jackson, Andrew, 52, 54
James, Henry, 152
James, John Angell, 31–2
Jim Crow laws, 128–9

K

Karafilis, Maria, 57, 58
Katherine Walton (Simms, 1851), 74
Kelly, R. Gordon, 32
Kennedy, John Pendleton, 11, 19, 49–52, 55, 66–73, 76, 170n22, 172n27
  Faulkner and, 153
  political career of, 66
  use of family as nation metaphor, 55, 58, 128
  see also Horse-Shoe Robinson

L

lateral attachment, 9, 15, 18, 24, 102, 107, 157
  contrasted with parent-child relationship, 18, 72
  in *Dred*, 20, 116, 152
  in *Ernest Linwood*, 20, 89–90, 93–4, 105–7

lateral attachment—*continued*
  in Hopkins's fiction, 146–7
  limitations of, 118, 121, 123–4, 126
  in *The Linwoods,* 65
  Nullification Crisis and, 54–5
  in post-Reconstruction fiction, 129, 146
  psychotherapy and, 175n19
  in Revolutionary War fiction, 65, 69, 76, 82–3
  slavery and, 119–24, 126
  slavery debate and, 110, 113
  see also opposite sex sibling relationships
lateral conflict, 121
lateral dysfunction, 4, 126
lateral solidarity, 15, 21, 54, 73, 82, 111, 146
Latham, Harold, 150
Levine, Robert S., 16
Lewis, Arthur, 145
Life at Home (Aikman, 1870), 115
The Linwoods (Sedgwick, 1837), 15, 25, 51–2, 56–66, 82–3
  family as nation metaphor in, 58, 62, 65
  gender differentiation in, 65
  parent-child relationships in, 60–2
  sibling relationships in, 63–5, 170n21
Little Women, 37–8, 167n21
Locke, John, 7–8, 162n15
  antipatriarchial principles of, 25, 56, 60–2
The Lofty and the Lowly (MacIntosh, 1853), 113
Longfellow, Henry Wadsworth, 38
lynching, 129, 140

M

Marion, Frances, 66
marriage, 25
  in *Ernest Linwood,* 87, 91, 97–101, 103–4, 106
  in Hegel's philosophy, 162n19
  as metaphor for national politics, 4, 73, 130, 159n4, 161n9, 167n19
  parent-child relationship and, 68, 72–3, 78, 80, 82–3
  race and, 131, 141–2
  reconciliation marriage, 16n9, 130
  sibling relationships and, 8, 14, 28, 79–80, 85–6, 94, 99–100, 114–17, 141, 166n3
May, Leila S., 157, 164n29
McIntosh, Maria, 113
Means and Ends, or Self-training (Sedgwick, 1839), 25–30
melancholia, 175n17
Melville, Herman, 16, 89, 149–50, 153–4, 157, 182n13
Merry's Museum (periodical), 35, 167n22
Millichampe (Simms, 1836), 74
Mintz, Steven, 6, 24–5, 165n2
miscegenation, 120, 150
Mitchell, Juliet, 18, 95, 100, 102, 165n30, 175n19
Mitchell, Margaret, 149–51, 165n31
mixed-race sibling relationships, 20–1, 111, 113–14, 118–25, 152
  incest and, 130, 149
Morrison, Toni, 17, 152, 173n7
Moss, Elizabeth, 90
Mozart, W. A., 80
mutual identification, 9–10, 106
mutuality, 4, 27, 29–30, 38, 40, 98, 119, 158

N

national affiliation, 4, 128, 146–7, 149
nationalism, 16, 49, 52, 169n4
  literary, 50
  of Sedgwick, 170n15, 170n16
  see also black nationalism

national kinship, 3, 15, 29
  sibling relations as metaphor for,
    3–4, 7–8, 15–16, 37–8, 54–5,
    57–8, 127–8
A New-England Tale (Sedgwick,
  1822), 56, 58, 62
non-biological family, 112, 177n8
Nullification Crisis, 19, 52–4, 57–8,
  82, 169n7, 172n33
  family dynamics and, 169n8
  novels published during, 11, 25,
    49–50, 66
  Simms and, 75
  Southern paternalism and, 90

O
opposite sex sibling relationships
  adoptive, 85–6
  in advice literature, 5, 19,
    24–32
  in American history, 160n7
  in *Antigone*, 8–11
  in *Battles at Home*, 38–42
  brother as protector in, 3, 5, 24,
    29–32, 36, 44, 64–5, 70, 79,
    88, 95, 115, 121–3, 170n21
  in children's literature, 19, 32–46
  in Civil War Stories, 19, 37–8
  codes of conduct for, 24, 28,
    29–31
  in *Contending Forces*, 141, 146
  contrasted with parent-child
    dynamics, 7–8, 18, 30, 72
  contrasted with same-sex sibling
    relationships, 5
  in *Donald and Dorothy*, 42–6
  double standards in, 116
  in *Dred*, 111, 113–26
  in *Ernest Linwood*, 14, 20, 87–8,
    92–6, 98–107, 112
  in Hawthorne's fiction, 155–6
  Hegelian philosophy of, 8–10,
    63–4, 116, 156, 163n22
  in *Horse-Shoe Robinson*, 67–73

in *The House Behind the Cedars*,
  135–9
importance of confidence in, 5, 12,
  29–31, 71, 80, 101, 115
incest and, 149–54, 161n14
innocence of, 165n2
in *Iola Leroy*, 130–1
in *The Linwoods*, 60, 63–5,
  170n21
marriage and, 8, 14, 28, 79–80,
  85–6, 94, 99–100, 114–17,
  141, 166n3
in *Means and Ends, or Self-Training*,
  25–9
in Melville's fiction, 153–4
as metaphor for national politics,
  3–4, 7–8, 15–16, 37–8, 54–5,
  57–8, 127–8
mixed-race, 20–1, 111, 113–14,
  118–25, 130, 152
mutuality in, 4, 27, 29–30, 38, 40,
  98, 119, 158
nineteenth century expectations for,
  1–2, 5–6, 115–17
Nullification Crisis and, 19
in *The Partisan*, 74–83, 85
in Poe's fiction, 157–8
portrayals of Reconstruction and,
  129–31
in post-Reconstruction fiction, 21,
  128
in Revolutionary War fiction, 51–2,
  82–3
self-esteem and, 95, 102
sister providing moral guidance in,
  5, 24, 28, 30–1, 38, 63–4,
  115, 155
in Southern gothic tradition,
  107
utopian potential of, 146
see also lateral attachment
Orestes, 164n24
O'Sullivan, John L., 57
Our Young Folks (periodical), 35, 38,
  167n22

P

parent-child relationships, 7–8
  contrasted with sibling relationships, 18, 30, 72
  as inappropriate metaphor for nineteenth century fiction, 57
  Lockean perspective on, 7–8, 56, 60
  in *The Partisan*, 76–7
  as primary trope of Revolutionary War discourse, 23–4
  in Revolutionary War fiction, 60–2
  see also filial loyalty
Parille, Ken, 36
The Partisan (Simms, 1835), 51–2, 67, 74–83, 85, 172n32
  relative obscurity of, 17
paternalism, 7–8
  hypocrisy of, 125
  slavery and, 86, 90, 113, 121–3, 128
  Southern, 89–90, 111, 174n12
periodicals, *see* children's literature
Phenomenology of Mind (Hegel, 1807), 8
Phillips, Michelle H., 32
Pierre (Melville, 1859), 89, 153–4, 182n13
Pinckney, Henry Laurens, 75
Plain Words to Young Men (Woodbury, 1858), 115
The Planter's Northern Bride (Hentz, 1854), 20, 86–7, 89–90, 106–7, 174n11
  contrasted with *Uncle Tom's Cabin*, 112
Poe, Edgar Allan, 11, 16, 66, 150, 152, 157–8, 164n29
post-Reconstruction fiction, *see Contending Forces; The House Behind the Cedars; Iola Leroy;* Reconstruction
psychoanalytical theory, 18, 162n18, 165n30, 175n19

R

racial "passing," 135–9, 143, 180n23
racial segregation, 130, 136
reconciliation marriage, 130, 146, 161n9
Reconstruction, 15, 128–9
  African-American agency in, 21, 128, 132–5, 139, 179n8
  literary representations of, 128–30
  national unity prioritized over civil rights in, 21, 128–9, 130, 140, 144–6
  see also Contending Forces; The House Behind the Cedars; Iola Leroy
Revolutionary War fiction, 11, 49–51, 55
  see also Horse-Shoe Robinson; The Linwoods; The Partisan
Riss, Arthur, 110–12
"Ropa Carmagin" (Mitchell), 150–1
Rotundo, E. Anthony, 5–6, 114, 116

S

St. Nicholas Magazine (periodical), 32, 42–3, 46
same-sex sibling relationships, 5, 142, 160n5
Sanders, Valerie, 160n5
Sand, George, 12
Scott, Walter, 19, 57
sectionalism, 4, 8, 14–15, 57–8, 85–6
Sedgwick, Catharine Maria, 15, 49–52, 55–66, 76
  as author of advice literature, 25–30
  nationalism of, 170n15, 170n16
  Nullification Crisis and, 19
  political beliefs of, 55–7
  sibling relations of, 170n21
  use of family as nation metaphor, 55, 58, 128
  see also The Linwoods
Sedgwick, Robert, 170n21

Sedgwick, Theodore, 55
self-reliance, 133, 139
sentimental literature, 89, 150–4,
 159n4
 children's literature and, 36
 parent-child dynamic in, 73
 sibling dynamic in, 4, 16–17,
  43–4, 64, 85–7, 153–4
 slavery debate and, 111–13, 130
 Uncle Tom's Cabin as, 176n3
sibling equilibrium, 9, 11–13, 156
sibling relationships, *see* opposite sex
 sibling relationships
Sigourney, Lydia, 36, 39, 45
Simms, William Gilmore, 19, 49–52,
 55, 74–83, 172n28
 political views of, 74–5, 172n32
 use of family as nation metaphor,
  55, 58, 128
 see also The Partisan
sister-brother relationships, *see*
 opposite sex sibling relationships
slavery, 54, 90, 128
 definitions of family and, 111–14,
  118, 126
 literary debate over, 14, 20, 86–7,
  89–90, 109–13, 119, 176n2,
  176n3
 mixed-race siblings and, 118–24
 Nullification Crisis and, 169n7
 paternalism and, 86, 90, 113,
  121–3, 128
 in post-Reconstruction fiction,
  131–2, 134, 141–2
 see also abolitionism
Smith, Frances Foster, 131
Smith, Sidney, 50–1
Sophocles, 8–11, 13
Souls of Black Folk (DuBois, 1903),
 133
South Carolina, 52–4, 90
 see also Nullification Crisis
states' rights debates, 15, 19, 50,
 52–3, 57–8, 169n6
 see also Nullification Crisis

Steuben, Freidrich von, 69
Stewart, James Brewer, 54
Stowe, Harriet Beecher, 20,
 176n5
 abolitionist views of, 86,
  109–12
 contrasted with Harper, 178n4
 contrasted with Hentz, 89, 109
 published in children's periodicals,
  38
 use of family as nation metaphor,
  128
 see also Dred; Uncle Tom's Cabin

T
Thayer, Abbott Handerson, 1–3,
 159n1
Twain, Mark, 152

U
Uncle Tom's Cabin (Stowe, 1852), 20,
 110, 112–13
 mother figures in, 176n6
 sentimentalism of, 176n3
 treatment of family in,
  118–22

V
vertical paradigm, *see* parent-child
 relationships

W
*Warcus Warland; or, the Long Moss
 Spring. A Tale of the South*
 (Hentz, 1852), 107
Warner, Susan, 85–6
Weinstein, Cindy, 110
white supremacism, 129, 132, 136,
 138–40, 143–6
Whittier, John Greenleaf, 38
The Wide Wide World (Warner, 1850),
 85–6
Wieland (Brown, 1798), 89
Williams, Heather, 139
Wilson, Matthew, 138
Winthrop, John, 4–5

Wollstonecraft, Mary, 12
Woman in the Nineteenth Century (Fuller, 1845), 11–12, 28
"women's fiction," 17, 173n7
women's rights, 11–13, 26–8, 164n28
Woodbury, Augustus, 115

Y
The Young Man's Guide (Alcott, 1834), 30–1
The Youth's Companion (periodical), 33
The Youth's Dayspring (periodical), 34

Z
Zender, Karl, 152

Printed in the United States of America